Urban Design Governance

Urban Design Governance

Soft powers and the European experience

Matthew Carmona, João Bento and
Tommaso Gabrieli

This project has received funding from the
European Union's Horizon 2020 research
and innovation programme under grant
agreement n° 831704

First published in 2023 by
UCL Press
University College London
Gower Street
London WC1E 6BT

Available to download free: www.uclpress.co.uk

ISBN: 978-1-80008-427-8 (Hbk)
ISBN: 978-1-80008-426-1 (Pbk)
ISBN: 978-1-80008-425-4 (PDF)
ISBN: 978-1-80008-428-5 (epub)
DOI: https://doi.org/10.14324/111.9781800084254

Contents

List of figures and tables   vii
List of case study boxes   xxi
Preface   xxiii
Acknowledgements   xxv

1   Urban design governance in Europe   1
        Design yesterday and today   1
        National and European policies on design   17
        Moving on …   41

2   Exploring European urban design governance   43
        Systems of urban design governance   43
        The Urban Maestro method: a tools-based analysis   61

3   A European typology of tools   65
        Surveying Europe   65
        A typology of urban design governance tools   74
        Urban design governance landscapes and their tools   80

4   Understanding the informal tools   114
        Building a panorama of European practices   114
        Analysis tools   115
        Information tools   123
        Persuasion tools   136
        Rating tools   149
        Support tools   167
        Exploration tools   178

5   The financial dimension   195
        Finance and design   195
        Adding design strings   208
        Finance and design: chickens and eggs   218

6   Interrogating the tools   221

    Knowledge transfer (in both directions)   221

    The culture and commitment to design quality   223

    Building the toolkit for urban design governance   231

    The governance of urban design governance   241

    The power and people of urban design governance   246

    The economics of urban design governance   250

    How practices travel   259

    Twenty propositions   264

7   Landscapes, tools and fundamentals for delivery   268

    Bringing tools together within diverse urban design governance landscapes   268

    A comprehensive typology of urban design governance   277

    Six Cs: the fundamentals of urban design governance   282

References   289

Index   298

List of figures and tables

Figures

1.1 Building types were determined by the nature of the street they fronted. Here the second sort is shown that fronted 'streets and lanes of note and the River Thames' (image: Matthew Carmona). 3

1.2 From place quality to place value (a virtuous loop) (image: Matthew Carmona). 6

1.3 Unsustainable sprawl characterises much of Europe's post-war urban fabric, here (a) Berlin (b) London (c) Paris (d) Madrid (e) Rome and (f) Warsaw (images: CNES/Airbus MGGP Aero Maxo Technologies 2021 Google). 8

1.4 Different developers have constructed standard apartment block types on both sides of this street in Rome, applying a standard road and footpath typology. Height and set-back controls have been respected but provision of parking (on the left in a podium creating a blank frontage onto the footpath, and on the right in a relentlessly hard street-level parking area) undermines any quality in the public realm (image: Matthew Carmona). 11

1.5 For decades Paris operated a simple height limit within its city limits of 37 metres. The policy followed the negative reaction to the 59-storey Montparnasse Tower, completed in 1973 (as seen on the skyline in this image taken from the Sacré-Coeur). While the limit has since been relaxed in defined outer areas such as La Défense, with its towering skyline, the historic city maintains its horizontal skyline and the dominance of key historic landmarks (image: Matthew Carmona). 12

1.6   In Copenhagen, a city known for its careful nurturing
       of urban quality, almost everything that can be seen in
       the image has been carefully controlled by a complex
       combination of planning and construction regulations.
       The result, however, despite the best intentions and
       high-quality materials, is a scheme that feels dull,
       sterile and desolate (image: Matthew Carmona).   12

1.7   The state largely took on the role of rebuilding Polish
       cities damaged during the Second World War, and
       subsequently that of housing the country's growing
       population. Although the historic centre of Gdansk
       (a) in the north of Poland (which had been 90% destroyed)
       was reconstructed on its original plan with neo-traditional
       façades that replicate those of the former burgher houses
       (in spirit if not always in detail), new housing areas to
       accommodate the city's industrial workers (b) often took
       a very different form. Both were driven by centralised and
       largely unaccountable state power, but also by very strong
       public-sector visions of what these different places should
       be (images: Matthew Carmona).   13

1.8   New large-scale housing schemes in England vary hugely
       in their quality. Research has shown that those which
       benefit from the use of design codes (a form of site-specific
       design guidance) are around five times more likely to be
       designed well or very well than those that don't (Carmona
       et al. 2020). Similarly, those that use design review
       (the project-based peer review of design) are four times
       more likely to score in these categories. Another finding
       is that regions with the poorest-rated housing design were
       those with the lowest use of these tools of urban design
       governance, tending to favour the use of more generic
       design policy and guidance instead. The differential
       results, as shown in images (a) and (b), are very clear to
       see (image: Matthew Carmona).   14

1.9   The changing Dutch institutional infrastructure for
       architecture (image after Kresse 2016).   20

1.10   At the turn of the century relatively few cities in Europe
       were pursuing architectural and environmental quality
       as a coherent political objective; Gothenburg was one
       of them (image: Matthew Carmona).   25

1.11 Winner of the EU Mies van der Rohe award 2013,
the Harpa – Reykjavik Concert Hall and Conference
Centre (image: Matthew Carmona).   26

1.12 Countries with an architectural policy, or planning to
produce one, 2011 (image: Bento 2012).   31

1.13 Types of architectural policy, 2011 (image: Bento 2012).   32

1.14 The eight criteria for a high-quality *Baukultur*
(image: Swiss Federal Office of Culture 2021b).   35

1.15 The three inseparable values of the New European
Bauhaus (image: European Union 2021).   39

1.16 In England, the Building Better, Building Beautiful
Commission argued for the foregrounding of beauty leading
to revised national policy, the greater use of design codes
to guide new housing development and the establishment
of the Office for Place from 2022 to lead a larger culture
change (image: Building Better, Building Beautiful
Commission 2020).   40

1.17 A timeline of Europe-wide initiatives demonstrates
the increasing sense of urgency that design and place
quality are receiving (image: adapted from OMC 2021).   42

2.1 The carefully structured urban framework of Penya-roja,
a post-industrial regenerated area in Valencia, is marred
by the over-engineering of its roads, making walking and
cycling more challenging than they should be
(image: Matthew Carmona).   45

2.2 Frank Gehry's Dancing House in Prague, completed in
1996, draws praise and criticism in equal measure. It is
clearly a creative and very contemporary building in a
historic setting, but while it contrasts with its surroundings,
it also fits in through the use of materials, proportions,
and height and massing parameters that respects its
neighbours. In this case not only did the site create its own
constraints, but so also did the fixed zoning system of
Czech cities where development quantum and heights are
controlled; in this case courtesy of the *Plan of the Stabilized
Zones of Prague*, produced by the Chief Architect's Office
(prior to the abolition of that position) in 1994 in order
to guide the post-communist restructuring of the already
built-up sections of the city (image: Matthew Carmona).   46

2.3 Styles of government intervention (image: adapted from
Policy Lab in Siodmok 2017).   51

2.4　The scales of policymaking (and design)
　　　(image: Siodmok 2017). 52
2.5　The America's Cup Pavilion in Valencia was designed
　　　by David Chipperfield Architects in collaboration with
　　　b720 Arquitectos. Completed in 2007, the building had
　　　previously won a limited competition organised by Consorcio
　　　Valencia (a consortium of public-sector actors) with eight
　　　preselected teams. The need to prepare rapidly for the
　　　America's Cup once Valencia had been selected as the
　　　host city, while delivering architectural excellence at
　　　the same time, suited a design competition
　　　(image: Matthew Carmona). 54
2.6　Formal and informal tools compared (image: Matthew
　　　Carmona). 54
2.7　Urban design governance landscapes across scales
　　　(image: Matthew Carmona). 59
2.8　Bringing the key concepts together: an analytical
　　　framework (image: Matthew Carmona). 61
2.9　The Urban Maestro method (image: Matthew Carmona). 64
3.1　Classification of informal design governance tools
　　　used by CABE (image: Matthew Carmona). 66
3.2　Countries with an official publication, memorandum or
　　　policy on architecture/urban design or who were
　　　anticipating adopting one in the near future
　　　(image: Urban Maestro). 69
3.3　Categories of urban design governance tools
　　　(image: Matthew Carmona). 76
3.4　A typology of urban design governance tools
　　　(image: Matthew Carmona). 79
3.5　Financial mechanisms in the typology of urban design
　　　governance tools (image: Matthew Carmona). 81
3.6　Lisbon's urban design governance landscape
　　　(image: Matthew Carmona). 83
3.7　A deliberately broad definition of architecture is adopted
　　　in Portugal's National Policy for Architecture and
　　　Landscape, encompassing 'outdoor spaces that comprise
　　　the design of the city and the territory' (here at Portimão)
　　　as well as buildings, their interior spaces and all other
　　　built structures (image: Matthew Carmona). 85

3.8   Heritage issues can trump other design factors, including
       in a redevelopment scheme for three empty buildings in
       Lisbon city centre on the Avenue Fontes Pereira de Melo.
       While the redevelopment of these buildings was designed by
       Souto Moura, a Pritzker-winning architect, the scheme was
       rejected by the municipality after receiving a negative review
       from the Ministry's advisory body (image: João Bento).   86
3.9   A particularly complex area is the Port of Lisbon, covering
       11 municipalities and an overarching port authority and
       requiring coordination of projects on both the Lisbon
       (see Figure 3.10) and the more challenging Setúbal
       peninsula sides of the Tagus. The latter is now undergoing
       some rehabilitation in which small-scale, informal
       place-making has been key to the early regeneration
       projects (image: Matthew Carmona).   88
3.10   The Lisbon Waterfront has seen huge, sustained investment
       in transforming former industrial port areas into a new
       leisure environment (image: Matthew Carmona).   90
3.11   In 1998 the Lisbon Oceanarium by Peter Chermayeff was
       awarded the Valmor award, followed up by an honourable
       mention in 2011 for an extension by Pedro Nuno Campos
       da Costa to house its collective equipment (image: Matthew
       Carmona).   91
3.12   London's urban design governance landscape
       (image: Matthew Carmona).   94
3.13   Ten 'Characteristics of Well Designed Places' from
       the National Design Guide (image: Ministry of Housing,
       Communities and Local Government 2020).   95
3.14   The forerunner of Homes England was influential in
       establishing high-quality design aspirations for the
       Greenwich Peninsula. Since 1997 these have continued
       to inform development outcomes, now spanning 25 years,
       despite the organisation itself (like central government)
       wavering in its commitment to design over that period
       (image: Matthew Carmona).   96
3.15   Blue House Yard in Wood Green was commissioned by
       the London Borough of Haringey with funding from
       the Mayor of London to create a new space for local small
       businesses who might otherwise be priced out of the area
       (image: Matthew Carmona).   98

3.16 Design review panels in London (image: adapted from
      Urban Design London 2020).   101

3.17 'The Tulip' by Foster and Partners (a 300-metre-high
      visitor attraction) was called in by government and rejected
      in 2021. The decision confirmed an earlier rejection of
      the scheme by the Mayor of London, in contravention of
      an initial decision to approve the project made by the City
      of London – within whose boundaries it would have stood
      (image: Foster and Partners).   102

3.18 Vienna's urban design governance landscape
      (image: Matthew Carmona).   104

3.19 The proposed *Baukultur* ecosystem. The planned agency
      would act as a coordinating partner between the spheres,
      and where there was deemed to be insufficient exchange
      it would act to stimulate contacts (image: adapted from
      Platform Baukulturpolitik 2021).   106

3.20 In 2013 BIG launched an international design competition
      for the master plan of the new campus of Vienna University
      of Economics and Business, which was won by
      BUSarchitektur (image: João Bento).   107

3.21 Quarter Two (Viertel Zwei) is an office and residential area
      in the 2nd district of Vienna. After a cooperative planning
      process between the City Council and landowners involving
      several architecture and urban design competitions,
      the project was built between 2007 and 2010
      (image: João Bento).   109

3.22 In Vienna 62 per cent of residents live in social housing,
      which has a reputation for the quality of its environments,
      space and amenities (Ball 2019), including here at
      the Alt-Erlaa Social Housing complex (image: Matthew
      Carmona).   111

4.1 Scope of the 2020/21 *Baukultur* report (image: Federal
      Foundation of Baukultur 2021).   118

4.2 *Baukultur* report production process (image: Federal
      Foundation of Baukultur 2021).   119

4.3 Housing design audit headline results, national and
      regional (image: Place Alliance).   121

4.4 Summarising analysis tools (image: Matthew Carmona).   123

4.5 The Architecture Navigator provides information on
      contemporary and historic architecture across Finland,

and allows searches by function, location, design team and other criteria in this example, housing in Helsinki (images: Matthew Carmona). 125

4.6 Urban Design London's 'Code school' supported a larger national drive to promote design coding as part of more design-focused housing development processes in England (image: Urban Design London). 128

4.7 Using models to explore the built environment, Arkki Greece (image: Natalia Pantelidou). 132

4.8 Coverage of the 17 UN Sustainable Development Goals (image: KADK). 135

4.9 Summarising information tools (image: Matthew Carmona). 136

4.10 The annual Madrid Architecture Week involves a wide range of organisers (6), sponsors (9), media partners (5) and collaborators (56) to deliver the complex programme, including the Caixa Forum, Madrid (image: Matthew Carmona). 139

4.11 Winner, European Prize for Urban Public Space 2008, the Norwegian Opera House, Oslo (image: Matthew Carmona). 145

4.12 The Pavillon de l'Arsenal, Paris (image: Matthew Carmona). 146

4.13 A digital screen is laid out on the floor of the Pavillon for visitors to interact with (image: Matthew Carmona). 147

4.14 The economic collapse towards the end of the first decade of this century left city authorities in Dublin struggling to continue the city's regeneration of the decade before. The solution was found in a renewed appetite to forge collaborative alliances both within and beyond the city, so 'while the City Council has displayed leadership, it sees the role of facilitator as being critical in prompting collaboration and harnessing capacity' in order to continue the regeneration of the city with 'an urbanist's sensibility' (Gleeson 2015), for example here in Dublin's Docklands (image: Matthew Carmona). 148

4.15 Summarising persuasion tools (image: Matthew Carmona). 149

4.16 Sustainability was a large part of the design of the Quartiere delle Albere's regeneration project by Renzo Piano in Trento, Italy. MuSe (the Science Museum)

achieved a LEED Gold certification, and all of the residences
and offices have a level B CasaClima classification, a local
system used in the Autonomous Province of Bolzano.
They were among the winners of the 2013 CasaClima
Awards (image: Matthew Carmona).   152

4.17 Example of Place Standard final spider diagram
      (image: www.placestandard.scot).   154

4.18 In preparing their City Plan for 2017–26 the City of Dundee
      used the Place Standard tool to deliver 504 online returns
      focused on understanding the qualities of the city that
      respondents valued or felt undermined their experience
      of place. Among the range of concerns this process
      revealed were issues of pedestrian accessibility and
      conflict with traffic (image: Matthew Carmona).   154

4.19 The competition culture in selected European countries
      in 2017 (image: after Architectuur Lokaal).   157

4.20 Distribution of Spatial Quality Teams
      (image: Sandra van Assen and José van Campen).   158

4.21 The Q-team set up to review projects in the Almere new
      town was described by Van Ginneken (2008) as the
      'conscience of the city centre', helping to guide the diverse
      projects that make up this new central area into a
      coherent place (image: Matthew Carmona).   159

4.22 One of the winners of Europan 15, this scheme by an Italian
      team for the Uddevalla site in Sweden (image: Jalla!).   163

4.23 Model of the prize-winning scheme for Florenc
      (image: Matthew Carmona).   164

4.24 Summarising rating tools (image: Matthew Carmona).   166

4.25 Completed projects based on design competitions in
      the Czech Republic between 1993 and 2019
      (image: Tomáš Zdvihal).   170

4.26 The location of twenty years of open call projects
      1999–2019 (image: Liefooghe and Van den Driessche 2019).   173

4.27 Map of the 95 départements covered by CAUEs
      (https://www.fncaue.com/?page=home).   174

4.28 The observatory of the architectural quality of housing,
      collected by the Île-de-France association, provides
      learning from regionally significant projects such as
      the Quartier Massena in Paris (image: Matthew Carmona).   175

4.29 Summarising support tools (image: Matthew Carmona).   178

4.30 The central but deprived neighbourhood of Mouraria has benefited from the Bip/Zip programme (image: Matthew Carmona).   182

4.31 Temporary projects in Aarhus have ranged from new uses for abandoned shops to festivals, container cities, and the infinite bridge, here seen from above, which allows people to walk onto and over the sea. Originally a temporary structure, the bridge is now re-assembled each year between April and October as a meeting place for citizens (image: Aerodata International Surveys, CNES/Airbus, Aero Maxo Technologies Scankort Map data 2022).   184

4.32 Berlin has hosted two IBAs thirty years apart, each exploring innovative urban typologies of their time as represented in the two images. The first (a), in 1957, explored new models for a future city in a context of the post-war divided city being rebuilt. The second (b), from 1979–87, explored new healing typologies with a focus on building new residential perimeter blocks (images: Matthew Carmona).   186

4.33 Poster for the documentary *Les grands Voisins: le cité rêvée* (great neighbours: the dream city) by Bastien Simon (image: Les Grands Voisins).   188

4.34 Praga district, Warsaw: creative interventions in a heritage context (image: Matthew Carmona).   193

4.35 Summarising exploration tools (image: Matthew Carmona).   194

5.1   Gated development in Gdynia, Poland, as an expression of development solely guided by the market/profit motive (image: Matthew Carmona).   198

5.2   In this major new development in Helsinki, the roads infrastructure (bottom left), public transportation infrastructure (right) and private investment (top left) are all in place, but fail to integrate to create a place that is more than the sum of its parts (image: Matthew Carmona).   199

5.3   The buildings and public spaces of Bjørvika, in Oslo, reflect the public/private delivery model that gave the municipality an inside seat on all key decisions. Seen here are the distinctive 'barcode buildings' that featured in an early development phase (image: Matthew Carmona).   203

5.4   In recent years a major beneficiary of the Timbrul
      de Arhitectură fund has been the Street Delivery festival
      in Bucharest, where for three days key central streets are
      closed to cars and opened to pedestrians and a series
      of activities designed to connect the public to artists,
      architects and artisans and to celebrate street culture
      (image: Matthew Carmona).   207
5.5   Vision for Het Hof van Cartesius (Utrecht), an early
      investment by the fund in a cooperative providing
      workspace for circular and green entrepreneurship.
      Starting in 2017 with two pavilions and 25 members,
      by 2021 eight had been completed, housing 110 members
      (image: Het Hof van Cartesius).   215
5.6   Evaluation matrix used for the Olga plot joint venture,
      Stuttgart (image: after Temel 2020).   216
5.7   In the Olga plot concept tendering exercise, design
      and environmental aspects received a 60% rating
      (image: Google map data 2022).   217
5.8   The high design ambitions for Bo01 in Malmö were first
      established by the 2001 European Housing Exposition
      held in the city, with prototypes explored for the remainder
      of the Western Harbour area, which was designed as a
      carbon neutral mixed-use neighbourhood. Sixteen
      developers worked alongside the city drawing on 250 million
      Swedish Kroner to incentivise delivery of the highly
      sustainable ambitions established by the *Quality
      Programme*, a tool setting out standards and guidelines
      for sustainable urban design (Madureira 2014)
      (image: Matthew Carmona).   219
5.9   Summarising financial mechanisms (image: Matthew
      Carmona).   220
6.1   Today Copenhagen's waterfront is a haven for walking,
      relaxation, contemplation and exercise (of all sorts),
      providing the city with an animated blue lung
      (image: Matthew Carmona).   228
6.2   Samoa île de Nantes, diverse projects across the island
      (image: https://www.iledenantes.com; https://www.
      samoa-nantes.fr/).   230

6.3 The ladder of architectural culture in which quality moves through five steps: step one, architecture and design is not part of the everyday public conversation, practices or priorities; step two, architecture is valued but seen as simply part of a final form-giving, 'styling' stage of the development process; step three, architecture is integrated into all stages of the multi-disciplinary development process; step four, architecture is integrated more deeply across governance scales with design professionals inputting directly into policymaking across a wide range of sectors; step five, knowledge of architecture and design fundamentally informs planning, forecasting, procurement and the full range of development practices that the public sector engages with or influences – design quality is widely aspired to and celebrated (image: OMC 2021). 233

6.4 In Geneva, the need to build new housing to tackle an affordability crisis has led to major expansion plans, including here in the huge Acacias Bâtie redevelopment area. This has been accompanied by a realisation that major growth needs to be underpinned by a consistent emphasis on high-quality *Baukultur*, something that has not always been the case in the past (image: Matthew Carmona). 235

6.5 Temporary pandemic-inspired public-realm interventions became commonplace in 2020/21 such as in Greenwich, London (a), allowing more space for pedestrians to pass each other safely, and in Dublin (b) where feet painted on the ground every 2 metres offered a visual reminder of the safe distance to queue (image: Matthew Carmona). 236

6.6 Porto's Praça de Lisboa now contains a new high-level park (above retail and parking) in the centre of an area formerly in decline. The site was subject to two competitions organised respectively by the municipality and by a citizens' collective who launched the 'No rules, great spot' competition to encourage debate about the future of the space. The final scheme was carefully controlled, being immediately adjacent to the boundary of the UNESCO World Heritage site, yet establishes an innovative green space within which relaxed informal activities occur with users shaping the space daily to their own ends (image: Matthew Carmona). 237

6.7 At the largest scale – planning for whole cities – informal approaches are being favoured by cities such as Birmingham, Malmö and Hamburg as means to explore complexity and risk and competing visions for change while promoting dialogue among citizens and other actors over future directions. This is the role of plans such as Birmingham's *Big City Plan* (published in 2011), which are designed to be propositional and flexible rather than restrictive and regulatory (Barth 2015). While the *Big City Plan* sits alongside a formal development plan that guides the city's development management decision-making, it remains an ambitious vision document, containing both high-level principles and concrete plans for local transformations, such as to the city's principal station – New Street – and its surroundings (now realised). In 2021 work began on rolling the *Big City Plan* forward to 2040 (image: Matthew Carmona).   240

6.8 The Marble Arch Mound (a), installed in an attempt to lure shoppers back to the West End of London following the pandemic, was poorly executed, doubled in cost (to £6 million) and was poorly received by visitors following a failure by Westminster City Council to manage the project properly and a rush to open the mound before it was ready. By contrast, the Carlsberg City development in Copenhagen employed a range of temporary diverting public-space strategies to help create a 'brand' on the city's former Carlsberg brewery site, following the financial crisis of 2008 when private development came to a halt. These, including the Rope Forest (b), quickly disappeared when the market recovered, leading to a public debate over the value of such temporary projects (images: Matthew Carmona).   242

6.9 Changing the image of social housing through small-scale environmental intervention, San Basilio quarter, Rome (image: Matthew Carmona).   246

6.10 This hastily constructed sign and the planters denote this as a pedestrian street, instigated in Malmö following the wave of vehicles-as-weapons-of-terror attacks that hit Europe from 2016 onwards (image: Matthew Carmona).   249

6.11   From the late 1990s onwards, Cambridge had structures and
       tools in place to deliver a much-needed planned expansion
       of the city. One such tool is the informal Quality Charter for
       Growth, which was drawn up following study tours to
       exemplar developments elsewhere in the UK and around
       Europe. The Charter focuses on the four 'C's of Community,
       Connectivity, Climate and Character, which have become
       the template against which new projects, such as here at
       Trumpington Meadows, are evaluated by the Cambridgeshire
       Quality Review Panel (image: Matthew Carmona).   252
6.12   Vauban, a sustainable urban neighbourhood
       (image: Matthew Carmona).   256
6.13   Today, the City of Sydney (the central area of the
       Australian metropolis) runs a unique formal competitions
       process for large-scale developments. Developers agreeing
       to take their developments through this competitions
       process can benefit from an additional 10% floor area or
       height bonus and – in the case of a fully open competition –
       a 50% reduction in the Heritage Floor Space requirement
       (the need to purchase transferable development rights from
       heritage buildings). Through their exhaustive study of the
       process, Freestone et al. (2019: 311) conclude that it offers
       an effective means of prioritising design quality, delivers
       generally better-designed outcomes, and 'enable[s]
       the public interest to be prioritised if not guaranteed in
       more creative, cooperative and productive ways'
       (image: Matthew Carmona).   259
6.14   Vancouver and Toronto condominium blocks compared
       (image: Matthew Carmona).   261
6.15   In 2005, an invited international competition was won by
       consultants West8 for the design of the reclaimed area above
       the then-proposed new tunnel for the M30 ring road around
       Madrid (the tunnel is below the pedestrian/cycleway on the
       far bank in this image). As well as a new strategic landscape,
       the proposals envisaged a family of smaller projects including
       squares, boulevards and parks, and a family of new bridges
       to connect up the urban districts along the new Madrid Rio
       (image: Matthew Carmona).   264
7.1   IPR's guidance focuses on making Prague a pleasant city
       for pedestrians, with space for people, trees and commercial
       activities (a). A focus on the detail helps to reinforce

Prague's unique character (b, bottom half of image) but as its
guidance is informal, it is not always implemented (b, top
half of image) (images: Matthew Carmona).   271

7.2   The Swedish National Architect will build upon the
      enviable reputation that the country already has as
      reflected in well-known projects such as Hammarby Sjöstad
      in Stockholm. This project is based on a clear but flexible
      urban design framework and detailed design codes to 'fix'
      the key design parameters at each phase, all delivered by a
      public-sector team with the means and capabilities to
      proactively engage through the full range of tools available
      to them. These include: powerful incentives vested in
      enlightened land ownership; the use of design competitions
      at each phase of the development; a rigorous design review
      and evaluation process; and partnerships between the city
      and local development teams (image: Matthew Carmona).   272

7.3   The influence of stakeholders over the course of
      the Co-City project Cumiana 15, Turin
      (image: Urban Maestro Masterclass).   274

7.4   The Hamburg Kesselhaus in HafenCity is an information
      centre for the area and its regeneration, including a
      1:500 scale model of the entire development
      (image: Matthew Carmona).   276

7.5a Deploying tools across the urban design governance field of
      action: quality-culture tools (image: Matthew Carmona).   279

7.5b Deploying tools across the urban design governance field of
      action: quality-delivery tools (image: Matthew Carmona).   280

7.5c Deploying tools across the urban design governance field
      of action: finance mechanisms with design strings
      (image: Matthew Carmona).   281

7.6   Comprehensive typology of urban design governance
      tools (image: Matthew Carmona).   283

7.7   The six Cs of effective urban design governance
      (image: Matthew Carmona).   284

Tables

3.1   Comprehensive architectural policies (table: Urban Maestro).   70

5.1   Financial mechanisms and urban design governance
      tools compared (compiled by Matthew Carmona).   209

6.1   Urban Maestro workshops (table: Urban Maestro).   224

List of case study boxes

Chapter 4

1. Assessing quality: Germany's biennial *Baukultur* reports (Germany)   117
2. Campaigning for quality: Place Alliance (England, UK)   120
3. Enhancing professional knowledge: Urban Design London (England, UK)   127
4. Inspiring the next generation: Arkki School of Architecture for Children and Youth (Finland)   131
5. Guiding with a social purpose: *An Architecture Guide to the UN 17 Sustainable Development Goals* (Denmark/international)   134
6. Engaging the community: Madrid Architecture Week (Spain)   138
7. Rewarding excellence: European Prize for Urban Public Space (Europe)   144
8. The value of architecture centres: Paris Centre for Architecture and Urbanism (France)   145
9. Inspiring conversations: Place Standard (Scotland, UK)   153
10. Delivering focused expertise: Spatial Quality Teams (Netherlands)   158
11. Raising standards competitively: Europan and Florenc (Europe/Czech Republic)   162
12. Subsidising architectural and urban competitions (Czech Republic)   170
13. The multiple roles of the Flemish State Architect (Flanders, Belgium)   172
14. Nationwide support network: Councils of Architecture, Urbanism and the Environment (CAUEs) (France)   173
15. Reshaping the public realm: Lisbon's BIP/ZIP Programme (Portugal)   181

16. Injecting innovation: IBA International Building
    Exhibitions (Germany)   185
17. Temporary occupation: Les Grands Voisins, Paris (France) 187
18. Top-down and bottom-up in Warsaw (Poland)   192

Chapter 5

19. Financing and guiding transformative investment in
    Oslo (Norway)   202
20. 0.05% for architecture: architectural stamp duty (Romania) 206
21. Investing in place-making: Citymaker Fund (Netherlands) 214
22. Balancing quality and price using concept tendering
    (Germany)   215

Chapter 6

23. Sustained commitment to quality: By&Havn, Copenhagen   227
24. Capturing value in Freiburg   255

Chapter 7

25. Arms-length, but not: IPR Prague (Czech Republic)   270
26. Co-governing the urban commons in Turin (Italy)   273
27. Development-focused urban design governance in
    Hamburg (Germany)   275

Preface

This book takes a deep dive into the governance of urban design across Europe. It examines interventions in the means and processes of designing the built environment that have been put in place by public authorities and other stakeholders across the continent in order to shape both processes and outcomes in a defined public interest. In particular, the focus is on the use of soft powers to influence design quality with the aim of understanding the scope, use and effectiveness of the range of informal (non-regulatory) urban design governance tools that governments, municipalities, and others have at their disposal.

The book brings together work from the Urban Maestro project, which used a tools-based analysis and a five-stage process – i) framework, ii) survey, iii) panorama, iv) case studies and v) workshops – to gather, capture and progressively understand the diverse approaches to urban design governance across Europe (see Chapter 2). Much of the evidence on which the book is based is compiled and collated at www.urbanmaestro.org.

The book consists of seven substantive chapters. Chapter 1 places the discussion in the context of Europe's long history and contemporary policy context for urban design quality. Chapter 2 introduces the approaches used in the Urban Maestro project and situates the initiative in larger discussions about urban governance. Chapter 3 presents the first and second stages of the project, the analytical framework and European survey that informed it. An important and longer Chapter 4 dives deeper into the urban design governance toolbox and, drawing from the third and fourth stages of the work, presents a systematic analysis of the key informal urban design governance tools used in Europe. The linked Chapter 5 examines the use of allied financial mechanisms and discusses their interrelationships with the design tools. Chapter 6 focuses on the final stage of the project, the outcomes from a sequence of workshops that ran throughout the duration of Urban Maestro. These discussions are summarised in twenty propositions. Ultimately, in Chapter 7, the notion of diverse urban design governance landscapes are discussed and the propositions are boiled down further into six 'C's that should inform practices everywhere. These are the critical prerequisites for high-quality urban design governance in Europe and, arguably, anywhere.

Acknowledgements

Urban Design Governance: Soft powers and the European experience stems from the Urban Maestro project, a unique collaboration between the United Nations Human Settlement Programme (UN-Habitat), the Brussels Bouwmeester Maître Architecte (BMA) and my own institution, University College London (UCL). I was first approached by Frederic Saliez of UN-Habitat in the summer of 2018. Frederic had seen my work on Design Governance, which resonated with conversations he was having with colleagues in the European Commission.

From the start, the project was genuinely collaborative, with colleagues at BMA – notably Frederik Serroen and Kristiaan Borret – joining Frederic Saliez, Tommaso Gabrieli and myself to develop a proposal and work programme that aimed to play to the strengths of each organisation. This meant the policy reach and expertise of UN-Habitat, the practice know-how and network of BMA, and the theoretical underpinning and research expertise of UCL.

In late 2018 the project, now named Urban Maestro, received funding from the European Union's Horizon 2020 research and innovation programme. It was launched in January 2019 and ran until April 2021, with this book taking a further year to write. This was a tumultuous period for such a project. Not only did it span the run up to and delivery of Brexit, but also the first year of the Covid-19 pandemic. The project's successful completion on time and to plan (more or less) was therefore all the more remarkable and could not have been achieved without the input, enthusiasm and wisdom of my fellow authors at UCL – João Bento and Tommaso Gabrieli – and all our Urban Maestro collaborators:

Kristiaan Borret (BMA)
Cecilia Bertozzi (UN-Habitat)
Terpsithea Laopoulou (UCL)
Colm Mac Aoidh (BMA)

Simona Paplauskaite (BMA)
Frederic Saliez (UN-Habitat)
Frederik Serroen (BMA)
Emilia Syvajarvi (UN-Habitat)

We are indebted to them, as well as to Ugo Guarnacci at the European Commission for his unfailing support, Paulius Kulikauskas and Laura Petrella at UN-Habitat for theirs, and Elena Marchigiani for her work reviewing the completed project. Finally, like all such work, it would not have been possible without the unsung inputs of countless practitioners, policymakers, academics, students, and other interested parties who gave up their time to share their thoughts, practices and experience with us. Thank you!

Matthew Carmona
London
April 2022
More information about the project can be found at
www.urbanmaestro.org

1
Urban design governance in Europe

In this first chapter, the experiences of Europe are seen through two lenses. First, a historic one, in which the governance of design has long played a part in shaping Europe's urban landscape, and second, the contemporary one, in which aspirations and means of engaging in design have rapidly developed and evolved. Setting the scene for this recent evolution, we explore the development of high-level national and related Europe-wide policy, marking a shifting context in which design quality is now firmly on both national and internationals agendas, if not always – yet – reflected in development practices.

Design yesterday and today

Europe has a long history of urbanisation, with the first cities dating back some 8,000 years. While the formal means of decision-making (if any) used to shape the form of these settlements are lost in the mists of time, it is highly likely that from the earliest times some form of control was enacted on where and how people could build. Inadvertent controls would certainly have dictated much of what was built: building technologies would have constrained building heights; the choice of building materials would have been determined by what was available locally; building form and spacing by climatic factors; the positioning of buildings by where routes and flows of people had already been established; and factors such as privacy distances, building orientation, ornamentation, and so forth might have been dictated by culture and tradition.

Such unwritten codes would undoubtedly have been highly influential, in different places leading to Europe's hugely diverse vernacular traditions that changed only very slowly over time and led to a uniformity that still characterises traditional settlements. However, from the earliest times there would also have been a need to address collective needs such as defence, access to water, places to congregate and trade, facilities for worship, safe disposal of waste (human and otherwise), and so on. Whether dictated by a ruler, religious authorities, or agreed collectively, rules on building would have been formalised from the earliest times.

The reforms of Solon the lawgiver from around 600 BC in ancient Greece are some of the earliest recorded. These included guidelines for the spacing and placement of houses, walls, ditches, wells, beehives, and certain types of trees (Harris 2005). Ancient Rome, similarly, had its regulations determining what were appropriate forms of development, typically for very functional reasons. The appropriate width of Roman roads – around 14 Roman feet (4.16 metres) – was laid out in order to allow two vehicles to pass each other, and restrictions were placed on the height of buildings primarily because of the fear of collapse – 70 Roman feet facing a public street under Augustus and 60 under Trajan (Harvey 2013). By contrast, while the architects and philosophers of the ancient world readily espoused the principles and importance of aesthetic considerations, such matters were rarely written into law. An exception was the Roman law of AD 45 that forbade the demolition of buildings in the countryside purely for aesthetic reasons, namely because wealthy countryside dwellers didn't like to view the ruins that were left behind (Phillips 1973).

The medieval world in Europe also had its controls on what we now know as urban design, which multiplied in the modern – and exponentially in the contemporary – worlds. The first Lord Mayor of London, for example, introduced an Assize of Building in 1189 to encourage construction in brick (among other things) as a defence against fire following the first 'Great Fire' of 1133. This was strengthened following the Great Fire of London of 1666 when the London Building Act of 1667 set a comprehensive set of rules that determined factors as diverse as the use of materials, building height, façade design (only four types were allowed – see Figure 1.1) and construction. With surveyors employed to police it, this eventually gave rise to the particular look and feel of Georgian London and continued to influence the patterns of building regulations for the next 250 years (Boys Smith 2018: 57). During this period, cities across Europe increasingly enacted formal controls of one form or another upon themselves as urban populations expanded and safety and functional concerns increasingly needed to be addressed.

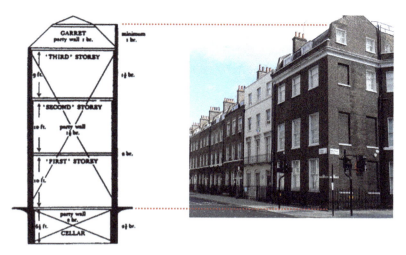

Figure 1.1 Building types were determined by the nature of the street they fronted. Here the second sort is shown that fronted 'streets and lanes of note and the River Thames' (image: Matthew Carmona).

Aspirations and challenges today

During the twentieth and into the twenty-first centuries, new policy positions and associated regulations multiplied alongside a greater willingness and expectation that the public sector could and should intervene to shape the built environment in the public interest. This meant either directly itself through funding and constructing infrastructure and development or intervention through systems of urban governance which became ever more sophisticated as a result. The trends also reflected better scientific understanding and greater cross-jurisdictional learning – locally, nationally and internationally – that easier travel and communications allowed. A case in point was zoning, which had its origins in Napoleonic France before spreading to parts of modern-day Germany (Metzembaum 1957). However, it wasn't until its systemisation in 1916 in New York City that the system spread like wildfire across the United States and from there around the globe, including back to Europe – warts and all.

Today, a much wider range of 'public interest' motivations are apparent for intervening in the design of new development. These will vary both in their scope and relative prioritisation from place to place, depending on local circumstances and identity (Gospodini 2004), but in the sophisticated policy environment that Europe has become, goals have increasingly swung towards urban areas that support the common good, in other words, places that support the needs of all groups (and the environment) in a mutually supportive and non-rivalrous manner (Berni and Rossi 2019). Carmona (2016: 707) conceptualises nine such primary motivations that to varying degrees will inform the operation of urban design governance:

- Welfare concerns relating to health and safety: one of the longest established of design-related policy goals is to prevent the spread of fire and disease, traditionally enacted through such means as density and road-design standards but which in recent years have expanded to broader aspirations for greener and more walkable and cyclable environments.
- Functional considerations to ensure built environments are fit for purpose: including a wide range of prosaic factors such as the penetration of natural light, space for movement, or that infrastructure is properly sized, all of which impacts on the day-to-day experience of using places.
- Economic motivations though the stimulation of higher returns on investment: because as well as having social goals, most public-sector players will have regard to how their decisions impact on the market, and in particular on stimulating local economies, for example by encouraging the right mix of uses. A further economic consideration relates specifically to public spending, notably whether development is likely to create management liabilities that will fall on the public purse, and how large these might be.
- Projection rationales concerned with how images project identity and meanings: particularly in a globally competitive environment where cities compete with one another for investment and where the quality and image of the built environment provides a very real and visible means through which to compete.
- Fairness objectives tied to agendas around a more equitable built environment: beginning with aspirations that environments should be accessible to those with disabilities, and extending to all those who for various reasons find the built environment either threatening, disabling, or otherwise challenging.
- Protection against harms to man-made or natural assets of recognised importance: protection of heritage assets goes back as far as the earliest welfare concerns, and today gives rise to sophisticated systems of protection with their own legislative underpinnings that also inform all other built environment systems.

- Societal goals focused on a broad basket of social benefits around the liveability of places: beyond fairness objectives, goals of establishing a more pleasant built environment in which people feel happier and more secure, and in which they consequently wish to spend more time, are a key objective of urban design.
- Environmental imperatives in the light of climate and ecological crises: these have impacts across the scales and associated regulatory regimes, from the strategic design of cities and decisions over where new development is located, to the detail of building and landscape design and construction.
- Aesthetic factors focused on creating a more beautiful environment in which to live: while often seen as subjective and intangible, the visual quality of environments has long been a concern of politicians and the public and therefore of policy, with early systems of planning unapologetically pursuing 'beauty' among other aims (Reynolds 2016), reflecting an intrinsic awareness that what places look and feel like impacts on every other aspiration in the list.

These diverse motivations have at various times and in various ways been 'written into' the public policy agendas of the multiplicity of related, but often separate, governance regimes that help to shape the built environment, including economic investment, development and regeneration; housing; planning; transportation; construction; heritage and cultural services; public health and safety; urban management; and sport and recreation, across the different scales and arms of government. Each, for better or for worse, impacts on the built environment and ultimately – alongside critical input from the private sector and crucial not-for-profit investors such as universities and cultural institutions – on how it is experienced by users.

Together, the motivations demonstrate that what is meant by 'design quality' in any one place is no narrow concern focused simply on what places look like – indeed even if limited to architectural quality, the meaning is far broader than aesthetic (Forte 2019: 37–40). Instead, it encompasses a broad and holistic set of considerations that impact on how places (from buildings to cities) are used, experienced and appreciated by society at large, as well on how interventions subsequently impact on the local economy, society, environment and health. Carmona (2019: 3) characterises this as 'place value', arguing that there is (potentially) a virtuous loop, with the degree to which environments deliver economic, social, environmental and health value determining whether they are intrinsically high-quality or not (see Figure 1.2). Or, in

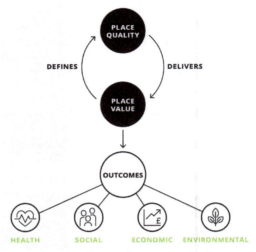

Figure 1.2 From place quality to place value (a virtuous loop) (image: Matthew Carmona).

reverse, design quality can be directly measured through 'the diverse forms of value generated as a consequence of how places are shaped'.

Yet, as aspirations grew and proliferated over the 75 years since the Second World War, critiques of what was being produced also proliferated. Nine critiques, corresponding directly to the nine motivations listed above, suggest that the urban fabric is too often:

- Unhealthy: an extensive literature and much empirical evidence has developed to demonstrate that built environments have become progressively unhealthy given the post-war move to drivable rather than walkable urbanism with its attendant ills of pollution, passive rather than active travel, road accidents and so forth.
- Fragmented: much has been written about the fragmentation of the built environment into islands of development connected only by roads that isolate functions, making it difficult to conduct multiple activities through single journeys.
- Commercialised: because, many argue, in the neoliberal era the role, functions and assets of government have increasingly been privatised or otherwise become subservient to private interests, including how the built environment is shaped in private rather than public interests.
- Homogeneous: as cities increasingly look to compete and, as a result, become more similar, as ideas and global capital become less

rooted in localities and investments are made to serve international capital rather than local interests, and as a public realm is created to minimise public maintenance liabilities instead of to maximise place potential.

- Exclusionary: sometimes due to their over-management (securitisation) and sometimes their undermanagement (neglect), urban areas have been critiqued as inequitable, creating places that are hostile, for example to the homeless or teenagers, or threatening and/or inaccessible, for example, to women or those with disabilities.
- Acontextual: and unresponsive to the historic context, favouring development that fails to engage with, and may even undermine or remove, built or natural assets of historic significance that contribute to the distinctive character of places.
- Unliveable: particularly for those without wealth or private means of transport because the public realm is too often harsh, sterile or uncomfortable and not conducive to social interchange or simply the enjoyment of being in a valued place.
- Unsustainable: in two senses, because environments have been produced for carbon-hungry modes of living and consequently use excess energy and generate excess heat and waste, and because in doing so they have become ecologically impoverished, feeding both ecological and climate crises.
- Ugly: because all the above tend to lead to environments that fail to nourish the senses, and that few find either attractive or otherwise stimulating, at least in a holistic sense, and because beauty is seen as a luxurious commodity that is only prioritised when it is paid for.

While some of the most persuasive literature setting out these critiques comes from a North American perspective, in fact the evidence is truly international, both as regards the challenges represented by the critiques and the 'place value' inherent in overcoming them through good urban design, or 'place quality' (Carmona 2019). In this, Europe is no exception, as arguably the majority of post-war planned development falls foul of the critiques, including the continent's ubiquitous peripheral office, retail, and leisure parks; inner-urban estates; residential sprawl, and urban arterial corridors and ring roads (see Figure 1.3).

In turn the critiques have fed the motivations and led to ever greater attempts among at least some governments (national, regional and local) to reinforce their policy positions and shape their urban design governance infrastructure to more effectively address their policy aspirations on

Figure 1.3 Unsustainable sprawl characterises much of Europe's post-war urban fabric, here (a) Berlin (b) London (c) Paris (d) Madrid (e) Rome and (f) Warsaw (images: CNES/Airbus MGGP Aero Maxo Technologies 2021 Google).

design quality. Although this has led to a good deal of innovation in the governance of design across Europe (as this book explores), the continent has nevertheless predominantly been building urban areas in a manner that is profoundly unsustainable (European Environment Agency 2019) and, social attitudes surveys suggest, is often disliked by European citizens (see for instance Baukultur Bundestiftung 2015: 20; Ministry of Housing, Communities and Local Government 2019: 6). This is locked into how urban areas are shaped and is in turn informed by an inertia built up over decades in which interlinked systems of investment, knowledge and regulation have produced patterns of development that continue to inform professional, political and policy responses and societal aspirations, and which cannot easily be turned around (European Environment Agency 2019: 367).

The politics of design

The profoundly political nature of design decisions relating to the built environment is strongly confirmed in the international literature (Netto 2017; Tonkiss 2013; Vale 2013), but, despite this, Carmona (2016: 715) argues that the notion of achieving design quality is essentially apolitical given that few would disagree that a well-designed built environment has value and should be aspired to. The politics intervene when we ask, how and by whom is that best achieved? This question is highly political, although not straightforwardly so.

In answering the 'how' and 'who' questions, right-wing commentators have often favoured a more free-market orientation, eschewing state intervention in favour of market players delivering what the market wants, the argument being that the market – not regulators – are the best judge of what is appropriate in different localities. At the same time, right-wing commentators have been among the most vociferous campaigners for conservation controls, seeing them as protecting property assets. There is also a strong right-of-centre argument for a certain view of beauty in the built environment (Scruton 2009). Among such circles the simplified lines of 'modern architecture' are often associated with the post-war welfare state and globalisation while 'traditional design' is seen as more market-oriented and contextual (Scruton 1994; Adam 2013) and, therefore – across Europe – as more popular (even popularist) (Mathieson and Verlan 2019).

On the left, by contrast, although political discourse tends to favour a more interventionist state, in the field of urban design this has tended to come up against preconceptions that design in the built environment (and associated heritage concerns) is an elitist preoccupation, concerned with maintaining property values and driving gentrification, and thus is generally a low priority when set against other 'big-ticket' policy priorities (Lees 2008). The arguments that a concern for the design of the physical built environment risks being physically deterministic typically originate with left-of-centre commentators (Cuthbert 2006), as do concerns that controls over design can (intentionally or otherwise) discriminate against minority tastes (Lung-Amam 2013).

The results of these conflicting priorities on both right and left give way to a confused picture where proponents and opponents of a public design agenda can come from, or come up against, both camps.

Consequently, an over-simplistic political analysis of urban design – or at least its governance – can be misleading.

The governance of design (for better or for worse)

Although argument for and against increased intervention in design can be highly (if not straightforwardly) political, day-to-day practices are often more unwitting than political. American scholars have traced the role and influence of regulations in how places are shaped, with arguments advanced that almost every aspect of the built environment is, in some way or other, subject to regulations that have seemingly accreted over decades (Talen 2012). Many of these have simply been borrowed from one place by another, with standards becoming 'the definers, delineators and promoters of places, regardless of variations in landform, natural systems and human culture' (Ben-Joseph 2005: xiii). Given their ubiquitous nature, longevity and undoubted influence, the argument follows that such controls are culpable in, if not of course responsible for, the problems of urbanity critiqued above. Responsibility lies with the politicians, professionals and ultimately the communities who continue to use such controls, often as a substitute for a design process that has the characteristics and qualities of place at its heart. As Carmona (2016: 708) suggests, these forms of regulation – which prescribe everything from parking norms, to road widths and hierarchies, to land use relationships, to density requirements, to landscape and tree provision, to urban form and layout, to construction – are too often 'limited in their scope, technical in their aspiration, not generated out of a place-based vision, and are imposed on projects and places without regard to outcomes'.

Such regulation-based approaches are also global, including in Europe (Punter 2007). In Rome, for example, despite more than 2,000 years of experience in regulating design, new residential areas can be built without character or quality. While the *Carta per la qualità* (charter for quality) provides extensive guidance for developing sensitively in the historic city, the *Piano regolatore generale* (general urban development plan) and in particular the *Standard urbanistici* (urban planning standards) provide only relatively crude standards to guide design in the city's sprawling suburbs (see Figure 1.4). In this case (as in many others) two-dimensional zoning is simply not sophisticated enough to deal with all the complexities of urban design when faced with private developers intent on returning a short-term profit at the expense of long-term place-making. Equally there are circumstances where clear, simple and even crude rules can have a huge and beneficial impact, for example on

Figure 1.4   Different developers have constructed standard apartment block types on both sides of this street in Rome, applying a standard road and footpath typology. Height and set-back controls have been respected but provision of parking (on the left in a podium creating a blank frontage onto the footpath, and on the right in a relentlessly hard street-level parking area) undermines any quality in the public realm (image: Matthew Carmona).

preserving the Parisian skyline (see Figure 1.5), while the most sophisticated rules can fail to create places of distinction (Figure 1.6).

Based on the often unsatisfactory outcomes that result from the thoughtless application of design regulations, standards and codes to places, Carmona (2016: 716) has advanced the design governance conundrum: 'Can state intervention in processes of designing the built environment positively shape design processes and outcomes, and if so, how?'. In Europe, evidence of the power of the state to both define clear place-quality aspirations and to shape urban areas against a clearly defined vision is widespread. Most powerfully this is reflected in the manner in which, in the post-war world, states used powers in a far more interventionist way than ever before, in both East and West. They did so in order to conserve and enhance (and sometimes even completely rebuild) Europe's damaged historic urban centres, but also – as a more paternalistic politics took hold – to design, develop and manage large parts of cities themselves in the period of post-war Modernist urban renewal (see Figure 1.7).

Figure 1.5 For decades Paris operated a simple height limit within its city limits of 37 metres. The policy followed the negative reaction to the 59-storey Montparnasse Tower, completed in 1973 (as seen on the skyline in this image taken from the Sacré-Coeur). While the limit has since been relaxed in defined outer areas such as La Défense, with its towering skyline, the historic city maintains its horizontal skyline and the dominance of key historic landmarks (image: Matthew Carmona).

Figure 1.6 In Copenhagen, a city known for its careful nurturing of urban quality, almost everything that can be seen in the image has been carefully controlled by a complex combination of planning and construction regulations. The result, however, despite the best intentions and high-quality materials, is a scheme that feels dull, sterile and desolate (image: Matthew Carmona).

Figure 1.7 The state largely took on the role of rebuilding Polish cities damaged during the Second World War, and subsequently that of housing the country's growing population. Although the historic centre of Gdansk (a) in the north of Poland (which had been 90% destroyed) was reconstructed on its original plan with neo-traditional façades that replicate those of the former burgher houses (in spirit if not always in detail), new housing areas to accommodate the city's industrial workers (b) often took a very different form. Both were driven by centralised and largely unaccountable state power, but also by very strong public-sector visions of what these different places should be (images: Matthew Carmona).

As top-down paternalistic and hierarchical forms of post-war government increasingly gave way in Europe to market-driven and networked governance (in the West from the 1980s and in the East from the 1990s), the state had less direct control over the shape of urban areas, relying instead on the market to establish a vision that the state then regulates, or on working in partnership with private actors to create or shape places. While these relationships vary from country to country and even from municipality to municipality, a key feature of the neoliberal era has been a waning of direct power vested in the public sector, replaced instead by more diffuse and indirect means to secure public interests (Adams and Tiesdell 2013: 106). If previously government (national to local) played the decisive role, then now decision-making is negotiated and shared between key public and private actors, with the exact balance of power between parties endlessly shifting from place to place and over time.

Theorising this, Carmona (2016: 719) notes:

At this level design can be as much about shaping the environment within which decisions occur as with the process of designing;

or to put it another way, the more one moves away from designing actual things (buildings, roads, landscape features, etc.) the more considerations are with the way that decisions are made than with the making of design decisions.

This is fundamental because if the public sector can sufficiently shape the decision-making environment within which decisions on design and development are made, then without actually designing anything itself, it may be possible to secure design outcomes that meet all public-interest aspirations. Yet, as international experiences repeatedly demonstrate, this will not occur by chance or through crude regulation alone. Instead, it will require the construction of a sophisticated system of urban design governance with the achievement of holistic design quality at its heart (see Figure 1.8).

Figure 1.8 New large-scale housing schemes in England vary hugely in their quality. Research has shown that those which benefit from the use of design codes (a form of site-specific design guidance) are around five times more likely to be designed well or very well than those that don't (Carmona et al. 2020). Similarly, those that use design review (the project-based peer review of design) are four times more likely to score in these categories. Another finding is that regions with the poorest-rated housing design were those with the lowest use of these tools of urban design governance, tending to favour the use of more generic design policy and guidance instead. The differential results, as shown in images (a) and (b), are very clear to see (images: Matthew Carmona).

Europe's engagement with 'urban design'

Although there are no shortages of the sorts of critiques listed above directed at the state of the European built environment, that environment undoubtedly also remains a huge cultural asset, a magnet for visitors that is a major reason why Europe attracts 50 per cent of international tourist arrivals (UN World Tourism Organization 2018: 15). Europe's architectural and urban traditions, from classical and gothic to romanticism, garden cities and modernism have long been exported around the world (in part explained by its colonial history), as, over the centuries, have its practitioners, who have been marked by their migration, networking and the active publicisation of their work (Ottenhyem and De Jonge 2013).

In recent years, the continent's rich ecology of architectural education, practice and innovation has kept it at the forefront of global trends, most recently on sustainable urbanisation (Beatley 2012), while its preserved historic urban environments and vociferous heritage movement has kept development practices in the most sensitive locations tethered to their historical roots (Zeayter and Mansour 2017). Arguably the incarnations of these traditions have not always led to positive outcomes, with the worst excesses of neo-traditional pastiche, car-dependant suburbia and international architecture around the globe each showing a direct lineage back to earlier European ideas and practices (respectively the Arts and Crafts movement and garden cities, both from the UK, and Beaux-Arts and Modernist ideas hailing from continental Europe), even though incarnations in Europe itself have often been more constrained than elsewhere.

Despite the rich architectural and urbanistic heritage that unites Europe, the term 'urban design' is often lost in translation. Loew (2012: 326) notes that in the Romance languages urban design often translates simply to 'urbanism', but while qualified architects with an education in the Beaux-Arts traditions of France are automatically seen as urbanists (as well as architects – the term is *architecte-urbaniste*), elsewhere the term is reserved for town planners, who are likely to be in a different profession. In the Netherlands anyone involved in the design of the built environment is considered to be an urban designer, while in Germany the profession *Stadtplanning* (city planning) is sometimes used to similar effect, although further subdivides into those that create (design) and those that manage (plan).

In the UK, architects and planners are strictly different professions, although urban design spans both and also has its own home – the Urban

Design Group – offering a limited form of stand-alone professional recognition, and also the Academy of Urbanism, which provides a home for a wider range of professionals with an interest in urban quality. This, however, is rare, and typically urban design (however referred to) is not regarded as a profession in its own right – or indeed as something separate at all – but instead as part of something larger, typically architecture and less often planning. A comparative analysis of territorial governance and spatial planning systems across Europe (Nadin et al. 2018: 34) notes, for example, that of the 29 European countries investigated with explicit planning laws, just six explicitly cite design as a substantive issue for planning, and a further eight note design to be part of the procedural operation of planning.

Farther afield, places as diverse as Australia, Hong Kong, India, Japan, New Zealand, South Africa, and the United States each have associations of urban design professionals, yet in Europe such bodies are notable by their absence outside of the UK (and briefly in the Nordic countries, thanks to the Nordic Urban Design Association, which existed between 2005 and 2016). At the pan-European scale, the European Council of Spatial Planners was founded in 1985 to represent the professional planning institutes of 24 countries while the Architects' Council of Europe, since 1990, has represented 31 countries with a particular focus on cross-border mobility, professional membership and practice standards across Europe. Neither explicitly include or exclude urban design.

In 2017 Placemaking Europe was established as a non-profit network for place-makers in Europe, and since then it has run an annual 'Placemaking Week' and publishes a regular newsletter in order to promote the sharing of practice and innovation (https://placemaking-europe.eu). Drawing inspiration from the Project for Public Spaces in New York, place-making in this network tends to be associated with public-space interventions, participatory practices and ephemeral urbanisms, and does not extend across the larger remit of urban design.

Despite the history and the continued ambiguity, a simple web search reveals a wide range of university programmes across Europe with a focus on the broad subject-matter of urban design, with the term itself appearing directly in at least nine countries:

- urban design/urbanism (France, Ireland, Netherlands, Russia, Spain, UK)
- architecture and urban design/urbanism (Czech Republic, France, Italy, Sweden, UK)

- urban design and city planning (UK)
- urban design for healthy cities (Spain)
- international urban design (UK)
- interdisciplinary urban design (UK)
- sustainable urbanism/urban design (Spain, Sweden, UK)
- design of urban, architectural and mobility spaces (Spain)
- design for the urban environment (Spain)
- landscape architecture for sustainable urbanisation (Sweden)
- urban strategies and design (UK)
- urban and landscape strategies and design (Germany)
- landscape urbanism (UK)
- landscape, built heritage and design (Ireland)
- architecture, ambiences, urbanity (France)
- smart city design (France, Germany, Slovenia, Spain, UK)
- design for public space (Italy)

The spread of the term alongside the increasing isolation of the subject-matter as an explicit focus for postgraduate study suggests a growing awareness of the need to distinguish the domain as an important field of action in its own right. This is mirrored in European and national policies.

National and European policies on design

The first Europe-wide policy directive relating to architecture was the Architects Directive 85/384/EEC, adopted in 1985, which (like the beginnings of such policy in some member states, notably the UK and France) had more to do with professional recognition than design quality. The directive established the mutual recognition of diplomas and other evidence of formal qualifications in architecture, while noting that 'architecture, the quality of buildings, and the way in which they blend in with their surroundings ... are matters of public concern'. Thus, although the directive recognised the public interest inherent in architecture, its scope was restricted to safeguarding the freedom of movement of architects within the EU, and to ensuring that architects from the different member states had comparable skills and competencies (Meijer and Visscher 2005). In essence it was a single-market measure.

From the early 1990s onwards, countries began to adopt high-level policy statements on architecture and urbanism. While not possessing any specific authority in this area under the international treaties establishing the European Union, the EU began to show an interest in the subject, following national trends and spurred on by its competencies relating to the environment (specifically the urban environment), transport, and supporting competencies relating to culture, public health and tourism, all of which touch in different ways on the built environment and its quality. In turn this drove further national and trans-European action until in September 2020 the New European Bauhaus was inaugurated, bringing the shaping of the built environment centre stage for the first time in the face of global challenges such as climate change, pollution, digitalisation, and a demographic explosion predicted to increase the world's population.

National architecture policies (and architects)

The nations of Europe have long employed architects in prominent official positions, typically at the behest of their monarchs to oversee important construction projects. Sir Christopher Wren carried the title Surveyor of the King's Works between 1669 and 1718, a post that dated back to 1378 and lasted until its merger in 1940 into the Ministry of Works. In essence the role – retitled 'architect' from 1761 – involved overseeing the building and maintenance of the royal estate but also amounted to an informal advisory role on all things urban. In France, Baron Haussmann was famously appointed by Napoleon III to the role of Prefect of the Seine in 1853, and from that official position until 1867 was able to replan central Paris to address the emperor's ambitions for a healthier, grander, and less congested capital. The Netherlands has had a Royal Architect (now the Chief Government Architect) since 1806, a position that illustrates how such roles have transformed. Although originally established to oversee key construction projects, the role became increasingly an advisory rather than delivery one in the second half of the twentieth century, and today, from a position in the Ministry of the Interior and Kingdom Relations the postholder is charged to stimulate the quality of government buildings, protect cultural heritage, and give architectural advice on urban planning policy and projects.

In the democratic era, the exercise of royal prerogative on such matters gave way to the establishment of national policies and regulatory practices that have touched on aspects of urban design. In the UK, for example, the Housing and Town Planning Act of 1909 had as its objective, achievement of 'the house beautiful, the town pleasant, the city dignified and the suburb salubrious', while in 1931 the Architects (Registration) Act set up a register of qualified architects to ensure that standards of professional competency were maintained. Over the years policy and guidance was added on different sectorial aspects of design, for example, the 1966 Circular (28/66) on Elevational Control, and the suite of Design Bulletins published through the 1960s and 70s on all aspects of housing design and layout (largely aimed at the public sector).

In 1977 a more comprehensive Architecture Law was established in France. This attempted to raise the significance of architecture by proclaiming it to be a pre-eminent expression of culture and a matter of public interest (Champy 2001). However, like the British act, its content was mainly focused on the regulation of the architectural profession, establishing a mandatory minimum floor area above which a qualified architect needed to be employed, but also establishing the system of Councils for Architecture, Urbanism and the Environment (see Box 14, p. 173).

The Netherlands, a first architecture policy

While the British took a largely sectorial approach to design – issuing policy and guidance in an ad hoc manner for different sectorial responsibilities (such as transport, housing and planning) – and the French looked to primary legislation to establish the role and regulation of architecture from the top down, it was the Dutch who in 1991 set out the first holistic high-level policy on architecture. As with most innovations, this pioneering policy did not start from scratch. Ten years prior, a bottom-up movement of local initiatives had begun, giving impetus to an overall improvement of the architectural climate in the Netherlands. The movement reflected a broad dissatisfaction with the quality of buildings and urban spaces developed in the preceding decades, and notably the public housing developed during the 1970s and still influenced by post-war housing models, but also the production of the private sector (Figueiredo 2010). This coincided with debates about the location of the new Netherlands Architecture Institute (NAi) involving the merger of three overlapping bodies (Van Ulzen 2007: 171) and the restructuring of the Dutch cultural policy which led the then Minister of Culture and the Minister of Housing, Planning and Environment to work together on a joint architectural policy with the side aim of bringing building and cultural policy closer and providing a bridge between the two ministries (Bento 2017).

This first Dutch national policy – *Space for Architecture* – aimed to set high aspirations on architecture and urban design. The initiative was pioneering in adopting a comprehensive approach that aimed to bridge the gap between governmental responsibilities on the subject – for example in the different domains of culture, building policy and planning – with the intention of raising the quality by thinking holistically across different sectorial contributions.

This strategic policy defined two main objectives: to promote good practice among public authorities and to create a favourable climate for architecture and urban design in the Netherlands (Dings 2009: 133). The former advocated setting an example to society at large, and development actors in particular, by designing and constructing high-quality public buildings and urban projects (Ministry of Welfare, Health, and Public Affairs 1991: 13). The latter intended to improve the architectural climate and promote a culture of design, for which a set of design institutions and a wide range of measures was advanced: investing in architectural research and education, promoting the country's architecture and architectural services exports, encouraging the establishment of a network of architecture centres across the country, and funding to the tune of millions of euros annually a range of institutions to deliver on the ambitions, including Architectuur Lokaal (see Chapter 4). Over time, this has led to both a concentration of some responsibilities in a number of key organisations (for instance the NAi) but also to a diversification of these and new organisations into areas such as archiving and exhibiting, internationalisation, talent development and education and quality (Kresse 2016) (see Figure 1.9).

Since 1991 the Dutch government has revised and renewed its architectural policy every four years alongside approving a multi-year

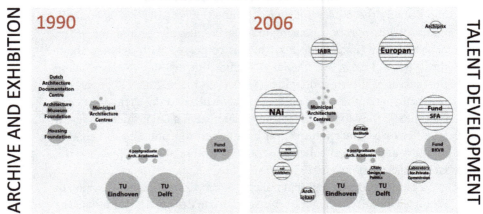

Figure 1.9 The changing Dutch institutional infrastructure for architecture (image after Kresse 2016).

policy budget, introducing new themes and updating its action plan. For example, its second policy – *Architecture of Space* – was adopted in 1996, widely expanding the scope of the policy arena with a focus on the idea of 'spatial quality' and cutting across a wider range of disciplinary areas, including architecture, urban planning, landscape and infrastructure design. Around this time, other European countries also began to develop their own high-level national design policy, including England (1994), Ireland (1996), Finland (1996) and Scotland (2001) (Bento 2012).

A first wave of architecture policies

In England, work began in the early 1990s on the government discussion paper *Quality in Town and Country* (published in 1994), following housing projections that threatened a major new wave of greenfield developments around English cities at a time when the market had become the sole provider of new homes, and their low density, suburban-standard products were being widely condemned (Carmona 2001). Although mainly an exhortation to others to do better, and with few binding commitments on government, the document and the wider initiative of which it was part put urban design (for the first time officially using the term) on the national agenda and led to an important tightening of planning policy on design three years later. It also led eventually to the work of the Urban Task Force, chaired by the architect Richard Rogers, to devise a national strategy to promote the urban revival of English cities, which concluded in 1999 with the report *Towards an Urban Renaissance* and in 2000 with government setting up the Commission for Architecture and the Built Environment (CABE). This new arms-length organisation represented a dedicated national champion for design quality with dedicated resources to match (Carmona et al. 2016) (see Chapter 2).

Both *Quality in Town and Country* and *Towards an Urban Renaissance* were highly influential, feeding into and informing policy at national and local levels, but neither had the status of policy themselves. This contrasted with the development of a Scottish architecture policy, which was an early priority of the first devolved Scottish Government, and in 1999, just four months after the new Scottish elections, the then Scottish Executive published a framework document for public consultation. Under the coordination of the Chief Architect's Office, a series of public meetings were then held across Scotland leading to approval of *A Policy on Architecture for Scotland* in 2001. In further contrast to practices south of the border it also led to a sustained governmental commitment to its principles ever since, with the first architecture policy followed up by a dedicated policy on urban design – *Designing Places* (also in 2001) – and leading in 2013 to *Creating Places: A policy statement on architecture and place for Scotland*, which brought the fields together.

In Ireland, the idea of developing a design policy was inspired directly by the Dutch example following an international conference held in Amsterdam in 1992 where board members of the Royal Institute of Architects of Ireland (RIAI) discussed the new Dutch policy and later persuaded the government to adopt an architecture policy, although the process was not quick. In 1996, a consultation document was published that resulted in the adoption of a very high-level national policy statement on architecture, but it wasn't until 2000 that an interdepartmental working group was established to define policy proposals and actions and, in 2002, Ireland's new policy on architecture was finally adopted under the title *Action on Architecture 2002–2005*. The document contained 29 concrete actions ranging from the merely aspirational to the administrative, to specific and funded proposals with a particular focus on raising standards within government-funded projects and recognising heritage values in design.

Finland was also directly inspired by the Dutch policy, a process that began with the appointment of a committee to prepare the first Finnish architectural policy, which produced a first draft in May 1997. After an extensive round of comments, the final policy was completed and officially adopted by the Council of State in December 1998. This policy was largely considered a reference (rather than action) document with a particular focus on younger generations and the importance of education for the creation of cultural values around architectural design for Finnish society (an emphasis that continues today – see Box 4, p. 131).

Within this wave of growing national commitments to design, some jurisdictions took a more formalised stance, reminiscent of the long-standing French approach. In 1998, for example, the Swedish parliament approved a bill on architecture entitled *Forms for the Future: An action plan for architecture and design*. The resulting Act put forward a number of objectives to improve the quality of architecture and introduced aesthetic clauses into the Planning and Building Act, Roads and Highways Act and the Railway Construction Act. Very tangibly it requires that all state agencies involved with the construction and maintenance of buildings had to develop and report on measures to improve the quality of the built environment in their respective fields of responsibility. In 1999 the Flemish government, within Belgium, took the decision to appoint a Chief Government Architect as an independent expert to support public clients and champion design quality across regional and local governments. The position operates as a partnership with the Architecture Institute of Flanders.

Reviewing the decade following the first Dutch policy of 1991, it is possible to observe a burgeoning growth of high-level architecture policies that has continued ever since. A Europe-wide survey conducted in 2003 identified six countries with an architectural policy, two more in preparation and five countries in which architecture formed a significant part of other national arts, culture or urban policies (Ford and Sawyers 2003). In these, 'architecture' was typically used as a catch-all term to describe a more holistic view of the built environment (incorporating the arena of urban design) than the use of the term in the Anglosphere would imply. In 2001 these forms of architecture policy began to be institutionalised as a pan-European concern, initially through a European network of policy experts that lobbied for the adoption of a pan-European architecture policy.

National to supra-national design policy

Following international interest in its approach, the Dutch government included an intention to organise an international conference on the topic in the second iteration of its policy. Consequently, under the Dutch presidency of the EU in 1997 the pan-European conference – *Policies on Architecture and Urban Design* – was organised in order to exchange views and experiences on the use of design policies. The event, in Rotterdam, gathered together delegates from ministries, governmental agencies, cultural institutions and professional bodies from across Europe, with a second *European Meeting on Architecture* taking place in Paris two years later during the Finnish presidency. The objective was to create a network between member states to share experiences and practices relating to the emerging design policies. The result was the European Forum for Architectural Policies (EFAP) and an agreed text highlighting the need to promote architecture and urban design quality at national and European levels, which was later presented to the Council of Ministers of Culture (European Forum for Architectural Policies 2007). Meeting every six months and hosted by the country holding the EU presidency, EFAP was influential in encouraging countries to prepare architecture policies, keeping them up to date and in spreading best practice around actions and implementation.

A Resolution for Architectural Quality

Year on year, a growing number of member states were engaged in the activities of EFAP, which in turn fed into and informed policy at the European level. The first official EFAP conference in July 2000 brought together representatives of the professions and authorities in charge of architectural matters from across Europe. During the event, a draft text for a European resolution on design quality was discussed and approved and in November of that year the European ministers of culture formally adopted the proposed policy: *A Resolution for Architectural Quality in Europe (2001/C73/04)*.

Although the negotiations on the text were led by the French, who held the presidency at the time, EFAP played a crucial role in helping to demonstrate and legitimise the shared public interest in design quality across Europe. Above all, the resolution represented a political recognition of the value of good architecture and urban design for the quality of life of European citizens, as 'one of the component parts of cultural identity and a vector of social cohesion and citizenship' (Ministers of Culture and Communications 2002: 6). It was also a proclamation of the cultural dimension of contemporary architecture and urbanism (and not just heritage) with the final resolution stating that 'architecture is a fundamental feature of the history, culture and fabric of life of each of our countries' and that it 'represents an essential means of artistic expression in the daily life of citizens and constitutes the heritage of tomorrow' (European Union 2001).

Specifically the Council resolution advocated for the convergence of cultural, spatial planning and environmental policies in order to focus on improving the living conditions of citizens and to encourage deeper citizen involvement in built-environment-related decision-making (Ministers of Culture and Communications 2002: 6). Like the national architectural policies that paved the way, it called for the active advancement of 'architecture and urban design quality by actions of promotion, dissemination and awareness of architectural and urban culture' (European Union 2001) and reminded member states of their responsibility to ensure that the commissioning authorities for the construction of public buildings and infrastructure demonstrated an awareness of quality concerns.

Although it was very high level and aspirational rather than binding in a concrete sense on the actions of member states, approval of the resolution represented a major milestone in the European journey towards a more universal and systematic regard for the governance of urban design. As a public policy concern, the interrelationship between

Figure 1.10 At the turn of the century relatively few cities in Europe were pursuing architectural and environmental quality as a coherent political objective; Gothenburg was one of them (image: Matthew Carmona).

architecture and the economic, intellectual, cultural and artistic life of Europe was formally recognised, legitimising the various national design policies in the process and encouraging others down that path. However, despite the emergence of sustainable development on the European agenda at the same time, including the *European Strategy for Sustainable Development*, which was approved in Gothenburg in 2001 (see Figure 1.10), an explicitly environmental dimension to design policy would have to wait.

The first resolution began the progress of more seriously developing a design-quality dimension at a pan-European scale. It related well to a second, more celebratory Europe-wide initiative. In early 2000, the European Commission (the executive branch of the EU) launched an international call for the creation of a European Union Prize for Contemporary Architecture. The winning proposal was submitted by the

Fundació Mies van der Rohe, from Barcelona, which since 1988 had run a biennial Mies van der Rohe Award for European Architecture. From 2001 this became the EU Mies van der Rohe Award and one of the EU's official prizes, looking back to reference the work of one of Europe's masters of Modernism – Mies van der Rohe – but in a new European award for the best architecture of today.

Now funded by the EU, this biennial prize is awarded by an Advisory Committee representing sixteen institutions from different countries. At this level the major decisions are made, including those relating to the composition of the jury, the appointment of independent experts to assist in the evaluation of entries and the detailed rules and regulations. The scheme relies on collaboration from 45 member organisations of the Architects' Council of Europe (ACE), who submit national entries.

Nominated works are publicised through the award website and, following a shortlisting process, jury members visit the work of finalists, and meet with users of the schemes. Following the final selection (see Figure 1.11) an award ceremony is held in the Mies van der Rohe Pavilion in Barcelona, with a catalogue and international travelling exhibition produced to celebrate all the nominated, shortlisted and awarded projects. Information on all of the works nominated is available online where, in line with the original mission of encouraging quality and

Figure 1.11 Winner of the EU Mies van der Rohe Award 2013, the Harpa – Reykjavik Concert Hall and Conference Centre (image: Matthew Carmona).

inspiring others, they act as a database of exemplary projects from across Europe (https://www.miesarch.com/).

Curiously, a second biennial Europe-wide prize, also organised in Barcelona, this time by the CCCB (Centre de Cultura Contemporània de Barcelona) was set up at almost the same time, in 2000. This was the European Prize for Urban Public Space (see Box 7, p. 144). That prize recognises not only the creative talent of designers, but also the importance of effective partnerships and underlying governance processes for the creation of successful places. Both prizes build on a longer history of pan-European design awards, notably the Europan competition which has run every two years since 1988 and has been open to young professionals under 40 years of age to submit proposals for sites across Europe (see Box 11, p. 162).

Conclusions on Architecture

The omission of sustainability from the 2001 resolution was all the more surprising given the establishment by the European Commission of an Expert Group on the Urban Environment in the early 1990s, and recommendations that flowed from this concerning the need to integrate an urban dimension into EU environmental policy. In 1997, following on from the publication of the *European Sustainable Cities Report* (1995), the Commission issued a communication – *Towards an Urban Agenda in the European Union* – that called on European institutions and member states to achieve more sustainable urban development. As part of the implementation of this work, in 2002 they supported the establishment of an Expert Working Group on Urban Design for Sustainability, with the main objective of delivering a set of recommendations to the European Commission. This marked an early – perhaps the first – use of the term 'urban design' in an official capacity within the EU.

In 2004 their conclusions – *Urban Design for Sustainability* – were finally published. The report explored redesigning and retrofitting existing urban areas, designing for greenfield sites, and knitting the urban fabric together to achieve an integrated city-wide vision. The report argued that achieving urban design and sustainability objectives were compatible and represented a win-win scenario, with better urban design also delivering more sustainable development. It thus set out a vision of sustainable urban design in a European context. It aimed for:

> an inclusive and participatory planning, design and management process that aims at creating beautiful, healthy and socially integrated and inclusive places; promotes equitable economic

development; conserves land; looks at towns and cities in relation to one another and their hinterlands; ensures the strategic location of new developments in relation to the natural environment and transport systems; ensures development is mixed and of appropriate density; includes a well-developed green structure and a high quality and well-planned public infrastructure and respects and builds upon the existing cultural heritage and social capital. (Lloyd-Jones 2004: 3)

Among a wide range of recommendations were recognition of issues that underpin the present book, namely:

- The updating of the EU's own 'soft laws' with specific objectives around sustainable urban design;
- promotion of changes to national laws and strategies for land uses, planning, transport and procurement to incorporate the agenda;
- developing urban design for sustainability guidelines to inform existing subsidy systems, including subsidies for urban regeneration and those for environmental, transport and cultural heritage programmes;
- promotion of environmental and integrated planning and urban design tools and methods; and
- improved mechanisms for sharing good practice.

Over the years that followed, issues of sustainable development came increasingly to the fore, beginning with the approval in May 2007 of the *Leipzig Charter of Sustainable European Cities* following a long process of meetings and negotiations. In effect, this was the first European Union-wide initiative for developing sustainable strategies for improving quality of place (Wesener 2011) and set out the EU territorial agenda. The charter introduced a set of common objectives on sustainable urban development and, in pursuit of integrated urban development, argued that 'quality public spaces, urban man-made landscapes and architecture play an important role in the living conditions of urban populations' (European Union 2007). Among these, it promoted the concept of *Baukultur* (building culture) as the sum of all the cultural, economic, social and ecological aspects influencing the quality and process of planning and construction. This German concept has continued to gain traction ever since.

Reflecting the foregrounding of sustainability in European policymaking, two EFAP conferences in 2008 were dedicated to the role of architecture in sustainable development. In the first, a declaration was approved emphasising the need to adapt architectural values to the increasing problems of urban regeneration and climate change. In the second, a *Manifesto about European Cities* (European Forum for Architectural Policies 2008) was approved addressing the vital importance of architecture in achieving sustainable urban development. These two documents informed the development of a second EU resolution adopted in November 2008, *Conclusions on Architecture: Culture's contribution to sustainable development* (2008/C 319/05) (European Union 2008).

Based on the 2001 resolution, this second policy continued the same holistic vision about the contribution of a well-designed built environment but placed a new emphasis on the contribution of culture to sustainable development. The text emphasised that architecture crosses a variety of public-policy remits – not just cultural policies – and has the potential to play an integrating and innovative role in implementing sustainable urban development, for example by seeing 'high-quality architectural creation as an economic stimulus and tourist attraction for towns and cities'. It was also seen as a means to reconcile 'the sometimes differing requirements of building and landscape conservation and contemporary creation' (European Union 2008). It called on member states to:

- Make allowance for architecture and its specific features in all relevant policies, especially in research, economic and social cohesion, sustainable development and education;
- encourage innovation and experimentation in sustainable development in architecture, urban planning and landscaping, particularly within the framework of European policies or programmes and when commissioning public works; and
- raise public awareness of the role of architecture and urban planning in the creation of a high-quality living environment, and encourage public involvement in sustainable urban development.

The resolution also invited the European Commission to 'ensure that architectural quality and the specific nature of architectural services are taken into consideration in all its policies, measures and programmes', and to 'encourage innovation and experimentation in sustainable development in architecture, urban planning and landscaping'. In response, the Commission published its own architecture policy setting out quality aspirations for all its facilities and buildings (European Commission 2009). The document largely constituted ten fundamental elements for evaluating the design quality of buildings that the Commission itself would occupy, with a noticeable reference to the lifecycle of buildings:

1. Urban integration
2. Accessibility and mobility
3. Respect for the environment and energy efficiency
4. Quality of construction and well-being
5. Innovation
6. Clarity of purpose and comprehensibility of buildings
7. Aesthetic aspect and image
8. Functionality, modularity and flexibility
9. Costs
10. Cohesion

It further espoused two guiding principles, namely, that a proper briefing process should be put in place to define the architectural programme and that architectural competitions should be used as the tool to guarantee a proper and systematic consideration of quality. In doing so it demonstrated at least a degree of naivety, concluding that 'the adoption of this approach should not give rise to additional costs' (European Commission 2009: 8).

Getting serious about design quality

In the years that followed the pan-European resolutions, the number of member states with architectural policies increased significantly. In the ten years between 2000 and 2010, Estonia (2002), Luxembourg (2004), Lithuania (2005), Northern Ireland (2006), Denmark (2007) and Latvia (2009) all adopted a policy. To take stock of this trend, in 2011 EFAP launched and published a European survey on architectural policies to map the progress of design policies across the continent (Bento 2012), a survey that was updated by the Urban Maestro project in 2020 (see Figure 3.2, p. 69). In 2011, 18 administrations (including Iceland and Norway outside the EU) had an official architectural policy, with an additional 14 administrations in various stages of producing one or actively considering producing one (see Figure 1.12).

The study concluded: 'Looking at the progression of national architectural policies in the European Union, like other public policies a process of Europeanization is occurring, where, through bench-marking, each country learns from the other and makes a greater convergence between the policies possible. Nevertheless, the nature and content of the

Figure 1.12 Countries with an architectural policy, or planning to produce one, 2011 (image: Bento 2012).

policies cannot be divorced from the constitutional, administrative and political framework in which the policy was developed' (Bento 2012: 86). As such, the pan-European resolutions were having an impact on encouraging states to promote architectural quality as a precondition for improving the quality of life of their citizens, although if and how this was leading to enhanced delivery on the ground was unknown.

Mapping the countries and semi-autonomous regions who had already produced an architectural policy revealed a bias to Northern Europe, but also that no two policies were the same. Not only were they produced by a diversity of different governmental departments – most often culture or environment and less often public works or interior – but even within individual jurisdictions, responsibilities for production were often not clear cut, in England for example cutting across culture, communities and transport. This simply reflected the reality of a diverse range of cross-cutting impacts, but also some of the challenges of implementation that such a fragmentation could bring. There was also a differentiation between those jurisdictions where a truly integrative policy was in place (a 'comprehensive policy' in the terminology of the report) and those where, in practice, the policy was either split sectorially (as in England) or reflected a more limited range of legislative (rather than policy) provisions, such as in France and Sweden (see Figure 1.13). Nevertheless, it was clear that the quality of the built environment was on the agenda across much of Europe, and increasingly governments were taking note of their important role in encouraging the management or delivery of high-quality places.

The Davos declaration on Baukultur

The next significant moment in the pan-European story relating to the governance of design came with the increasing foregrounding of the *Baukultur* concept, which had featured in the 2007 Leipzig Charter. This time the initiative largely came from the national level, and from outside the EU (from the Swiss). EFAP, which had been established as a not-for-profit organisation based in Brussels with more than seventy members at its height, was dissolved in February 2015 due to financial difficulties, leaving an advocacy gap at the pan-European scale. While less

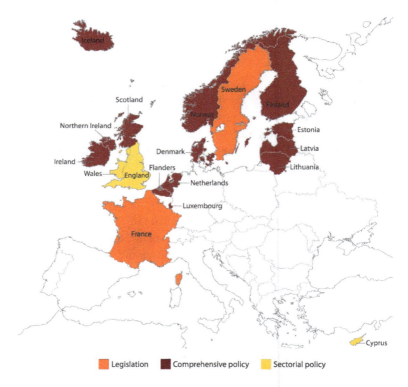

Figure 1.13   Types of architectural policy, 2011 (image: Bento 2012).

regular European Conferences on Architectural Policies (ECAP) continued, into this gap stepped the Swiss.

After two previous initiatives promoted by the Swiss Society of Engineers and Architects, in December 2015 the Swiss federal government announced its decision to develop a national policy for *Baukultur*. The word literally translates as 'building culture' and encompasses a view of the built environment that sees what is created – both in the past and the future – as a cultural construct with a value that should be recognised in design, management and development decision-making. Thus, shaping the built environment shapes culture, but *Baukultur* is also established through a particular culture of building that will vary from place to place. Both, it is argued, are worthy of refining to deliver better outcomes (Trigg 2017).

The concept was not new. Wesener (2011: 431) recounts how, in the Germanic world, it had been used and exploited in Nazi propaganda, then (as a result) disappearing from political discourse until its revival in the 1970s under a very different guise. Like the origins of the term 'urban design' (Carmona 2021a: 9), this time the concept was used in an attempt to reconnect the disciplinary fragmentation of the Modernist world and address dissatisfaction with the post-war built environment. In the early 2000s, both in Austria and Germany, these discussions started to bear fruit. In Austria, the Platform for Architectural Policy and Building Culture was established in 2003 and later succeeded in obtaining a parliamentary resolution to create a *Baukultur* report, now produced on a five-yearly cycle (https://www.baukulturpolitik.at) (see Chapter 3). In 2006 a law establishing a Federal Foundation of *Baukultur* (https://www.bundesstiftung-baukultur.de/en/) passed the German Federal Council, with the organisation setting up in Potsdam a year later with a remit to monitor and support the development of the country's *Baukultur*, notably by producing a biannual *Baukultur* report (see Box 1, p. 117).

In January 2018, at the Davos World Economic Forum, the Swiss Federal Office of Culture invited the European ministries of culture to an international conference on how to achieve a high-quality *Baukultur*, with the aim of promoting the concept beyond German-speaking countries. The two-day conference culminated in the adoption of the *Davos Declaration on Baukultur* by the European ministers of culture, calling for the embrace of building culture as a primary political goal.

The declaration itself is a short document of just six pages, and begins with an awareness of the damage across Europe caused by 'a trend towards a loss of quality in both the built environment and open landscapes all over Europe, evident in the trivialisation of construction, the lack of design values, including a lack of concern for sustainability, the growth of faceless urban sprawl and irresponsible land use, the deterioration of historic fabric, and the loss of regional traditions and identities'. At the same time it recognised 'the crucial contribution that a high-quality built environment makes to achieving a sustainable society, characterised by a high quality of life, cultural diversity, individual and collective well-being, social justice and cohesion, and economic efficiency'. It declared that 'we urgently need a new, adaptive approach to shaping our built environment; one that is rooted in culture, actively builds social cohesion, ensures environmental sustainability, and contributes to the health and well-being of all. This is high-quality *Baukultur*' (Office Fédéral de la Culture 2018).

The Davos declaration was largely an advocacy document and is therefore short on details about how its lofty aspirations might be delivered. Among its few concrete suggestions we can summarise the following assertions:

- High-quality *Baukultur* must form part of the relevant legal instruments in which the central goal of a high-quality built environment is made obligatory in all activities with a spatial impact. To do this, applicable standards and norms should also be compatible with the goal of high quality.
- High-quality *Baukultur* can only arise in the context of interdisciplinary discourse and through multilevel and cross-sectoral cooperation between policymakers, competent authorities and professionals, with all relevant disciplines and professionals taking part on an equal footing – perhaps through the use of design competitions – and engaging the participation of civil society and an informed and sensitised public.
- High-quality *Baukultur* requires the engagement of education and awareness-raising, with a view to enabling better judgements regarding *Baukultur*. In this, all those involved – both public and private sector – bear responsibility for the quality of the built environment, which will be passed on as a legacy to future generations.

Inevitably some states showed a greater commitment to the Davos declaration than others. While for some it reinforced plans already in place, including Sweden's plans for a state architect (established in 2018), for Italy it highlighted the repeated failure to get a bill with architectural quality as its objective into national legislation, something that Italian parliamentarians have tried and failed to do four times since 1999 (Forte 2019: 40). For Switzerland, which drove the process forward, the commitment followed a growing national determination to address issues of quality across government, with a team in the Federal Office of Culture tasked to take this forward. Two pillars were identified, the first to develop the content of *Baukultur* – what did it actually mean (scientifically and in practice) and how should it be used – and the second on spreading the message through international conferences and debates (https://davosdeclaration2018.ch).

An early output from the first of these was the Davos Baukultur Quality System (Swiss Federal Office of Culture 2021a), a tool aimed at better defining and communicating the concept, as well as allowing users to make assessments about the quality of their own *Baukultur*. To devise the system an international review of the literature and approaches to measuring quality in the built environment was conducted (Swiss Federal Office of Culture 2021b) and eight criteria were selected to encompass the different dimensions of a quality *Baukultur* (see Figure 1.14), each linking back to the original declaration, to a principle (explanation of the concept) and to a series of questions. In turn the questions are made available in a proforma that users can fill out to evaluate their own place and the extent to which it meets the objectives of a high-quality *Baukultur*.

Figure 1.14 The eight criteria for a high-quality *Baukultur* (image: Swiss Federal Office of Culture 2021b).

The system concludes: 'A place is of high-quality *Baukultur* if all eight criteria solidly meet the quality requirements' (Swiss Federal Office of Culture 2021a: 29), although the broad and very diverse nature of the criteria – from governance to beauty – arguably make them very difficult to evaluate or to relate to each other.

New European Bauhaus

Building on the momentum of Davos, in 2018 the *European Plan for Culture 2019–22* announced the establishment of an OMC (Open Method of Coordination) Group of EU member state experts (39 experts from 23 member states, plus Switzerland and Norway) focusing on models for achieving a 'high-quality architecture and built environment for everyone'. The final report of the group, published in October 2021, made six key recommendations (OMC 2021: 12–13, reworded here for clarity and concision):

- High-quality procedures and solutions become best-practice models: routinely adopting best-practice principles as defined by the Davos quality criteria so that decision-making enhances and never reduces the quality of the built environment.
- Everyone has access to knowledge about quality: democratising knowledge on place quality through educating about qualities and challenges relating to the built environment and spreading knowledge through awards and other initiatives.
- Decision-makers subscribe to quality: enhancing skills and knowledge in administration so all decisions on the design and use of space that have a long-term impact on the living environment should benefit from the latest expertise and competences.
- Co-creation with quality in mind: relating to decisions on funding, location, design briefs, construction and so on, so that all people and organisations affected by decisions have an opportunity to contribute.
- Consistent planning to achieve quality: injecting a quality dimension into planning across all departmental and administrative levels from strategic planning decisions to architectural decisions relating to the building life cycle, regeneration and recycling.
- Regulations, standards and guidelines help to achieve quality: ensuring that all formal regulatory, public-procurement and related funding mechanisms fully reflect quality principles both in their preparation and throughout their subsequent use.

The OMC Group represented a precursor and a feed-in to a much higher-profile initiative on design quality than had been seen thus far from the European Union, marking a major new and proactive move into a territory that had previously been seen as a local and national responsibility and which, at the pan-European scale, had been marked by high-level aspiration only. In September 2020 the President of the European Commission, Ursula von der Leyen (2020), announced the creation of a 'New European Bauhaus'. The reference back to Europe as the cradle of architectural Modernism was no accident, and was designed to position Europe as the centre of a new cauldron of innovation in urbanism, this time to address the challenges of climate change rather than those of urbanisation faced by the original Bauhaus in the inter-war years.

From this point on, the New European Bauhaus has featured front and centre in the growing pan-European interest in architecture, with a new policy on architecture issued in December 2021 titled (not very snappily), 'Council conclusions on culture, high-quality architecture and built environment as key elements of the New European Bauhaus initiative'. The new policy combines advocacy for the New European Bauhaus with a reassertion of the idea of the built environment as a cultural resource, advocating member states to 'work towards a holistic, inclusive, transdisciplinary, high-quality-led and long-term vision for architecture and the built environment by integrating different policies and expert knowledge in all processes, guidelines and co-creation projects shaping our living environment' (European Union 2021: para 15).

The approach directly advocated the eight criteria in the Davos Baukultur Quality System as the basis for informed choices concerning the shaping of the built environment and argued for member states to create favourable frameworks for high-quality architecture including 'regulatory simplification and innovative procedures that foster a high-quality-based approach over a solely cost-based one' (para 22); following best practice in the conduct of design competitions; using available financing tools to facilitate the delivery of high-quality standards when shaping the built environment; raising awareness of a high-quality built environment in formal and informal early-age education; and the setting up of advisory expert groups 'such as State and City Architect Teams'. In other words, moving beyond a reliance on formal regulation.

Although slow to get off the ground, the New European Bauhaus was immediately connected to the EU's European Green Deal policy and Renovation Wave strategy, which together aim to improve the energy performance of buildings and double the rate of renovation of buildings in order to improve the quality of life of Europeans, reduce Europe's greenhouse gas emissions, promote digitisation and improve the reuse and recycling of materials. Consequently, the New European Bauhaus is presented as an environmental, economic and cultural project for Europe, combining design, sustainability and investment, which will bring the European Green Deal 'to life' and develop a new aesthetic for green transformation (https://europa.eu/new-european-bauhaus/index_en). To achieve this, it is anticipated that the New European Bauhaus will be, at one and the same time: a forum for discussion; a space for art, culture and technology; an experimental laboratory; an accelerator for new solutions; a 'hub' for global networks of experts; and a meeting point for citizens interested in the topic.

The New European Bauhaus represents an ambitious attempt to capture and advance a very broad agenda that recognises the central role of the built environment if the continent's simultaneous climate-change and quality-of-life ambitions are to be met. With a budget of €85 million in 2021/22 to fund a wide range of contributory projects, the initiative aims to inspire a movement towards 'three inseparable values' (https://europa.eu/new-european-bauhaus/about/delivery_en):

1. Sustainability, from climate goals to circularity, zero pollution, and biodiversity.
2. Aesthetics, quality of experience and style, beyond functionality.
3. Inclusion, from valorising diversity to securing accessibility and affordability.

In contrast to previous initiatives but building on the *Baukultur* principles (see Figure 1.14), beauty is front and centre of these values, with creative design seen as the key means to deliver innovation (see Figure 1.15). Commenting on this transition, Kononenko (2021) wrote: 'Never before did the European Commission place beauty so high on its policy agenda', although he adds that this needs to move, first, beyond the aesthetics of Modernism that defined European cities in the second half of the twentieth century (focused on the economic conditions of post-war economic growth and a car-centred way of life), and second, 'beyond the neo-modernism that ... is often criticised as profit-driven, generic and soulless' in the twenty-first century. He concludes: 'In this post-Covid global ecosystem, Europe should be ready to act as a design powerhouse and a place where beauty truly is a public good'.

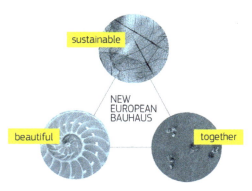

Figure 1.15 The three inseparable values of the New European Bauhaus (image: European Union 2021).

Interestingly, the emphasis also echoes post-Brexit built-environment policy ambitions in the UK (Ministry of Housing, Communities and Local Government 2021) which from 2020 was no longer part of the larger European governance landscape but is nevertheless pursuing its own related agenda with the somewhat intangible notion of beauty at its heart (see Figure 1.16) (Carmona 2021b). Curiously, it also echoes one of President Donald Trump's last acts in office, namely Executive Order 13967, which stipulated that all new federal buildings should be 'beautiful' – although in that case rather narrowly defined as 'traditional' in style, and preferably classical. That order was revoked by President Biden just 69 days later (Block 2021), although the collective embrace of beauty narratives by governments in Europe and beyond demonstrates a new-found confidence to venture even into the more subjective areas of design policymaking, although its interpretation will vary hugely.

Reflecting the scope of its agenda, the new European Bauhaus attracted criticism during the early stages of its development over its lack of clarity and focus (Naujokaitytė 2021). In early 2022, in one of the first tangible outcomes from the initiative, a suite of New European Bauhaus (annual) prizes were awarded to twenty projects from some two thousand applications that reflected the values of the initiative (ten of which were from 'rising stars'). A *Communication on the New European Bauhaus* (European Commission 2021) was formally adopted at the same time and marked the transition of the initiative from a 'co-design' to 'delivery of transformation' phase that aimed to put some meat on the bones of the idea. This included:

Figure 1.16 In England, the Building Better, Building Beautiful Commission argued for the foregrounding of beauty leading to revised national policy, the greater use of design codes to guide new housing development and the establishment of the Office for Place from 2022 to lead a larger culture change (image: Building Better, Building Beautiful Commission 2020).

- Announcing the establishment of a new European Bauhaus Lab as a 'think and do tank to co-create, prototype and test new tools, solutions and policy recommendations'.
- Development of self-assessment and labelling tools for use to determine and advertise if projects are meeting the values represented by the New European Bauhaus (see Figure 1.15 above).
- A request to member states to reflect their commitment in their own national initiatives, including those related to recovery and resilience planning.

Marking the mainstreaming of the initiative, and therefore of built-environment quality in EU work programmes, other strands of the work were in large part to be delivered through existing funding streams such as the Horizon Europe, Erasmus, and Life programmes.

Moving on ...

This chapter has introduced the field of urban design governance in Europe (and further afield), setting the subject in its historical context, addressing the question of why society should collectively seek to engage in the design of development, including some of the challenges, and discussing the recent development of the subject in policy at national and pan-European scales. From this it can be seen that, although the way in which the built environment is shaped has always been a concern of Europe's leaders – ever since we had them – in recent decades it has become an increasingly prominent focus of dedicated policy at the highest levels (see Figure 1.17). While this policy is largely aspirational, it is the hope of policymakers that it will eventually drive a Europe-wide change in practices whereby the quality of development – resulting in places that are healthy, integrated, vital, distinctive, inclusive, contextual, liveable, sustainable and attractive – becomes a routine consideration in day-to-day investment, development and management decision-making. In other words, in *Baukultur*, or what we might also refer to as urban design.

Most recently (between January 2019 and April 2021), the evolving Davos process and the New European Bauhaus formed part of the larger context into which the Urban Maestro project fitted (https://urbanmaestro.org). The extent to which such high-level initiatives will impact on the sorts of practices explored in this book is yet to be seen. The range of initiatives discussed in this chapter nevertheless reveal a gradual but increasingly committed drive to place design quality at the heart of European urban governance. The chapters that follow move beyond high level aspirations to examine key tools for delivery on the ground.

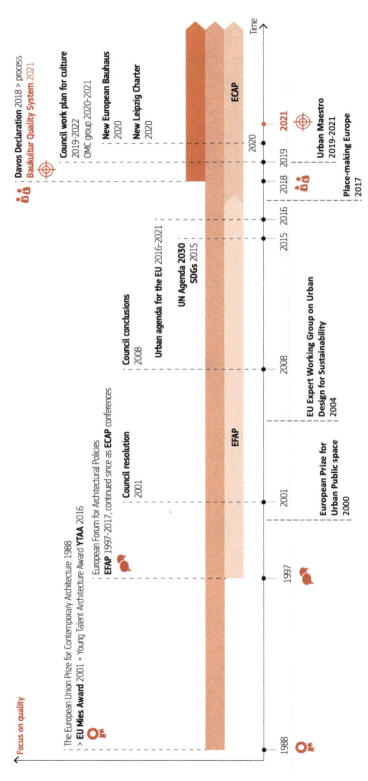

Figure 1.17 A timeline of Europe-wide initiatives demonstrates the increasing sense of urgency that design and place quality are receiving (image: adapted from OMC 2021).

2
Exploring European urban design governance

In this second chapter, the discussion takes a step back to examine systems of urban design governance conceptually. Given the diversity of practices across Europe, this is vitally important to understanding the differences and commonalities and means of comparing systems. The ultimate aim of the chapter is to devise an analytical framework as a lens through which to explore the governance of design in Europe, but also briefly to set out the methodological approach – a tools-based analysis – taken in the Urban Maestro project that underpins this book.

Systems of urban design governance

Today, right across Europe, local, regional and national administrations have established sophisticated urban management 'systems' that are meant to ensure the compliance of urban development, investment and management decisions with basic urban design qualities. Underpinning these are the wide range of motivations discussed in the previous chapter, from protection of the historic built fabric to the promotion of urban areas to attract investment and encompassing a variety of economic, societal, environmental and aesthetic drivers. The systems define the rules through which development interests, communities, the public and third sectors can all express their aspirations and seek to protect their interests, but are also multiple and complex, encompassing often separate processes of:

- Spatial planning
- Development management
- Heritage protection

- Environmental management
- Transport and infrastructure planning/investment
- Public realm/street management
- Construction control
- Open space management
- Urban regeneration/public investment and subsidy
- Social housing provision
- Public arts and culture

Each subsystem, to greater or lesser degrees, impacts on how the built environment is shaped, but the questions of how they operate, and what the motivations (values) are that underpin them, are determined locally across Europe, leading to huge variation in practices, including how these different roles are organised and related (or not) across tiers of government.

In its broadest sense, this is the realm of urban design governance where, even in the same country, practices may differ decisively from region to region, city to city, or municipality to municipality, with different subsystems controlled at different scales from Europe-wide down to neighbourhoods and communities. To add to the complexity, for every built environment intervention, the line-up of stakeholders, leadership and power relationships will also be different, although design remains a common and constant means through which the built environment is negotiated and renegotiated, shaped and reshaped over time in what Carmona (2014a) has referred to as a place-shaping continuum. Furthermore, quality in design will not be universally prioritised, or it may be prioritised in one subsystem but not another, leading to conflicts and to compromised outcomes. The story of carefully designed new neighbourhoods being let down by the application of over-engineered highways standards, for example, is a common tale across Europe (see Figure 2.1).

Direct and indirect design, process and product

Within this context, the governance of design is primarily concerned with establishing and shaping the decision-making environment within which choices about the design of particular projects (large or small) are made. In other words, it is not concerned with actually designing projects, but instead with setting the constraints within which others design. This can be discussed in terms of 'direct' and 'indirect' design (Carmona 2016: 724). Thus design professionals – architects, landscape architects,

Figure 2.1 The carefully structured urban framework of Penya-roja, a post-industrial regenerated area in Valencia, is marred by the over-engineering of its roads, making walking and cycling more challenging than they should be (image: Matthew Carmona).

engineers and urban designers – will be seen as designers of 'things', from buildings to landscapes, roads, or whole urban systems, but rarely do they have a free hand in that work. Instead, they react to and design within constraints established by the context within which they are building, by their clients, by local regulations, and so on.

While some have argued that designers need freedom to be able to express themselves fully (Imrie and Street 2009), others suggest that it is how they bring their creative thinking to bear to optimise design solutions within the constraints they are given that marks the true test of the best designers (Rybczynski 1994) (see Figure 2.2). Arguably, there is in any case no such thing as a free hand, since even sites that have not been previously developed 'will always be in, over, or under an existing landscape, which – more often than not – will be part of an existing urban fabric' so that 'we shape and reshape places over time' (Carmona 2021a: 1). In Europe, they will always be subject to at least some of the regulatory regimes listed above.

Although all forms of indirect design will shape the decision-making environment of designers – limiting and directing the scope of their design efforts – not all will be determined by the public sector or necessarily made in the conscious awareness that design

Figure 2.2 Frank Gehry's Dancing House in Prague, completed in 1996, draws praise and criticism in equal measure. It is clearly a creative and very contemporary building in a historic setting, but while it contrasts with its surroundings, it also fits in through the use of materials, proportions, and height and massing parameters that respects its neighbours. In this case not only did the site create its own constraints, but so also did the fixed zoning system of Czech cities where development quantum and heights are controlled; in this case courtesy of the *Plan of the Stabilized Zones of Prague*, produced by the Chief Architect's Office (prior to the abolition of that position) in 1994 in order to guide the post-communist restructuring of the already built-up sections of the city (image: Matthew Carmona).

outcomes will be impacted. Different forms of indirect design can be envisaged:

1. Spatial planning: before urban designers get to work envisaging possible futures for areas and sites, the process of spatial planning will frequently determine which locations are appropriate for development and which are not. This very act is one of strategic urban design, although one often made by non-designers for pragmatic rather than design reasons (for instance favouring sites that are available, easy to develop, owned by the public sector, and

so on) in the absence of a strong holistic vision of what the place should be.

2. The site and its constraints: stemming in part from spatial planning decisions, but also from land ownership factors (such as site fragmentation) and the associated aspirations of landowners, from physical constraints on sites and their surroundings (topography, hydrology and so on), and from regulatory constraints (for example, built heritage or natural environmental), the act of allocating/zoning sites for development and placing boundaries around them is itself an act of indirect design.

3. Design parameters: the parameters set in policy, codes, ordinances, standards, guidelines, and so forth, are typically established by the public sector as a conscious means to shape design outcomes, but they are often designed either i) as generic guidance in isolation from specific sites or ii) for particular sites or places but prior to a unifying design vision (such as a master plan) being prepared. How they are to be applied (and even by whom and when) is therefore unknown at the time of setting the parameters.

4. Financing: establishing the budget for a project, by a private or public client, in turn sets limitations on what can be achieved, though arguably, and within reason, good design can be achieved whatever the budget. Although budget will have profound design impacts, it will typically be set for other reasons relating to the local market, affordability, or to the business model of developers.

5. The brief: responding to the first three factors in this list, the combination of land uses and the desired quantum of development will be set out in the brief for a project by the client (public or private). These factors will, to a large extent, dictate the aspirations for a site and will fundamentally determine design outcomes, yet they will often be set without a single line being put on paper to suggest what form the development should take.

For urban designers working in a direct manner, on possible design solutions for key sites or areas, all these forms of indirect design influence and constrain their options and are typically determined before designers are appointed to give shape to the possible outcomes. Collectively they represent the indirect design context to which designers should respond and which – for the best designers – will inspire them to optimise their design propositions within the given constraints.

This means that many key decisions will be made by non-designers, some – accountants, financiers, land agents and so on – perhaps even unaware of the impact their decision-making will have on final outcomes. Most built-environment professionals, by contrast, will be aware of the part they play in shaping places: planners will attempt to allocate development sites in sustainable locations; site promoters will be concerned to put together development packages that are viable and likely to gain regulatory permissions; development partners will be aware of market and other constraints and the impact they will have on what is possible; and so on. For public-sector actors within this mix, normatively this implies a belief in the potential of such intervention to help deliver better outcomes, the ultimate expression of which would be the establishment of a culture where the quality of place is routinely prioritised (Carmona 2016). The use of indirect design to achieve this, backed by the authority of the state, represents a critical opportunity to secure such a culture.

A further distinction is important here, that between process and outcomes. While both direct and indirect design will focus on particular tangible projects or places as the ultimate 'outcomes' or products of development, they might also focus on the 'process' of getting there. This is reflected in the definition of urban design governance included at the start of the book: 'Intervention in the means and processes of designing and managing the built environment in order to shape both processes and outcomes in a defined public interest', which in turn reflects a long-held assertion within the urban-design literature that adoption of good process leads to good outcomes and poor process to poor outcomes (Carmona 2021a: 38).

This is an assertion that numerous studies have supported. To take a particularly well-documented example from outside Europe (Freestone et al. 2019), Central Sydney has long distinguished its approach to the governance of design through the mandated use of design competitions as part of the city's statutory planning process. Although such competitions do not ipso facto guarantee high-quality outcomes, their use sends a powerful message that: first, design quality is being prioritised (routinely in the case of Sydney); second, that the selection of development teams will not be automatic but is dependent on producing designs capable of winning a competition; and third, that the design team needs to be good enough to succeed within the constraints of points one and two. In Central Sydney, the process is 'consistently producing development projects that deliver on the City's design objectives whilst also satisfying the commercial requirements of property developers and having the support of the design profession' (Freestone et al. 2019: 306). In other words, there is a direct link between a defined 'good design process' – systematically forcing a greater focus on design – and better design outcomes than would otherwise be produced.

In Europe, also, studies have demonstrated the relationship between process and outcomes, including in the UK where a large-scale assessment of the quality of new housing developments against urban design governance tools concluded that schemes subject to design codes and/or design review routinely scored more highly in terms of outcomes (Carmona et al. 2020 – see also Figure 1.8, p. 14). Like the competitions in Sydney, these tools, when routinely used at the local level, seemed to signal a higher commitment to achieving design quality and to ensuring that developers employ suitably skilled and committed design teams capable of crafting contextually appropriate projects as opposed to simply applying standard house and road types in a repetitive manner. Resulting national guidance on design coding attempts to ensure that an increasing number of development teams follow good process to achieve better outcomes (Ministry of Housing, Communities and Local Government 2021b).

Good or bad, there is an ongoing and continuous process of change. Influencing this change will ultimately influence the outcomes it shapes. Seen through long-enough time horizons, this can be viewed as a cyclical process in which change in a locality builds on change that has come before and will, in time, change again (Carmona 2014a). In the shorter term, and with regard to individual development proposals, urban design governance interventions will impact across three distinct development phases:

- Pre-development: the period prior to any formal development interest in a locality/site.
- Development: the period following development interest being expressed and actioned, which in turn is subdivided into two phases:
  - pre-consent considerations: the period during which defined development options are being formally or informally discussed and/or negotiated; and
  - development delivery: the period of formal development consents and delivery of projects/proposals.
- Post-development: the period following the completion of development.

Together, these phases can be seen as the urban design governance 'field of action', and different tools will be more or less influential at different times during the process (see Figures 7.5a–c, pp. 279–81).

Hard and soft powers, formal and informal tools

Ultimately governments in democratic capitalist countries face limits on their powers, both on what they can and can't do and on how they go about doing it. As argued in Chapter 1, these limits are highly (if not straightforwardly) political with different strands of public policy rubbing up against individual freedoms including, in the case of the built environment, against private property rights. A large literature exists that examines the 'tools' of government, namely on the range of instruments, approaches and actions that policymakers deploy in order to steer the contexts, actors and organisations for which they are responsible towards particular policy outcomes.

As the exercise of government has become ever more multi-layered and complex and has moved away from either top-down, command-and-control approaches or hands-off free-market ones, an industry of consultants, journalists, professional politicians, and academics has challenged governments to innovate, reinvent, decentralise and de-layer themselves, and subject themselves to new performance regimes (Salamon 2000: 1612). To do this, governments need to familiarise themselves with the tools available to them, a basket of approaches that range from the application of softer influencing powers – 'carrots' – to harder law-making powers – 'sticks' – increasing in intervention through the following sequence of roles: i) steward, ii) leader (influencing and informing), iii) customer, iv) provider (of services), v) funder, vi) regulator, and vii) legislator (Siodmok 2017). Rather than the objects of government (what government is trying to achieve), these represent the operating processes by which it plans to get there – the means rather than the ends, according to Tiesdell and Adams (2011: 11).

The Policy Lab (a research group within the UK civil service) placed the seven vectors (or 'styles') of government intervention listed above in a matrix against different stages of maturity to identify 28 different ways that policymakers operate (see Figure 2.3). The exercise provides a valuable reminder that there are many more modes of government action than may at first be apparent, and, as these journey from soft-power to the hard-power end of the spectrum, they activate tools that move from informal (encouraging) to the increasingly formal (directive). Importantly, at the softer end of the spectrum and over recent decades, these modes of action have been increasingly implemented through arms-length government agencies or through engaging private, third-sector and community actors directly in the delivery of government.

Figure 2.3 Styles of government intervention (image: adapted from Policy Lab in Siodmok 2017).

None of these are exclusively the province of design, and in fact relate to the full range of state roles and responsibilities. Applied to design, all can be used to shape the decision-making environment within which design occurs by influencing, cajoling or encouraging other parties towards particular ends in the public interest. Siodmok (2017) directly relates the worlds of government and design, arguing that the creation of policy requires problem-solving and creativity (or design thinking) that moves from the creation of the right policy environment to guide decision-making, through the stage of system (or process) design to the delivery phase where the impacts of policy are felt. She equates this to 'design of context', 'designing context' and 'design in context' (see Figure 2.4) and argues that just as designers '"zoom in" to the detail and "zoom out" to the context when exploring new ideas, shaping both the brief and the solution together', so should policymakers.

Relating this specifically to the governance of urban design, the decision-making environment, design processes and design outcomes are inextricably interrelated (or should be). Thus, for systems of urban design governance to be responsive to changing circumstances they need to be capable of working through the scales and being 'smart' in the sense that they continually learn from the experience of implementation and refine practices and the decision-making environment accordingly. Arguably, this is both easier and quicker, and therefore more responsive at the softer end of the spectrum.

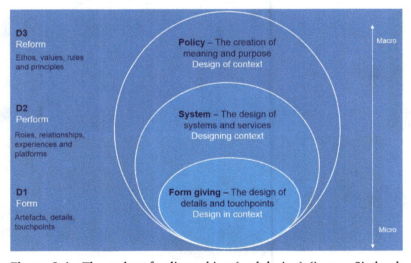

Figure 2.4 The scales of policymaking (and design) (image: Siodmok 2017).

'Formal tools' such as zoning ordinances (in the 'government as regulator' category of Figure 2.3) are legally defined in statute as 'required' roles of the state and typically have to go through a range of statutory adoption processes to ensure that they are fully compliant with other legislative regimes (environmental, human rights and so on), are politically sanctioned (for instance by a minister, mayor or municipality), have been subject to any statutory public engagement or consultation requirements, and are fully legal and robust, as set down in any enabling legislation. This all takes time, sometimes many years, and is difficult to change once it comes into force, making it somewhat inflexible. Set against this are the advantages of its statutory weight (which is difficult to challenge) and the transparency and democratic authority of its path into existence.

By contrast, 'informal tools', which are discretionary and therefore optional for authorities to use (or not), will still have to meet key public-sector standards of probity and fairness, but can be chopped and changed far more rapidly and with less public and political scrutiny. Design competitions, for example (in the 'government as customer' category of Figure 2.3), will sometimes be required in legislation but are more often simply recommended in certain circumstances (as in the Davos Declaration and in the second EU resolution on architecture – see Chapter 1). They can be organised speedily and flexibly (see Figure 2.5), although often less transparently and democratically than formal tools, albeit that is not always the case.

As the discussion suggests, and as summed up in Figure 2.6, the qualities of formal and informal tools are often contrasting. Arguably, therefore, overreliance on one category of tool over another can be challenging, but equally, they can be used together in a complementary way, as Meijer (1999) illustrates through the cases of Rotterdam and Le Havre, where informal monitoring alongside formal regulation act together to ensure that cultural value is properly weighed against economic value in areas of heritage value.

The different subsystems of urban design governance already listed will rely on different combinations of hard and soft powers and formal and informal tools. In the UK, for example, while highways adoption and building control are largely fixed formal systems with a minimum of discretion for professionals working within them, the operation of spatial planning and heritage protection gives professionals much greater latitude for discretionary action, using combinations of tools from the formal (such as adopted local plans) to the informal (such as negotiation). Throughout Europe the variation and resulting combinations of different approaches across different subsystems is huge.

Figure 2.5 The America's Cup Pavilion in Valencia was designed by David Chipperfield Architects in collaboration with b720 Arquitectos. Completed in 2007, the building had previously won a limited competition organised by Consorcio Valencia (a consortium of public-sector actors) with eight preselected teams. The need to prepare rapidly for the America's Cup once Valencia had been selected as the host city, while delivering architectural excellence at the same time, suited a design competition (image: Matthew Carmona).

Taking just one subsystem – spatial planning – a range of reports have examined the differences in practice across the continent. A 1997 study commissioned by the European Commission notes that while land-use planning systems across Europe have common roots in the

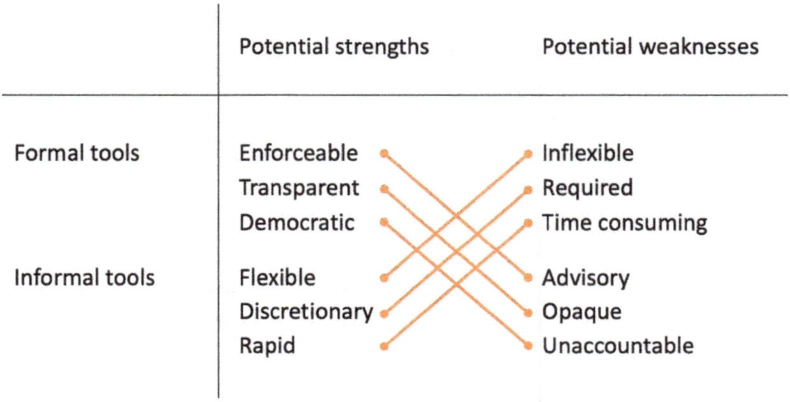

	Potential strengths	Potential weaknesses
Formal tools	Enforceable Transparent Democratic	Inflexible Required Time consuming
Informal tools	Flexible Discretionary Rapid	Advisory Opaque Unaccountable

Figure 2.6 Formal and informal tools compared (image: Matthew Carmona).

early-twentieth-century concern for housing and health and the problems that arose from dense and disorganised development, a complex mixture of factors have ensured that different arrangements have emerged in each country. These factors include historical and cultural conditions; geographical and land use patterns; the constitutional, administrative and legal framework; levels of urban and economic development; and political and ideological aspirations (Nadin et al 1997: 34). The authors conclude 'such complex forces are deep seated, indeed they define the concept of planning for each member state'.

Several studies in the 1990s from Punter (1994; 1999) and Nelissen (1999; Nelissen and de Vocht 1991) attempted to compare formal systems of aesthetic/design control through planning across Western Europe, but concluded in each case that the complexities of the different systems rendered comparison difficult. Despite the challenges, common themes emerged from the comparisons:

- The sophistication of approaches to design varied substantially from country to country and from municipality to municipality, with the most sophisticated systems in the Netherlands and Germany contrasting with the established but inconsistent systems found in England, France and Sweden and the still evolving systems in Italy and Spain.
- The much tighter controls apparent in historically sensitive locations, and the much looser controls elsewhere, although also a move (except in England) to use detailed local planning to establish basic but precise dimensional controls on urban form and associated land uses.
- A move to broaden the definition of design beyond urban form and aesthetic concerns to encompass issues of the mix of uses, landscape (including hydrology and ecology), public-space quality and energy use.
- Recognising the value of government leadership and inspiration (even in a context – at the time – of the rise of neoliberalism) in delivering good design through the increasing use of informal tools such as government commissions, public education programmes, design-led planning, aesthetic/design control committees, informal design guidelines, and design competitions; the latter also reflecting a related desire to avoid unwanted uniformity and instead to encourage design innovation and creativity.
- The increasing public concern for securing design quality across Europe, frustrated by the resistance of the development industry in

some countries (England, Italy, the Netherlands and Sweden in particular) and a tendency to retrench on such concerns in times of economic recession and in economically depressed locations, with the result that poor-quality development in itself acts as a barrier to investment.

- Despite the differences in traditions, processes and contexts, the beginnings of a trend towards a convergence in systems and practices of design intervention as a result of benchmarking between countries.

Twenty years later, however, there had been very little convergence in systems of spatial planning (Nadin et al. 2018: ix), nor in all the other formal systems of government that impact on the built environment. Perhaps reflecting this, and the final point above, there has been significant learning and sharing of practice across the softer activities of government that are not tied to the same legislative traditions and are easier to copy, more adaptable to changing local circumstances and more amenable to encouraging collaboration (ESPON 2018: 5). We will return to this question of diffusing practice in Chapter 6.

The governance in urban design governance

The notion of soft powers leading to the use of informal tools of urban design governance is echoed at the wider governance level in the notion of 'soft spaces' and 'informal arrangements' of governance organisations. Soft spaces cover the idea of places that are not congruent with administrative boundaries but are nevertheless functional entities requiring particular policy approaches (Purkarthofer 2016), while informal arrangements relate to the establishment of entities outside the formal governance arrangements and their specific legal frameworks, for example Barcelona's Territorial Commission of Urbanism, which brings together key public, private and social sectors to discuss the city's inclusive management (UN-Habitat 2020).

The fact that such entities are not clearly defined by spatial, legal and institutional boundaries opens them up to less formalised modes of governance, as well as to partnerships across sectors and boundaries. According to Haughton and Allmendinger (2007: 307), these forms of governance are complementary to, and not substitutes for, the harder and formal modes 'providing a form of lubrication to the development process, acting outside some of the frictions of formalised processes, engrained expectations, and institutional and professional histories'. This idea of lubrication to either encourage existing processes to work more effectively or to bypass them if necessary is a valuable one that applies more widely to the use of soft powers and informal tools in the governance of urban design, which were the focus of the Urban Maestro project.

Across Europe – as elsewhere – many tools of urban design governance exist outside formal statutory systems and processes, and shape the design decision-making environment through educating, encouraging and nudging stakeholders towards better design practices. Sometimes this will be indirect, through shaping the culture of quality, and sometimes direct, with a focus on the delivery of particular projects and places. But which tools predominate where depends, in large part, on the regimes of governance that apply.

Salamon (2000: 1612) notes how in the neoliberal age, innovations in the governance of urban areas came along with processes of privatisation, downsizing (of the public sector) and deregulation in an attempt to make government more efficient and less costly, more responsive to the needs of residents, more effective at achieving clearly defined ends, and less self-serving of the bureaucracy itself. He observes, however, that modern government had already undergone a fundamental transformation not just in the scope and scale of government action, but in its basic forms, with the adoption of new tools and organisational arrangements representing a critical part of this. Thus, whilst neoliberalism is associated with a rolling back of the state, the use of soft powers (instead of hard) and informal rather than formal tools of governance – in design as in other policy areas – may be associated with a rolling out rather than a rolling back of the state. To that extent, the neoliberal experiment of the last forty years is highly variegated (Castree 2008: 137) both between jurisdictions and within them. Sometimes confusion can reign between the desire for deregulation on the one hand and tighter control on the other (Carmona 2021b).

Although the traditional view of public power was one of command and control, where authority was centralised and exercised hierarchically by government, today governance starts from the notion that governments are severely limited in their ability to effect change when acting alone and consequently power is dispersed, with government increasingly acting in an enabling role and seeking to deliver its policy agendas through other actors (Salet et al. 2003: 8). Instead, public power acts through different tiers of government, through a wide range of government and arms-length agencies/agents, and through the resources and activities of the private sector (Pierre 1999). Relating this to the built environment, it has long been argued that the most successful policy approaches come about through effective coordination between the many different actors involved in their production: public, private and community (Hack and Sagalyn 2011: 266–7), and therefore that this way of working is fundamentally beneficial.

Taking a step back to urban governance more generally, three broad types are apparent in the literature:

- Hierarchical governance: is top-down, centralised, and operationalised through different levels of government – national, regional, local. Governance at this level will have access to, and will often rely on, the more formal (regulatory) tools of government to control design outcomes. This was the traditional way that government was done.

- Networked governance: has become increasingly widespread across Europe where decision-making is distributed across a more decentralised network, including to arms-length agencies, private actors and the third sector. Urban Maestro partner Brussels Bouwmeester Maître Architecte (BMA) supports the delivery of urban quality in the Brussels region and is an example of this form of governance, with the Bouwmeester position independent but appointed and funded by the City of Brussels (https://bma. brussels/en/homepage/). Networked governance will tend to foster a more diverse range of governance tools because of the wider range of organisations involved, many of whom don't have direct access to hard powers or to formal tools.

- Public open governance: deliberately facilitates individual and group dialog and engagement in more collaborative ways whereby groups and citizens can themselves advance and initiate discussions. Sometimes this is facilitated by state actors and sometimes it is the result of bottom-up action, perhaps attempting to fill a gap in leadership. Urban Maestro partner UCL hosts such an actor in the form the Place Alliance, a loose network of interested parties with a mission to campaign for place quality in England, largely through the production and dissemination of research evidence (https://placealliance.org.uk – see Box 2, p. 120). Given their total absence of hard powers or even publicly bestowed authority, actors in this sort of governance will have to look beyond traditional means of top-down power if they are to have an influence.

The Urban Maestro project examined organisations and practices from across these different modes of governance. This simply reflects the reality that different modes of governance exist simultaneously, even in the same territory, as different problems and different contexts give rise to diverse local relationships and therefore to varied forms of governance.

Urban design governance landscapes

Seen in this way, any locality is likely to be subject to overlapping urban design governance processes depending on where and with whom competences lie. A city may be made up of various municipalities, each with their own processes, network of powers and of course physical and social contexts. Overlaying these might be a city or regional authority with separate competences relating to design. The nation-state itself might also exercise competences, such as the setting of policy or the allocation of public funding, that impact locally on design and its governance. In Europe an intergovernmental level is also increasingly apparent (as discussed in Chapter 1) and how such influences trickle down will be significant, as well as how private, community and non-governmental organisations influence practices across all levels.

This can be envisaged as the 'urban design governance landscape', in other words the sum total of all of the overlapping responsibilities, approaches and influences on urban design governance decision-making as they impact on any particular location (see Figure 2.7). In turn this reflects the broader notion of places being shaped over time as part of

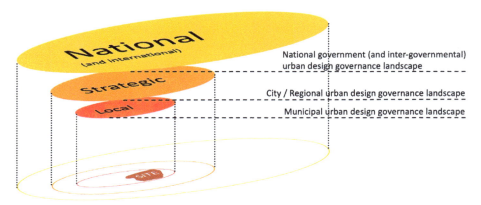

Figure 2.7 Urban design governance landscapes across scales (image: Matthew Carmona).

local place-shaping continua (Carmona 2014a: 33) in which practices and outcomes are constantly informed by:

- Historical place-based modes of operation (how things have always been done);
- the contemporary policy-influenced political-economic context (the political economy today); and
- the particular set of stakeholder power relationships (generally and in relation to each project or intervention).

Across Europe there will be many thousands of local urban design governance landscapes exhibiting wide variations in practices to meet local needs depending on the local organisation of government, the interactions across the different levels and how responsibilities are shared between them, the traditions of governance (the particular balance of and between the three types previously discussed), and the consequential engagement and sharing of responsibilities with other stakeholders – public, private, third-sector and community.

All this complexity implies that understanding the European urban design governance landscape (if such a thing even exists, given the variety of provision) represents a complex, perhaps even impossible, task. For this reason, the Urban Maestro project adopted an approach to understanding European practices of urban design governance based on the type of 'tools' being used for the governance of design, rather than seeking to understand (in detail) what forms of governance were leading to which tools.

An analytical framework

Reflecting on the discussion so far, it is possible to draw out some key concepts and diagrammatically represent their relationships as they define the field of urban design governance (see Figure 2.8). At the core of the diagram is the decision-making environment that is shaped by the governance regime and the particular landscape of stakeholders and powers (hard and soft). In turn, these inform the creation and use of particular combinations of formal and informal tools. Ultimately, through the design aspirations indirectly defined in these, and via their direct application to real projects and places, design processes – and finally design products – are shaped.

Urban Maestro lasted just over two years, from January 2019 to April 2021, and in that time represented a deep dive into practices of informal urban design governance across Europe (represented in the

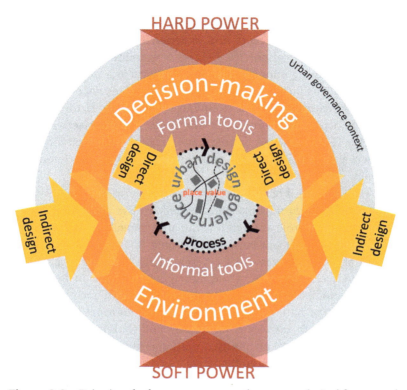

Figure 2.8   Bringing the key concepts together: an analytical framework (image: Matthew Carmona).

bottom half of Figure 2.8). However, as the diagram suggests, these are to a large degree dependent on, or otherwise inform the use of, formal processes. So, although the window into the subject was a relatively narrow if vitally important one – a sub-dimension of a sub-field of urban design, the field of investigation turned out to be wide. This is reflected throughout the remainder of the book, following a brief introduction to the project itself.

The Urban Maestro method: a tools-based analysis

The Urban Maestro initiative stemmed from initial conversations held in 2018 between UN-Habitat and the European Commission on how innovative governance practices might be applied to securing spatial quality in the built environment. Although pan-European studies on the subject were thin on the ground, research conducted at UCL offered a promising set of concepts and experiences that could inform a Europe-wide investigation. The UCL work examined the decade-long experience of using informal design governance at a national scale in the UK, and was published in the book *Design Governance: The CABE experiment* (Carmona et al. 2016). Alongside UN-Habitat, the inclusion of UCL as a research partner and the Brussels Bouwmeester Maître Architecte (BMA) as a practice partner – drawing from their long-term experience using informal tools of urban design governance – made up the team.

The UK analysis of the work of CABE (Commission for Architecture and the Built Environment) had focused on the tools used by the organisation in its role as English national champion for design quality in the built environment between 1999 and 2011. CABE was clearly influential, but its powers were severely limited and the organisation never had access to some of the most powerful tools in the design governance toolbox. Instead, CABE represented a unique experiment, exploring at the national scale the use of the informal tools – 'tools without teeth' – to advance a national agenda (in England) that from 1997 had increasingly emphasised the importance of design quality. CABE was established to lead that drive.

Within the tools of government literature, most studies still focus on the utility of single tools and their use in particular circumstances, rather than on the interrelationships between tools and on the decision-making processes used to distinguish when to use one tool rather than another (Linder and Peters 1989: 55–6). The demise of CABE in 2011 as a casualty of the austerity policies of the time represented an important moment and an opportune window through which to take a fundamental look at the full range of design governance tools that the organisation had used.

The exercise revealed that there are many more tools than are often recognised in the urban design literature, and certainly more than are typically used. Concluding the study, Carmona (2017: 32) argued:

Failing to utilise them more fully means that those who are responsible for shaping the quality of the built environment are typically doing so with one hand tied behind their back, particularly when it comes to shaping the all-important decision-making environment within which project and place-specific design decisions occur.

and that:

> Analysis of the CABE toolkit has forcefully revealed that those responsible should fully embrace the informal as well as formal modes of design governance and should consider such processes to be part of a long-term and necessary societal investment in place.

Drawing on the CABE analysis, Urban Maestro was a piece of qualitative cross-national comparative research and collective learning (Mangen 1999). Although concepts, contexts and practices vary hugely across Europe, enough commonalities exist to allow meaningful comparison, theorisation and analysis, all related through the robust analytical framework already presented (see Figure 2.8 above). To achieve its ends, the project used five research/learning approaches (see Figure 2.9) intended to gather and capture information about the diverse approaches to urban design governance across Europe:

1. Typology: utilising the earlier CABE research as a stepping-off point, a tools-based conceptualisation of urban design governance was constructed, tested and refined in order to establish a European typology of urban design governance tools (see Chapter 3).
2. Survey: a Europe-wide survey of informal urban design governance practices was conducted, primarily at the level of nation-states as a first means to test and refine this, and to begin the process of gathering experiences from across Europe (see Chapter 3).
3. Panorama: the systematic compilation of a Europe-wide panorama of innovative practices of informal urban design governance, and its publication at https://urbanmaestro.org. This formed the largest component of the work (see Chapters 4 and 5).
4. Case studies: chosen from the panorama, and focusing in greater depth on a range of innovative and representative practices of informal urban design governance in order to gain greater understanding and insight of their use and utility (see Chapters 4 and 5).
5. Workshops: examining the innovative practices further through a series of curated conversations with a diverse range of practitioner audiences across seven separate events spread through 2019 and 2020, some online and others in person (see Chapter 6).

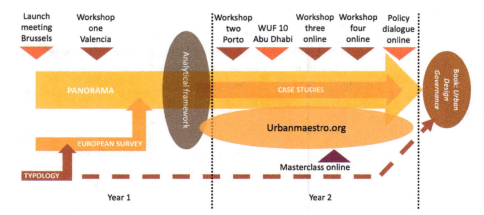

Figure 2.9 The Urban Maestro method (image: Matthew Carmona).

The five approaches ran simultaneously and were carefully coordinated, with the workshops providing opportunities to consider in greater depth, and in a comparative manner, practices that had been revealed in the survey, panorama and case studies. In turn, the workshops offered an opportunity to identify further practices and to critique and ultimately better understand those that other streams of the work had already revealed. Overarching findings from the project are brought together in Chapter 7.

3
A European typology of tools

In this chapter, the first two approaches adopted by the Urban Maestro project are explored: typology and survey. The chapter begins by setting out the result of a Europe-wide survey of informal urban design governance practices, examining, first, the spread and focus of high-level architecture policies across Europe, and second, the use of informal policy tools. The survey, in large part, was directed at national governments and institutions, and therefore the results are focused at that top-down scale. Together they helped to define and refine a European typology of urban design governance tools, and it is that which is presented in the second half of the chapter. To illustrate how this applies on the ground, the chapter concludes with three short case studies of cities – Lisbon, London and Vienna – setting out the full landscape of urban design governance practices in each of these complex urban contexts.

Surveying Europe

As already noted, there is a much larger toolkit available to the public sector than is generally realised through which to positively shape the built environment. Research introduced in Chapter 2 focusing on the period 1999–2011 in the UK identified a wide range of informal (non-statutory) tools that were in active use during the period (Carmona 2017). That research classified these approaches against five categories of informal tool: evidence, knowledge, promotion, evaluation and assistance (see Figure 3.1) and this classification was initially used in an unmodified form to structure the pan-European survey.

The survey represented the first attempt to establish a Europe-wide picture of how such tools are being used. It was conducted between March and December 2019 with personalised invitations sent by email to

Figure 3.1 Classification of informal design governance tools used by CABE (image: Matthew Carmona).

institutions in April and a follow-up in May and over a hundred telephone calls made to encourage participation in the survey. The questionnaire was sent to 124 governmental, local government and non-governmental/arms-length governmental agencies across Europe with responsibility for design covering 32 European countries (in the EU and EFTA) and separately to the three regions of Belgium and the four countries of the UK. A response rate of 51 per cent was received, including 31 national-level responses, giving invaluable information about the tools used and the structure of provision in each territory.

A series of open questions were asked relating, first, to the high-level architectural policies of Europe's nation states; second, to collecting information on the sorts of informal tools of urban design governance that were in use in each jurisdiction against the five-part classification seen in Figure 3.1; and third, to the use of financial mechanisms alongside design (see Chapter 6).

The spread of architecture policies

The survey confirmed the continuation of the cultural turn focused on prioritising a high-quality built environment across Europe (at least in policy), with many European countries and regions developing their own high-level architecture (and urban design) policies. Twenty-seven administrations stated that they have an official policy document of this type, seven stated that they do not have one, and three that it was not possible to collect this information.

In the intervening years since the last survey (Bento 2012), the French government, for example, had adopted its first *National Strategy for Architecture* with six clear objectives and thirty more concrete measures, including an aspiration to raise awareness and develop knowledge of architecture by the general public and all public and private urban stakeholders. In the same year (2015), after a long period of preparation, Portugal and Hungary also approved their policies, with the Austrian Council of Ministers following two years later with its *Federal Guidelines on Building Culture*. This argues that a comprehensive strategy is required at the federal level in order to anchor building culture across all departments and disciplines at the federal, provincial, and local scales. The policy aims to promote building culture and create a broader societal awareness of its principles, especially among leaders in politics, business, and public administration, including through promoting awareness and public participation, through research and the transfer of knowledge and expertise, and through coordination and cooperation across governmental layers.

Among the seven administrations that did not have an official policy document on design in the built environment, five – Germany, Romania, Italy, Spain and Switzerland – anticipated formally adopting one in the near future. Of these, Switzerland issued a national policy on *Baukultur* for public consultation in 2019 and formally adopted *Baukultur Strategy* in 2020, shortly after the survey closed. In the same year the Romanian Order of Architects and the Ministry of Regional Development and Public Administration in Romania signed a joint statement to work towards establishing a national architecture policy through an open decision-making process, and Germany announced its intention of developing its own national policy document on *Baukultur*, building on the extensive work of the Federal Foundation for Baukultur established in 2006 (see Box 1, p. 117).

In 2020 the Spanish Ministry of Transport, Mobility and Urban Agenda launched a public consultation to inform the legislative development of a future *Law on Architecture Quality in the Built Environment* (https://leyarquitectura.mitma.es/), although the Italian experience suggests that such efforts are not always rapid. The Italian Council of Ministers first approved a *Bill on Architectural Quality* in 2008, although this only made it as far as the Senate and was never approved. In 2018, after other initiatives, the Congress of the National Council of Architects approved a manifesto asking the government to develop an architecture law. This was followed by a civil movement led by the MAXXI National Museum of 21st Century Arts which promoted several debates on the subject (http://www.versounaleggeperlarchitettura.it/). In December 2020 the Higher Council for Public Works approved draft *Guidelines for the Quality of Architecture* (rather than a law) prepared by the Ministry for Cultural Heritage, which is expected to be adopted in 2022. The Spanish equivalent will enshrine in law the importance of achieving a high-quality built environment as a key means of securing people's well-being, environmental sustainability, social cohesion, and sense of identity. It will follow on the heels of a 2017 *Law on Architecture* enacted in Catalonia introducing a range of mechanisms and advisory bodies on urban quality across the province dealing with everything from procurement to design awards (Forte 2019: 43).

The recent additions, and those soon to be delivered, mean that Europe is largely covered by such high-level architecture policies (see Figure 3.2). This marks a significant step forward from the situation recorded in 2012 and discussed in Chapter 1 (see Figure 1.12). Digging deeper, the policy documents marked similar variations in type to those recorded previously:

- Twenty-one administrations had comprehensive policy documents of the type adopted in France and Austria, of a strategic nature and with a broad scope, crossing a wide range of departmental responsibilities and involving multiple actors in their implementation (see Table 3.1).
- Four – Cyprus, England, Malta and Wales – had sectoral policies involving fewer departments and functions within specific governmental responsibilities, such as urban planning, cultural heritage, or public buildings. Cyprus, for example, includes design policies in all statutory spatial development plans that are prepared under the Town and Country Planning Law, all of which include an annex with *Principles and Guidelines for the Aesthetic Improvement and Upgrading of the Quality of the Built Environment*. Most of these were introduced in the 1990s and significantly elaborated in the decade after 2010. In addition, a separate national policy on architectural competitions for public buildings has been adopted.
- The third type are official documents that cover only the activities of the public institution that developed them. The chief government architects (Bouwmeesters) appointed by the Belgian regions take this approach. The Flemish Bouwmeester, for example, was established to provide long-term support to the regional government in preparing and implementing an architectural policy for Flanders. Every four years, the Bouwmeester presents a policy document to be approved by government; that for 2017 is entitled *Creating Space for People and Nature*.

Have a policy
document

Anticipating a
policy document

Figure 3.2 Countries with an official publication, memorandum or policy on architecture/urban design or who were anticipating adopting one in the near future (image: Urban Maestro).

The dominance of comprehensive policy approaches ensures that the design of the built environment is seen as a strategic concern across the wide range of sectoral remits covered by the different 'systems' of urban governance listed in Chapter 2 and managed by varying governmental departments. By addressing the design of the built environment in this holistic way, governments can set high aspirations for design quality – albeit not legally binding – in such a way that the responsibility of all public authorities (and others) is made explicit.

Across Europe, with very few exceptions, this move to deal with design more comprehensively as a strategic (national) policy is being increasingly prioritised. In some countries this has been driven by the Europe-wide policy initiatives discussed in Chapter 1; elsewhere the benchmarking of neighbours has led to a convergence in practices, with administrations that have never previously developed a comprehensive policy framework on design now doing so. England, in recent years, has been a notable exception. During the 2000s the country developed one of

Table 3.1 Comprehensive architectural policies (table: Urban Maestro).

Year	Country	Policy document
1991	Netherlands	Space for Architecture
1992	Norway	Surroundings as Culture: Action Programme for Aesthetics in Public Environment
1996	Denmark	Architecture 1996
1997	Netherlands	The Architecture of Space
1997	Norway	Aesthetics in Government Building and Constructions
1998	Finland	The Finnish Architectural Policy
2001	Netherlands	Shaping the Netherlands
2001	Scotland	A Policy on Architecture for Scotland
2002	Estonia	The Architectural Policy of Estonia
2002	Ireland	Action on Architecture: 2002–05
2004	Luxembourg	Pour une Politique architecturale
2005	Lithuania	Architectural Policy Trends in the Republic of Lithuania
2005	Netherlands	Architecture and Belvedere Policy
2006	Northern Ireland	Architecture and the Built Environment for Northern Ireland
2007	Denmark	Nation of Architecture
2007	Iceland	Icelandic Government Policy on Architecture
2007	Scotland	Building our Legacy: Statement on Scotland's architectural policy
2008	Netherlands	Culture of Design
2009	Ireland	Towards a Sustainable Future: Delivering quality within the built environment
2009	Latvia	Architectural Policy Guidelines 2009–15
2009	Norway	Architecture.now
2013	Croatia	Architectural Policies of the Republic of Croatia 2013–20
2013	Netherlands	Building on the Strength of Design
2013	Scotland	Creating Places – A policy statement on architecture and place for Scotland

Year	Country	Policy document
2014	Denmark	Danish Architectural Policy Putting people first
2015	Hungary	National Architectural Policy
2015	Portugal	Política Nacional de Arquitectura e Paisagem
2017	Austria	Federal guidelines on *Baukultur*
2020	Switzerland	Strategie Baukultur

the most comprehensive and innovative approaches to design at the national level with the role of the Commission for Architecture and the Built Environment (CABE) at the centre (see Chapter 2), before largely dismantling it in the early 2010s (Carmona 2011; 2013), only to progressively revisit and reinvent it from 2020 onwards (Carmona 2021b).

Elsewhere in Europe, differences in political, legal, and administrative systems mean that variations in practice are large and despite the efforts of the European Union, there has been little alignment (Acampa 2019). Nevertheless, the leadership provided in recent years by the Germanic countries around the notion of *Baukultur* has clearly given new momentum to this broad policy arena at both European and national scales. While the same political concerns about place quality and its impact on everything from the quality of life to the vitality of economies and environmental impacts are present everywhere, the *Baukultur* policy initiatives have provided a very broad set of guiding principles concerned with extending design quality into the lifeblood of nations as part of both the cultural inheritance of Europeans and their future cultural health. The ideas are nothing new, but the concept and political drive behind it powerfully reasserts the case for design quality.

Following these policy commitments, several countries and regions have been making very significant efforts to implement a comprehensive approach to the governance of design. To do so, some have established dedicated institutions or appointed a state architect team to monitor implementation action plans tied to their architecture policies, often delivered through a range of informal tools. Bento and Laopoulou (2019) examine the role, instruments and impact of state architect teams and similar institutions in fostering spatial quality and a place-making culture across five European states. Some of these are vested in individuals with a team around them, notably Ireland's state architect and the Flanders government architect. Elsewhere the roles are more diffuse, for example the Scottish Chief Architect only has a small team in government with delivery of programmes largely taking place through the auspices of the arms-length body Architecture and Design Scotland. Through a series of in-depth interviews they conclude:

- Dedicated institutions such as state architects create the institutional conditions for improved public action on spatial quality, improving coordination and interaction between different stakeholders.
- Such positions provide leadership and strategic advice to government, cutting across the wide range of sectorial departments that are involved in design.
- Responsibilities vary from the design and construction of public buildings, to the establishment of cross-sector policy frameworks and related advice, to supporting cultural activities on design.
- Through these means, state architect teams have had a positive impact on design governance processes. The underlying belief being 'that, by improving the design process that leads to the public construction, we can also, in turn, improve the overall quality of the built outcome' (Bento and Laopoulou 2019: 90).

As with any policy arena, this concern for urban quality will only be delivered if properly resourced and effectively implemented, otherwise high-level policy statements on the value of good design will remain simply well-meaning aspirations. The range of tools (informal and otherwise) developed and used in different jurisdictions, as well as the organisational arrangements put in place for their delivery, offer a tangible demonstration of this commitment. The survey gave a first Europe-wide indication of what was being used.

Informal policy tools

The main focus of the survey was on the use of informal tools of urban design governance across Europe. Findings relating to particular tools are integrated into the discussion of informal tools in Chapters 4 and 5 (the latter relating to financial mechanisms) while the focus here is on overarching findings and on the categorisation of identified tools.

Respondents to the survey were provided with an open survey structure that advised them to add information about their policy tools where they felt they would fit best as regards the five categories included in Figure 3.1 and to provide as much information as they could about how they operate. An 'other tools' category was included at the end of the questionnaire for policy tools that respondents felt did not comfortably fit into any of the five pre-identified categories. This was particularly important given the need to test whether the categorisation fitted a pan-European context.

The survey uncovered an increasing number of administrations (national to local), developing an ever more diverse and sophisticated set of approaches to offer clear leadership on design quality. In doing this it was notable that governments across Europe are taking advantage of the informal tools of urban design governance to take the delivery of a better-designed built environment to new levels. But practices are far from consistent.

The survey revealed that some tools have been widely used and adopted across almost all administrations in Europe, for example design awards. Others are far more sporadic, including the use of design indicators, and have yet to be widely mainstreamed. Others still are well established, even routine, in a wide range of localities where they may no longer seem particularly innovative, but elsewhere are little used and their adoption would represent a significant innovation. The use of design competitions fell into this category.

All five forms of informal urban design governance tool explored in the survey were being actively and extensively used across Europe, with responses revealing two main purposes for the tools:

- Quality culture tools. First, tools were being used to develop a positive culture within which decision-making on design can occur. Such approaches seek to establish a positive decision-making environment in which a consensus gradually builds around the notion that a better-designed built environment is worth striving for and delivers what in Chapter 1 was described as 'place value' (see Figure 1.2, p. 6). Most evidence, knowledge and promotion tools fell into this category (discussed in Chapter 4 as analysis, information and persuasion tools).
- Quality delivery tools. Second, tools were being utilised to assist directly in the delivery of better-quality projects and places. These tools were being used to steer project- or development-related decision-making processes in a more focused manner, helping to ensure that from intervention to intervention in the built environment, design quality was being appropriately prioritised and delivered. Most evaluation and assistance tools fell into this category (discussed in Chapter 4 as rating and support tools).

The survey confirmed that informal tools were seen as important means to complement the formal side of local urban design governance landscapes, and greatly extend the means available to state actors to influence how the built environment is shaped. As part of this, there is the potential to use financial mechanisms alongside or as part of the urban design governance toolbox in such a way that design quality is encouraged, although the survey suggested that this potential connection often remains under-exploited. If the critical task for the state is not simply to incentivise development, but to incentivise high-quality development, the survey suggested that in 2020 many administrations were attempting to do this without using critical tools that were at their disposal (see Chapter 5).

Despite this, many administrations across Europe are proactive in promoting design quality and fostering a culture of place quality in order to raise standards of design and achieve better places. The survey identified a diverse range of collaborative processes and partnerships between public and non-governmental or arms-length organisations in order to deliver and use the informal tools of urban design governance. In particular, the most proactive administrations across the continent are taking this role seriously and have been setting up dedicated actors, institutes and initiatives to drive forward a culture of design.

If notions of governance embody the idea that a wide range of institutions, actors, tools and relationships are involved in the process of governing (Pierre and Peters 2000), then the survey confirmed that pursuit of design quality is no exception. Ultimately, however, although it acts with, for and among other stakeholders, it was clear that the public sector retains a special responsibility for creating the conditions within which a high-quality built environment can flourish and that in Europe informal tools of urban design governance are increasingly at the heart of this.

A typology of urban design governance tools

If the survey revealed that the types of informal tools used in the UK are common (in different forms, combinations and to different extents) across other European countries, it also suggested that the British classification that focused on the practices of the now defunct Commission for Architecture and the Built Environment (CABE) (Carmona et al. 2016) both omitted key tools and used terminology that did not lend itself easily to translation in a pan-European context. Based on the survey, and early work on a Europe-wide panorama of practices (see Chapters 4 and 5), the categorisation was refined, extended and developed into a conceptual European typology of urban design governance tools.

The starting point was to reflect two key conceptual and practical distinguishing features of the tools, both of which have already been discussed:

- Quality culture versus quality delivery tools. Some tools focus primarily on influencing the broad culture in which the quality of design is prioritised, indirectly shaping the processes of design. Others concentrate on directly shaping actual projects and places (the products of urban design). The two overlap and are not mutually exclusive, but nevertheless conceptually identify an important distinction.
- Formal versus informal tools. The most widely used tools focus on formally 'directing' decision-making processes relating to the design of projects and places. In doing so they use the hard powers of the state which are generally obligatory to use and to follow. Others informally 'influence' decision-making, ranging from the broad culture of design to the specifics of projects. These use the soft powers of the state to encourage and cajole development actors, but in a discretionary (non-obligatory) manner. Again, these categories are not hard and fast, with some types of tools being used in both categories, including design competitions or design review. Others can be used in different ways at different stages of the development process.

When considered together, these distinguishing features create three categorisations of urban design governance tool: i) informal quality culture tools, ii) informal quality delivery tools and iii) formal quality delivery tools. A fourth – formal quality culture tools – can also be envisaged. The inclusion of the built environment as a mandatory topic for children in schools, for example, might be included here. However, this was omitted from the framework as formal educational policy is beyond the remit of built environment policymakers and professionals, albeit that informal means of influencing (part of informal quality culture tools) are widespread (see Figure 3.3).

Formal quality delivery tools

While there is no hard-and-fast division between formal and informal tools in urban design governance, formal tools tend to encompass a range

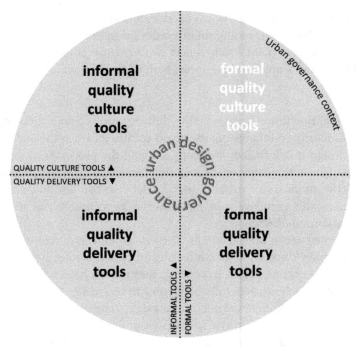

Figure 3.3 Categories of urban design governance tools (image: Matthew Carmona).

of more conventional instruments. They include development/zoning plans, design standards, state subsidies and investment, construction permits, development consent regimes, urban development charges, and so forth. Carmona (2017) has classified these as forms of guidance, incentive and control:

- Guidance tools: encompass a wide range of tools that in different ways formally set out operational design parameters to direct the design of development. Some are generic, relating to large areas such as whole municipalities, and some area-based or site-specific, often tied to particular projects or programmes. Some are highly prescriptive, such as design standards, design coding, or parameter plans, and others are performance-based and therefore subject to a good degree of interpretation, notably design policy or flexible design/development frameworks.
- Incentive tools: can be more or less interventionist depending on whether they involve the state directly inputting public resources to encourage better outcomes (for example through subsidy or direct

investment in infrastructure), or whether they are indirect and focused on rewarding defined 'good behaviour' with enhanced development rights. These include development bonuses, notably permission to build higher or denser than regulations would normally allow, or forms of process management, perhaps related to a streamlined route through a consent regime if certain rules are followed. Some forms of incentive focus on encouraging specific outcomes, others are process oriented, aiming to steer design-led development processes. Because they involve finance – either the giving of finance by the state or its receipt and reinvestment in the public realm – typically these tools are regulated and therefore lie within the formal side of the urban design governance toolbox.

• Control tools: are based either on fixed legal frameworks with pre-determined administrative decision-making, or on the discretionary professional interpretation of policy. They encompass both development and construction-related regulation and both pre- and post-development decision-making (including that related to enforcement). They can be differentiated by assessing to whom the benefit of the decision primarily accrues, for example whether a contribution from the developer to the state (where the public gets something, such as a developer contribution or infrastructure adoption), or an authorisation given from the state to the applicant (the applicant gets something, typically a development consent or warranty that the work has reached a defined standard).

If formal urban design governance instruments work well at preventing the worst forms of development, they are often less successful at stimulating the best (Ben-Joseph 2005; Talen 2012). Part of the problem may be that the sorts of tools predominantly used to guide the design of development are often limited in their scope and technical in their application. Frequently they are not generated out of any place-based vision that has been designed for a particular locality or project. Consequently, design quality in a holistic sense, and the issue of how quality is defined, may not be fully reflected in their operation.

Informal quality culture tools

Although formal tools also contribute to the culture of design through what they allow, what they deny, and the expectations that creates, informal tools often focus centrally on building a culture of design quality locally, regionally or nationally. Reflecting and updating the classification previously described (see the top three tiers of evidence, knowledge and promotion tools in Figure 3.1) with more widely understood and accepted terms, three forms of informal quality culture tool can be recognised:

- Analysis tools: help us understand how the built environment is shaped, through which processes and with what consequences. This evidence can then be used to underpin policy and guidance, to monitor design outcomes from the development process, or to evaluate the state of the built environment more widely.
- Information tools: act to disseminate knowledge about the nature of good (or poor) design practices and processes, as well as related development practices, and about why it matters. They help to raise design awareness and understanding among stakeholders.
- Persuasion tools: actively make the case for particular design responses in a proactive manner. Instead of waiting for organisations and individuals to seek out knowledge, for example in research or guidance, these tools take the knowledge to them physically or through the media, seeking to package key messages in a manner that engages attention and persuades audiences, notably important development decision-makers.

Informal quality delivery tools

Informal quality delivery tools focus on delivery in a similar manner to formal tools, but without the element of compulsion. They are typically concerned with providing the means through which projects and propositions can be discussed, enabled, promoted and tested. Again, reflecting and updating the classification previously described (see the lower two tiers, evaluation and assistance tools, in Figure 3.1) with more widely understood and accepted terms, and extending it with a new category that was revealed early on in the Europe-wide analysis, three varieties of informal quality delivery tools can be identified:

- Rating tools: allow judgements to be made about the quality of design in a systematic and structured manner, usually by parties such as professionals or community groups that are external to, and therefore independent from, the particular design process being evaluated.
- Support tools: are more directive within the design process itself as they involve directly assisting or enabling design/development teams with particular projects, or with the commissioning of

projects or the preparation of design guidance and other tools. They potentially encompass a range of financial means that can be used to encourage better design outcomes by providing financial support to key initiatives or delivery organisations or through the raising or transferring of funding focused specifically on delivering better design.

• Exploration tools: engage directly in the design process through mechanisms that investigate, test out and involve the community in particular design approaches. They are hands-on but exploratory in nature, either utilising temporary interventions or inputting into larger project- or place-shaping processes.

In total this leads to nine tool types (see Figure 3.4), although it is also important not to be overly rigid in how such a typology might be used. As already suggested, many tools have both culture and delivery implications, and the divisions between the formal and informal tools of the state are not hard and fast. The classification is instead a relational instrument,

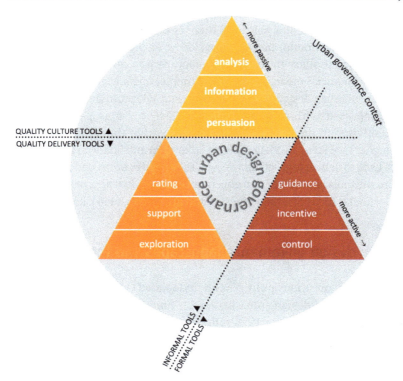

Figure 3.4 A typology of urban design governance tools (image: Matthew Carmona).

designed to understand and relate broad types, rather than to strictly classify them.

Within each category of tool there is also a transition from lesser to greater engagement, or from more passive to more active intervention with stakeholders and/or the specifics of projects and places. This implies that tools at the base of each category are more hands-on and often more forceful in their application. Again, while this may generally be the case, it will not always be so as the transition will not always be as clear cut as the diagram suggests.

Incentivising with financial mechanisms

As the discussion so far has suggested, urban design does not work in isolation. In particular, high-quality design solutions will be of little value if economic systems fail to allow for their implementation and long-term maintenance. For this reason, urban design governance outcomes and processes are shaped by the availability of economic resources and the nature of financing instruments for projects.

Whichever tool is selected, there is the potential to use financial (and other economic) means alongside or as part of the urban design governance toolbox to incentivise good design and discourage poor design. Financial means could, for example, encourage the production and use of urban design governance tools and also promote the aspirations encompassed within them. Typically this occurs as part of formal incentivisation processes, but also occurs within the informal support category (see Figure 3.5). Equally, in order to ensure financial mechanisms are used to deliver high-quality design, they need to be used in conjunction with the tools of urban design governance. These dual approaches formed a particular focus of Urban Maestro and are discussed in Chapter 5.

Urban design governance landscapes and their tools

Depending on their politics and associated view of government intervention on design (see Chapter 1), some might view the range of tools and associated practices reflected in the typology as a confusing diversity of potentially conflicting approaches needlessly imposed on design. Others would see them as a rich constellation of potentially complementary and beneficial practices from which to pick and choose.

In his international review of urban design practices, Loew (2012: 325) notes that even though the actual practices performed by urbanists in different countries are very similar, because the historical, geographical,

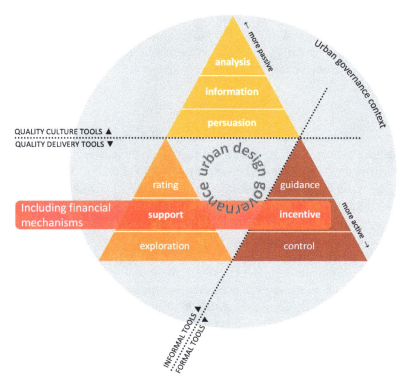

Figure 3.5 Financial mechanisms in the typology of urban design governance tools (image: Matthew Carmona).

social, economic and political contexts are very different, so inevitably are the systems through which they operate. This implies that the larger governance traditions within which urban design exists are among the major factors differentiating practices. While this generates difference, it also seems to allow for innovation, as professionals in each jurisdiction need to think through what is right for their particular location and set of contexts. This is reflected in the panorama of approaches discussed in the next chapter.

In Chapter 2 the notion of urban design governance landscapes was introduced (see Figure 2.7, p. 59), reflecting the idea that every country and, within its boundaries, every administrative area – regional, settlement-wide or local – is likely to have its own particular set of overlapping responsibilities, approaches and influences on urban design governance decision-making. To illustrate this variation and to apply the concept to the notion of tools of urban design governance, three landscapes reflecting different European legal and governance traditions are briefly sketched out and compared. These are: Lisbon in Portugal

(Napoleonic law, centralised government and fixed regulatory system), London in England (common law, centralised government and discretionary regulatory system) and Vienna in Austria (Germanic law, federal government and fixed regulatory system).

Lisbon

Lisbon is Portugal's largest city, with a population of around half a million within a metropolitan area approaching three million. It is the capital of Portugal and the westernmost city of continental Europe. Over the last three decades Lisbon has benefited from a period of economic growth, with modernisation and spatial quality prioritised across the city, which has become a trendy tourist destination. This boost was, in part, a result of a huge national investment in the regeneration of the city's large brownfield sites and riverfront areas along with Lisbon City Council's efficient urban management, careful rehabilitation of the old city centre and its public spaces renovation programme. Increasingly these achievements have been recognised internationally, including in the Academy of Urbanism's European City of the Year Award (2012), the Best European City Destination World Travel Awards (2019), and the EU's European Green Capital Award (2020).

Despite recent decentralising efforts, the Portuguese governance system continues to be strongly centralised with most legislation and public funding defined at the national level (Cravinho 2017). In the case of spatial planning, central government is responsible for the preparation and monitoring of national legislation to which municipalities need to comply through their development and management of local spatial plans. Lisbon City Council is the biggest local authority in Portugal. It is structured into 14 municipal directorates and further subdivided into around fifty departments, each with their own technical divisions, alongside several publicly owned companies with financial autonomy. Under this city-wide governance are 24 'parishes', Lisbon's smallest administrative division, which deal with matters such as the cleaning and the maintenance of public spaces.

Besides the public administration, non-governmental and professional organisations at national and local levels also contribute to the creation of a culture of design, notably in promoting an awareness among the general public and stakeholders about architecture and urban design. Although most are legally independent institutions, some are fully or partially funded by public funds. Lisbon's key urban design governance relationships are set out in Figure 3.6.

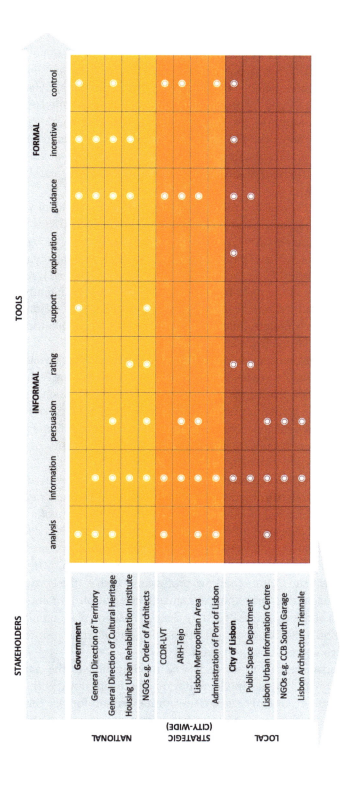

Figure 3.6   Lisbon's urban design governance landscape (image: Matthew Carmona).

Within the Ministry of the Environment, the Directorate General for the Territory (DGT) is responsible for public policies on land use and urban development, under the auspices of the principles, objectives and norms established by the *Spatial Planning, Urbanism and Land-use Act*. The Directorate is also responsible for updating the legal and regulatory framework, for the promotion of land management best practices, and for the development and dissemination of guidance and technical criteria that guide implementation locally (https://www.dgterritorio.gov.pt).

The DGT coordinated the development of the first National Spatial Planning Programme, which was enshrined in law in 2007 (Ministry of the Environment 2007), through which Parliament recognised architecture as a matter of public interest for the first time, embodying the EU Council Resolution on Architectural Quality (see Chapter 1). Among its ambitions was the need for a National Policy for Architecture and Landscape (*Política Nacional de Arquitectura e Paisagem*), alongside spatial planning policies addressing citizens' right to a healthy and ecologically balanced living environment.

After a long process and three formal working groups to develop the architecture policy it was finally adopted by a resolution of the Council of Ministers in 2015. In a European context, the Portuguese national policy is exceptional in combining architecture and landscape policy, aiming to protect the ecological function of the landscape, improve the heritage and quality features of built-up areas and promote the identity of place (Ministry of the Environment 2015) (see Figure 3.7).

Although the national policy established high-level design aspirations through five strategic goals, it did not contain a practical action plan, which only followed two years later in the form of a list of guidelines and measures for implementation spanning 2015 to 2020, to be monitored by an Architecture and Landscape Monitoring Committee. The Committee encompasses stakeholders from two Ministries (Environment and Culture) and two professional bodies (the Portuguese Order of Architects and the Portuguese Association of Landscape Architects) and is in charge of setting the policy action plan, monitoring its execution, developing annual progress and evaluation reports and issuing recommendations as requested.

Unfortunately, without dedicated funding tied to the national architectural policy, its implementation has been slow, with most measures still at an early stage (Directorate General for the Territory 2021). So far the main outputs have been an annual conference

Figure 3.7 A deliberately broad definition of architecture is adopted in Portugal's National Policy for Architecture and Landscape, encompassing 'outdoor spaces that comprise the design of the city and the territory' (here at Portimāo) as well as buildings, their interior spaces and all other built structures (image: Matthew Carmona).

(since 2017) on architecture and landscape, allowing the exchange of information on initiatives that are being delivered across the country, an online forum with a sequence of events, a National Landscape Award, and a dedicated portal for the initiative (https://pnap. dgterritorio.gov.pt).

Given the historic nature of much building stock in Portugal, the Ministry of Culture also plays an important national role in shaping the built environment, in this case through the Directorate General for Cultural Heritage, the public authority for classified buildings, protected areas and conservation zones. Under these provisions, for all projects covered by heritage status, municipalities are obliged to ask the Directorate for statutory advice on aspects such as layout, functions, materials, colours, and so forth. In exceptional cases with a high profile or importance, advice is sought from a national advisory body, the Architectural and Archaeological Heritage Section of the National Council of Culture (see Figure 3.8).

Figure 3.8 Heritage issues can trump other design factors, including in a redevelopment scheme for three empty buildings in Lisbon city centre on the Avenue Fontes Pereira de Melo. While the redevelopment of these buildings was designed by Souto Moura, a Pritzker-winning architect, the scheme was rejected by the municipality after receiving a negative review from the Ministry's advisory body (image: João Bento).

The Housing and Urban Rehabilitation Institute is also an important national player through its management of the National Building Rehabilitation Fund. To access the fund, applications need to satisfy a range of assessed criteria, which includes design quality. The Institute also promotes, in partnership with identified municipalities, design competitions for the development of affordable housing projects and the Public Housing and Rehabilitation Award, an annual prize for the best social housing and rehabilitation projects.

From the non-governmental sphere, the Portuguese Order of Architects regulates the architecture profession, spreading its influence further through a number of informal tools of urban design governance. Initiatives aim to promote a national culture of design, lobbying for designers and better legislation at national level, while its regional branches provide specialised training and support services for design competitions to public and private promoters. Other cultural institutions that deliver exhibitions or educational activities include the House of Architecture in Matosinhos.

Lisbon-wide governance of design

While there are two main governmental levels in Portugal – national and 308 municipalities – the Commission for Regional Development and Coordination of Lisbon and Tagus Valley (CCDR-LVT) is one of five regional structures (of the national tier) utilised for spatial planning coordination, management and the distribution of regional funds. As such, the commission is responsible for the implementation of environmental and spatial planning policies in the Lisbon region and coordinates the Lisbon Regional Spatial Planning Programme, a strategic planning instrument used to inform the development of inter-municipal and municipal spatial plans.

Special spatial planning programmes are also developed at this level, aimed at safeguarding national interests in environmentally sensitive or significant territorial areas, such as the coastline, parks and reserves (Campos and Ferrão 2015: 23). In these cases, schemes situated in a classified area will need additional permission from the competent regional agency alongside the municipal building permit, including separate context-specific criteria for the physical realisation of projects.

As part of its decentralisation strategy, in 2013 the Portuguese government set up a legal framework for the establishment of intermunicipal bodies to better coordinate and articulate municipal local policies. The largest of these, the Lisbon Metropolitan Area agency, was created with a strategic role at the Lisbon metropolitan scale, coordinating actions across its 18 municipalities and central administration services. In essence the agency is an advisory body, developing strategic studies and establishing scenarios, such as its *Metropolitan Plan for Adaptation to Climate Change of the Lisbon Metropolitan Area,* to inform policies and practices at the municipal level (Crespo and Cabral 2010), informing strategic design matters but with less influence on detailed urban design (see Figure 3.9).

Local governance of design

Similar to most Western European countries, municipal land-use plans (Plano Director Municipal – PDM) are a mixture of legally binding zoning provisions and design guidance, which provides clear development

Figure 3.9 A particularly complex area is the Port of Lisbon, covering 11 municipalities and an overarching port authority and requiring coordination of projects on both the Lisbon (see Figure 3.10) and the more challenging Setúbal peninsula sides of the Tagus. The latter is now undergoing some rehabilitation in which small-scale, informal place-making has been key to the early regeneration projects (image: Matthew Carmona).

rights, densities/floor space limits and often general development forms. This means that the PDM (in Lisbon, as elsewhere) is the main formal regulatory tool to guide local development and is binding on all parties, whereas plans and policies at the scales already discussed are only binding for public bodies and advisory for others.

In this context, Lisbon City Council is empowered by law to exercise the functions of a local planning authority and to issue planning and building permits, within the parameters established by its PDM, to guide the transformation of the city. For each zone covered by the plan, the Lisbon PDM specifies the main function and type of building allowed, including the maximum floor space and general building envelope (height, building line, plot depth and width). This creates a high level of certainty – guaranteed in law – for all parties, including for developers, the municipality and the affected public.

This comes at the expense of criteria controlling the realisation of urban design and architectural schemes, detailed parameters for which are not covered in the zoning plans, confirming the reputation of such formal tools as too often being a 'blunt instrument' for shaping an appropriate response to context (Carmona 2021a: 509). Because of the limited influence of the plan, Lisbon's local planning officials utilise a more discretionary process of development management to control the design quality of projects. Before receiving a building permit, proposals are reviewed by the local planning authority, which makes a decision about whether or not to grant permits, having taken advice from technical planning staff and drawing from guidance on design features published within the PDM alongside its zoning provisions (Mélice Dias and Marat-Mendes 2020: 171).

For certain areas of particular importance for the city's development, the City Council may decide to develop a Detailed Plan, the most local level of land-use plan used in Portugal. These are also regulatory plans focusing on particular neighbourhoods and, because they override higher-level plans, have a significant impact on the architectural design of those areas through the control of the mix of uses, morphological characteristics and the three-dimensional form of development. Detailed Plans, however, are only developed for specific cases where there is a strong political will to do so in order to guarantee a high level of design quality, for example for sensitive conservation contexts or town and city centres. In part this is because the approval process is complex and time consuming (OECD 2017).

A major dimension of the City Council's engagement with design quality relates to their 20-year-old public space programme, run by a dedicated Public Space Department and guided by Lisbon's *Public Space Design Manual*, which establishes principles to guide interventions in public space. Among other tasks this unit prepares and coordinates studies and projects for regenerating and enhancing a wide range of public spaces, from the city's grand avenues to its parks, local streets and squares. Some of these interventions have involved the organisation of design competitions and often sit side by side with prestigious new buildings designed by renowned Portuguese and international architects, including Charles Correa, Paulo Mendes da Rocha, Amanda Levete, Renzo Piano, Aires Mateus and Carrilho da Graça, following a strategy of giving the waterfront a new iconic status that is distinctive in its own right (see Figure 3.10). Design, in this sense, has deliberately been used as a place-branding tool, an approach advocated in the informal (non-binding) *General Plan for the Lisbon Waterfront* dating from 2008. This

Figure 3.10   The Lisbon Waterfront has seen huge, sustained investment in transforming former industrial port areas into a new leisure environment (image: Matthew Carmona).

plan was followed by a number of Detailed Plans and Masterplans for different areas along the Tagus, and by successive rounds of public investment (Medeiros et al. 2021).

Through this work the Department of Urbanism developed the 'Square in Every Neighbourhood' programme in order to promote citizen involvement in shaping the city's public realm. In a first phase, interested parties were asked to say what they would like to change in their neighbourhood by completing an online form or by attending a dedicated session for each place. In a second phase, new designs for selected spaces in each neighbourhood were discussed with local populations with the aim of creating high-quality public space and encouraging walking and cycling.

In addition, and to complement formal processes of public participation, Lisbon City Council promotes several informal participation initiatives, including (since 2008), the *Lisbon Participatory Budget* – the first in a European capital. Inspired by this tool, the Council sub-sequently developed Lisbon's BIP/ZIP programme to support small-scale, community-driven projects in deprived neighbourhoods, allowing bottom-up experimentation in the form of co-governance models, design solutions and cultural initiatives (see Box 15, p. 181). More recently, the

Lisbon Citizens' Council was created through which citizens can participate in a whole day of debates about the development of new proposals for the city.

In 2001, the City Council established the Lisbon Urban Information Centre to promote the dissemination of knowledge about the city and to encourage engagement around urban issues. The intention has been to foster a community of practice and a place-making culture by providing workspace for students and researchers, hosting meetings, workshops and other events, and through making available its collection of information, digital cartography and technical data about the city. This includes access to all spatial plans produced by the City Council and publications on urbanism, architecture and the history of Lisbon. The City Council also supports the oldest municipal architecture award in Portugal. Established in 1902, the Valmor Architecture Award celebrates the design of new buildings built in the city of Lisbon (see Figure 3.11)

While the City Council is, by far, the dominant player promoting design quality in Lisbon, others are also involved. Foremost amongst these is the Centro Cultural de Belém, a major cultural centre that was

Figure 3.11 In 1998 the Lisbon Oceanarium by Peter Chermayeff was awarded the Valmor award, followed up by an honourable mention in 2011 for an extension by Pedro Nuno Campos da Costa to house its collective equipment (image: Matthew Carmona).

initially built for holding the Portuguese EU presidency in 1992. After hosting several ad hoc exhibitions, it was decided to devote space (in its former parking garage) to a dedicated architecture centre. Since 2012, the South Garage has promoted a programme of architectural temporary exhibitions, lectures, debates and publications. In addition, its educational service offers a regular schedule of guided tours and workshops designed for children, schools and families (https://garagemsul.ccb.pt).

There has also been a growing number of architectural festivals and events across Lisbon, including Lisbon Open House and the Lisbon Architecture Triennale which was established with the support of the municipality and a wider group of partners in 2007. The Lisbon Triennale attracts a high number of participants and usually includes a diversity of activities – street installations, exhibitions, debates, guided walks, design workshops and so on – focusing on architecture and urban design. It is now part of a growing and well-established urban design governance landscape which, while still relying heavily on formal tools, is increasingly experimenting with informal means to reinforce the culture of design quality that is now part of Lisbon's future vision.

London

London is democratic Europe's largest city with a population of around nine million inhabitants and global city status. It is the capital of England and the United Kingdom, but, following Brexit in 2020 is no longer within the European Union. Since 2000 it has benefited from strategic city-wide government in the form of the Greater London Authority (GLA), the executive branch of which is the Mayor of London. By European standards the Mayor's powers are limited and most major public investment decisions in the city are still made by central government. The Mayor also has to follow national policy set down by the government in Westminster, including on matters of planning policy and infrastructure.

Under national government, the GLA has responsibility for strategic planning, economic development, and transport (among other things) and provides the strategic framework within which London's 32 boroughs and the ancient City of London (the Square Mile) operate. Borough responsibilities include local planning, development management, housing, open spaces, and street management and maintenance. Responsibilities for the governance of urban design in London are split between these three tiers of government, although in some parts of the city, Neighbourhood Forums have been set up and have the right to prepare a neighbourhood plan, in effect creating a fourth formal tier of governance (if not government), once plans are 'made'.

Other national and city-based organisations also play an important role in shaping a system that has developed in an ad hoc manner and which remains subject to London's governance traditions – 'Neoliberal before neoliberalism was invented' (Carmona 2014b: 377). Through much of its history the state has shied away from making 'big plans' for London, and instead has tended to look to the market and a succession of powerful investors and developers to shape the city in an incremental fashion (Hebbert 1998: 90–3). Its key urban design governance tools and relationships are represented in Figure 3.12.

London in its national context

Like local government across England, local authorities in London are subject to the policy of national government. In contrast to the devolved government in Scotland, the Westminster government has never felt the need for a national architecture or urban design policy to set out high-level design aspirations for the country. Instead, a series of sectorial policies cover the field in, arguably, a more fragmented manner, but also one with a more direct link to delivery, notably through town and country planning, housing, transport, and regeneration policy and practices.

These practices have also tended to lead to quite violent swings in the priority that successive governments give to design quality, with the post-war consensus that prioritised public-sector intervention giving way in the 1980s and early 1990s to a more 'hands-off' free-market philosophy. From 1994 onwards and until it was reversed once again in the austerity-driven policy context from 2008, increasingly government prioritised design quality, investing considerable resources and political capital in the Commission for Architecture and the Built Environment (CABE) to spearhead its delivery across England (see Chapter 2) (https://webarchive.nationalarchives.gov.uk/ukgwa/20110118095359/http://www.cabe.org.uk/). The organisation was mirrored in London through the auspices of the small but proactive Design for London, adviser on design to the Mayor (Bishop and Williams 2020).

CABE was swept away in 2011 (and Design for London before it) and for almost a decade, design quality was firmly off the national agenda until its revival once again in 2020 at the hands of a government looking to make new housing development more palatable to resistant local communities around the country through a new national drive for 'beauty', reflecting sustained advocacy from organisations such as the Place Alliance that brought national stakeholders together to argue for a greater national priority for design quality. Among other things, this included setting up, from 2022, an Office for Place (Carmona 2021b) (see Figure 1.16, p. 40).

TOOLS

STAKEHOLDERS

	INFORMAL					FORMAL			
	analysis	information	persuasion	rating	support	exploration	guidance	incentive	control
NATIONAL (ENGLAND)									
Government	●				●		●	●	●
Planning Inspectorate									●
National Infrastructure Commission		●		●					
Homes England				●				●	
Historic England	●	●	●	●	●				
Office for Place		●	●						
NGOs e.g. Place Alliance	●						●		●
STRATEGIC (CITY-WIDE)									
The Mayor (Greater London Authority)	●	●		●			●	●	●
Transport for London	●					●	●		
Urban Design London		●	●	●	●				
Mayor's design advocates				●	●				
Mayor's advocacy organisations	●	●							
Public Practice		●			●				
LOCAL									
32 Boroughs and City of London			●			●	●	●	●
Design-review panels				●					●
Community-review panels				●					
Neighbourhood forums							●		●

Figure 3.12 London's urban design governance landscape (image: Matthew Carmona).

While policy has come and gone, through much of this time the primary national vehicle for influencing design quality has been planning policy and guidance, currently in the form of the *National Planning Policy Framework* (NPPF), and associated national guidance, which includes a *National Design Guide* (2020 – see Figure 3.13) and a *National Model Design Code* (2021). Local policy, including *The London Plan* (the responsibility of the Mayor of London), has to be in conformity with the NPPF, although exactly how that is done is open to considerable discretion. The associated national guidance has the status of a 'material consideration' that local authorities, developers and others have discretion to use, but is not mandatory.

The centralised nature of government in the UK is confirmed by the ultimate authority vested in ministers to 'call-in' planning applications for the secretary of state to determine. Although typically this only occurs

Figure 3.13 Ten 'Characteristics of Well Designed Places' from the *National Design Guide* (image: Ministry of Housing, Communities and Local Government 2020).

for nationally significant or otherwise controversial development proposals (see Figure 3.17), the presence of many tall buildings in London ensures that higher proportions of schemes are called-in from London than elsewhere and when relations between City Hall and Westminster are strained, this can lead to more decisions called-in and decided in contravention to mayoral wishes (Harris 2019).

The dominance of national government is further reinforced by its range of arms-length agencies, including the Planning Inspectorate (to whom aggrieved applicants for planning permission can appeal); Homes England (funder of housing and regeneration and major landowner across England – see Figure 3.14); the National Infrastructure Commission (which establishes national infrastructure priorities for government); Historic England (an influential voice as a 'statutory consultee' on heritage matters) and, now, the Office for Place (tasked to assist government in transforming the local practices and priorities relating to design quality across England). Government funds and sets the policy framework within which each of these organisations operate, further limiting the autonomy of London institutions.

Figure 3.14 The forerunner of Homes England was influential in establishing high-quality design aspirations for the Greenwich Peninsula. Since 1997 these have continued to inform development outcomes, now spanning 25 years, despite the organisation itself (like central government) wavering in its commitment to design over that period (image: Matthew Carmona).

London-wide governance of design

Despite the limitations on their powers, the presence of successive mayors has acted as a counterbalance to the swings in the national commitment to design quality. Between 1986 and 2000 London had no strategic authority, and the period is generally regarded as one in which the quality of London's built environment suffered, so much so that some large private developers even took it on themselves to fill the gap, setting pseudo-regulatory frameworks on themselves (for instance at Canary Wharf) to ensure some consistency and quality, and thereby to safeguard their own investments (Carmona 2009).

From 2000 onwards, the presence of a mayor has tended to ensure a greater consistency in the delivery of urban quality and less reliance on, or reference to, national government. While the role of the mayor is a strategic one, with no specific powers relating to urban design or public-space quality in the legislation establishing the role, each of the three mayors elected since 2000 have been interested in these issues (Carmona 2012) and have used a series of soft and hard powers to drive a greater city-wide emphasis on design quality. This has been reflected in a comprehensive range of formal design policies in *The London Plan* and associated Supplementary Planning Guidance outside it, including guidance on: 'Character and context', 'Housing design quality and standards', and 'Small housing developments and design codes', among others.

The London Plan sets out strategic policies, including on design quality, that the 32 boroughs and the City of London are required to be in conformity with in their own Local Plans. In addition, the mayor is consulted on all applications of strategic significance – developments of more than 150 housing units, or over 30 metres tall (150 metres in the City of London) or on the greenbelt or metropolitan open land. These referable applications are decided, first, by the boroughs, and then referred to the mayor for consideration and final determination. All such schemes are required, by the mayor, to have been the subject of design review. By these means the mayor has a further opportunity to set and deliver clear design aspirations, although what is or is not considered good design is sometimes contested between the two tiers of local government, particularly over what is the right scale of development outside of urban centres (Local Government Lawyer 2021).

Successive mayors have also required that funding from Transport for London (the city's strategic transport authority) be directed towards improving the quality of London's streets and public spaces through a range of initiatives, including:

- Establishing *Streetscape Guidance* (street design standards) for across the city (tied to funding that boroughs bid for) based on the relative priority given to 'movement' and 'place' in each street and a range of other guidance, for example for sustainable drainage systems, and cycling design standards.
- Driving the link between street quality and health through the *Healthy Streets for London* initiative including its range of ten Healthy Street Indicators to guide a Healthy Streets Check on every Transport for London-funded public-realm scheme.
- Investing in a range of public spaces projects across the city, typically delivered by the boroughs (see Figure 3.15), particularly under the first two mayors – Ken Livingstone and Boris Johnson – who established, respectively, the '100 Public Spaces' and 'London's Great Outdoors' programmes.
- Since 2009, schemes over £1million have been required to undergo design review conducted by Urban Design London before funding is released.

Each mayor has instigated their own informal initiatives on design, with the latest mayor – Sadiq Khan – establishing an advisory panel of

Figure 3.15   Blue House Yard in Wood Green was commissioned by the London Borough of Haringey with funding from the Mayor of London to create a new space for local small businesses who might otherwise be priced out of the area (image: Matthew Carmona).

fifty Mayor's Design Advocates to conduct design review of relevant development projects, advocate for design quality across the city, deliver training, and so forth, all as part of the 'Good Growth by Design' initiative (https://www.london.gov.uk/what-we-do/regeneration/advice-and-guidance/about-good-growth-design). The mayor also keeps a list of Mayor's Advocate Organisations that play a major role in supporting a culture of design quality across London. These include the London Festival of Architecture, New London Architecture (an independent forum for discussion, debate and information about architecture, planning and development in London) and, most importantly, Urban Design London (see Box 3, p. 127).

Urban Design London is hosted, and part-funded, by Transport for London, but also operates a subscription model whereby the London boroughs (and others) pay a yearly subscription to access a diverse range of urban design training activities. In addition, the organisation plays an active role in advocacy around urban design, conducts design reviews and surgeries, and generally offers advice on design. The organisation is unique in England, giving the capital an advantage when it comes to upskilling development professionals and spreading best practice across the city (https://www.urbandesignlondon.com).

Local governance of design

The strategic drive across the city to prioritise design, backed up by structural advantages that the city has over other parts of the UK, notably, higher land values, higher densities supporting local services and public transportation, and a large pool of internationally renowned architects and urban designers, all contribute to the city scoring better than other parts of the country in terms of the design quality being delivered in new developments (Carmona et al. 2020). This is generally supported by practices at the local – borough – level, where the scale of development being delivered has meant that, generally (but not everywhere), London's boroughs have better-resourced planning and built-environment services, more-qualified urban designers, and conduct more design reviews than elsewhere (Carmona and Giordano 2021). This all contributes towards the better-quality design outcomes often seen across much of the city.

Despite the generalised situation in London, its boroughs are very diverse – socially, economically and politically – and their commitment to design quality also varies significantly. Data gathered by the GLA noted that 'capacity is not evenly spread across London and within teams, and not necessarily where most development pressure is' (Mayor of London 2020), with 'place-shaping' teams that vary in size between 40 and

144 people (including development management, urban design, highways and public-realm design, conservation, regeneration, planning policy and capital project delivery staff). It revealed that this capacity shrank by almost 20 per cent between 2014 and 2020.

The major barriers to improving this capacity include uncertainty over funding and the difficulties in recruiting and retaining staff in the public sector (Mayor of London 2020), arguably a particular problem in London where the buoyant and very large private sector often pays more and is more nimble in its recruiting practices. In an attempt to address the issue and to attract more dynamic and creative individuals into the place-shaping services of London's public sector, the not-for-profit social enterprise Public Practice was set up in 2018 with support from the Mayor of London and other partners. Public Practice operates, in effect, as a specialist recruitment agency, with 'associates' offered a year-long placement in public sector organisations that pay a placement fee. In its first four years, 26 of London's boroughs used its services, alongside the GLA and other authorities in the south-east of England, with seven cohorts of around 25 associates recruited (https://www.publicpractice.org.uk).

At the top of solutions to addressing the city's capacity needs, boroughs place the sharing of best practice (Mayor of London 2020). The relative geographic proximity of boroughs and various active networks between them across the city – notably through the auspices of Urban Design London – have acted to ensure that practices are shared more completely in London than outside of it. One such example is the spread of design review across the city.

Design review began in London over two hundred years ago with the establishment of the 1802 'Committee of Taste' by government to review the design of monuments to the fallen in the Napoleonic wars. It has come a long way since then, but many of the practices used today still closely resemble those developed by the Royal Fine Arts Commission, which was established in London in 1924 as the first national design review service. This morphed into the Commission for Architecture and the Built Environment (CABE) in 1999 with design review remaining a core part of its work until its funding was withdrawn in 2011 and a reduced design review function moved to the Design Council. When set up, 70 per cent of CABE's design review workload was in London, and when public funding was withdrawn in 2011, London still represented 45 per cent of a much larger workload (Carmona et al. 2018).

After 2011, for the first time in 90 years there was a complete withdrawal of national government involvement from design review and

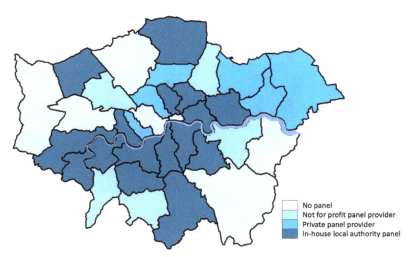

Figure 3.16 Design review panels in London (image: adapted from Urban Design London 2020).

the gradual emergence instead of a market in design review services across England. This was strongly endorsed in the wording of the National Planning Policy Framework (NPPF) in 2012 and has since received a further strong endorsement in the wording of *The London Plan*, now accompanied by a *London Quality Review Charter* produced and promoted by the Mayor of London.

Although, in the turbulent economic climate of 2011/12, a market in design review services initially struggled to establish itself in London, recently it has burgeoned. In 2021 there were 26 borough-wide design review panels and two development corporation panels (plus a small number of non-professional community review panels), with most panels funded directly by a charge levied for the service by local planning authorities or by private or not-for-profit panel managers retained by boroughs to run their design review services (see Figure 3.16). While there remain very significant gaps in the coverage of design review, Carmona et al. (2018: 14) note that 'there is a strong element of boroughs looking at each other in order to learn from and adopt the best practices of their neighbours'.

Much of the work of urban design governance is conducted at the borough level in London, with boroughs responsible for managing most non-strategic streets, most public spaces and the majority of parks across the city (notable exceptions being the Royal Parks). They are responsible for establishing local planning policy and conducting development

Figure 3.17 'The Tulip' by Foster and Partners (a 300-metre-high visitor attraction) was called in by government and rejected in 2021. The decision confirmed an earlier rejection of the scheme by the Mayor of London, in contravention of an initial decision to approve the project made by the City of London – within whose boundaries it would have stood (image: Foster and Partners).

management and are often major landowners with significant interests in large numbers of development and regeneration projects, including, once again, delivering social housing. Ultimately, the governance of design in London is a shared endeavour between tiers of government (see Figure 3.17), as well as with private and third-sector interests, but despite the slightly chaotic picture, in recent years this network of interests has often been able to leverage London's advantages, encouraged and cajoled by successive mayors, to deliver high-quality developments. Inevitably, given such a context, results are sometimes varied.

Vienna

Vienna is Austria's largest city, with a population of around 2 million inhabitants, within a metropolitan area with a population of around 2.6 million, approximately one third of the country's population. It is the capital of Austria and has long featured highly in international quality-of-life rankings, buoyed by its relative prosperity.

Similar to other Germanic countries, Austria's political and administrative structure is based on a federal system, organised in three levels: the federal government, the nine federal states (Bundesländer) and around 2,100 municipalities as the smallest units in the country's governance. There is no federal law on spatial planning as this is a competence of the individual federal states, which have their own legislative and executive powers, including spatial planning, construction regulation and housing policy (OECD 2017). Despite this, in 2017 the federal government adopted a country-wide *Baukultur* policy promoting high-quality environments across Austria.

Vienna is a particular case within this system because it is a federal capital. This means it combines two administrative levels: as a federal state in its own right and as a municipality. Thus the City Council (municipal body) also exercises the functions of the Vienna State Parliament (regional body) while the mayor also serves as the state governor, somewhat simplifying the urban design governance landscape for the city (see Figure 3.18). In 2014 Vienna's City Council adopted its own *Baukultur* policy establishing clear design-quality principles for the realisation of urban projects.

Vienna in its national context

Austria's constitution attributes spatial planning policy to the federal states and local planning to the municipalities. Despite this, since the early 2000s a range of national actors have been promoting initiatives focused on architecture and the built environment under the concept of *Baukultur* (see Chapter 1), integrating not only the remit of architecture but also other contributions to built-environment quality and culture, including urban design, engineering, heritage, planning, landscape, interior design and art for public buildings.

Although Austria already had a tradition of supporting design-quality culture initiatives, in 2002 a bottom-up movement promoting *Baukultur* emerged, involving a wide range of non-governmental actors in the field, including the Austrian professional bodies, design centres, and universities. Initially labelled the Platform for Architectural Policy and Building Culture, and later the Platform for Building Culture Policy (http://www.baukulturpolitik.at), the initiative led to a parliamentary debate in 2004 and to a resolution identifying a special responsibility of federal and regional administrations to promote better living environments and requiring that a report on building culture should be submitted to Parliament within a year (Platform Baukulturpolitik 2017). This led to the publication of the first Austrian *Baukultur* report in 2006.

A year later the Austrian Parliament agreed to the establishment of an Advisory Board for Building Culture as a consulting body for the federal government. The board's office was located within the Federal

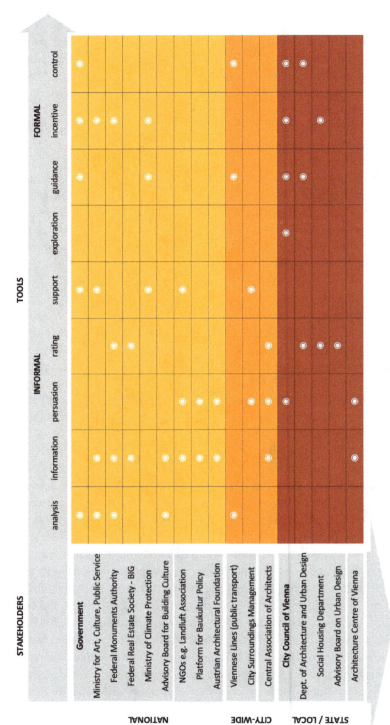

Figure 3.18 Vienna's urban design governance landscape (image: Matthew Carmona).

Ministry for Art, Culture, Public Service and Sport and constituted 28 members, including representatives from all federal ministries, the federal real estate company, the federal monuments office, cities and municipalities, and ten external experts. Meeting at least twice a year, from 2009 the board advises government on measures to improve design and planning processes as well as on initiatives to strengthen public awareness of building culture. It is also responsible for preparing Austrian *Baukultur* reports that are published every five years (a second report was published in 2011, a third in 2017 and a fourth in 2021).

There was a ratcheting up of Austrian *Baukultur* efforts in 2017. Following the Advisory Board's recommendations, the Austrian Council of Ministers adopted its first *Austrian Federal Guidelines for Baukultur*. According to the guidelines, the federal government should 'promote building culture and create a broader societal awareness of its principles, especially among leaders in politics, business, and administration' (Federal Chancellery of the Republic of Austria 2017: 5) across all departments and disciplines at the federal, state and local levels. The document encompassed 20 guidelines, each accompanied by specific stimulus measures setting out specifically what the national government aimed to do. The guidelines themselves ranged across the stewardship of the national estate and infrastructure, to new process measures (such as expanding the use of design competitions and design advisory committees), to addressing matters of skills and knowledge (for instance building research capacity around building culture), to the establishment of building culture guidance tools.

Building on this, the fourth Austrian *Baukultur* report in 2021 proposed the creation of an Agency for *Baukultur*. Among other roles, this would implement a dedicated new funding framework with a focus on stimulating contacts between actors in the existing broad ecology of *Baukultur*-related initiatives and organisations, thereby further strengthening the culture (see Figure 3.19) (Platform Baukulturpolitik 2021).

Within the federal government itself there are several departments with sectoral policy competences related to architecture and urban design. Prominent among these are the Department for Visual Arts, Architecture, Design, Fashion, Photography and Media Arts within the Ministry for Art, Culture, and Public Service. This department is responsible for the financial support of related projects, grants, scholarship programmes and so forth, and for the promotion of architecture within the broad field of the arts. They fund architecture centres and other institutions with architecture programmes, exhibitions, and prizes for architecture. They are also responsible for the organisation

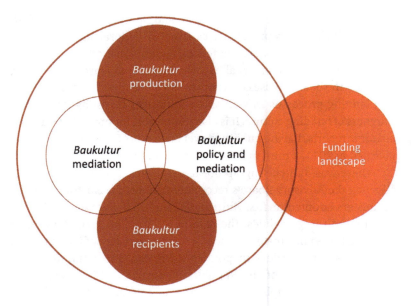

Figure 3.19 The proposed *Baukultur* ecosystem. The planned agency would act as a coordinating partner between the spheres, and where there was deemed to be insufficient exchange it would act to stimulate contacts (image: adapted from Platform Baukulturpolitik 2021).

of Austrian entries to international exhibitions, including to the Venice Biennale of Architecture, while the Austrian Ministry of Climate Protection promotes an annual State Prize for Architecture and Sustainability which, since 2006, has rewarded schemes that combine sophisticated architecture with resource-saving construction (https://www.bmk.gv.at/ministerium/staatspreise/staatspreis_architektur.html).

An additional important actor – nationally and locally – is the Federal Real Estate Company (BIG – Bundesimmobiliengesellschaft), Austria's largest public property owner, responsible for the planning, construction and conservation of most state buildings including government offices, universities, schools, social housing, and so on. With *Baukultur* as one of its key priorities, BIG promotes a number of design competitions to obtain preliminary design concepts for public buildings (see Figure 3.20), provides an online library of case studies, promotes debates about its building activity, and since 2007 has maintained an Architecture Advisory Board to advise on development projects, alongside an Art Advisory Board and Advisory Board for Building Culture with a particular focus on the public understanding of *Baukultur* (https://www.big.at).

Figure 3.20 In 2013 BIG launched an international design competition for the master plan of the new campus of Vienna University of Economics and Business, which was won by BUSarchitektur (image: João Bento).

On the non-governmental side, the Austrian Architectural Foundation (Architekturstiftung Österreich) is a joint initiative of the architecture centres of Austria's federal states, the Austrian Society for Architecture (ÖGFA) and the Central Association of Architects. The Foundation's goal is to get people interested in architecture and to make them ambitious partners in the design of their built environment. The LandLuft association has also been very active across rural Austria since 1999, promoting building culture. Landluft provides research capacity, showcases exemplary building culture projects through films, publications and leaflets, hosts lectures and events across the county, and offers design training for municipal decision-makers through the Landluft Academy. It also gives the Baukultur Municipality Prize every 4–5 years to the most outstanding municipalities in Austria (http://www.landluft.at/).

Vienna-wide governance of design
At the metropolitan scale, there is no strategic planning body encompassing the state of Vienna and its surrounding municipalities within the State of Lower Austria (Patti 2013), although there are several public organisations that operate at this scale with an impact on the city-wide built environment. These include the metropolitan

public transport company – Viennese Lines – which is wholly owned by the City Council of Vienna.

To improve cooperation and coordination at the metropolitan scale, in 2006 an association of municipalities was created, named City Surroundings Management, to promote cooperation and inter-municipal planning processes, and facilitate better communication among agencies across the city region, including on quality aspirations. However, without any formal planning tools or decision-making powers, the impact on the processes of urban design governance are minimal.

A number of relevant NGOs have regional branches covering Vienna, including the Chamber of Architects and Engineering Consultants and the Central Association of Austrian Architects. Besides representing their members, the Chamber regulates the profession and provides support for design competitions. The Association advocates for design quality to wider audiences through conferences and debates on architecture and urban design.

Local governance of design

Vested with its own regulatory planning framework and dual status, Vienna City Council is both the state and local planning authority. The local development concept is Vienna's main strategic plan defining the spatial development objectives for the city (OECD 2017: 57). Below this, there are zoning and development plans that are binding for landowners and which contain general zoning regulations defining the permitted types of land use. In addition, the City Council develops concept plans for major development projects that are not binding but inform the public and test concepts at an early stage. Besides these formal tools, the council has several informal tools, among which are its *Baukultur* policy, urban design competitions (see Figure 3.21), a design advisory board and a wide range of design cultural initiatives.

In 2005 the city organised the Vienna Year of Architecture and, after a public consultation process, adopted a design policy laying down the city's vision for architecture and urban design, entitled the *Vienna Architectural Declaration* and aimed at documenting the position of the city in relation to architecture and construction. Building on this foundation, in 2014 the City Council adopted a city *Baulkultur* policy – *Baukultur Wien* – establishing clear design-quality principles for the realisation of urban projects. In particular it advocated that the City Council, in its own projects, should act as a role-model for private investors encompassing quality of life, usability, sustainability and participation (Stad Wien 2014).

Figure 3.21 Quarter Two (Viertel Zwei) is an office and residential area in the 2nd district of Vienna. After a cooperative planning process between the City Council and landowners involving several architecture and urban design competitions, the project was built between 2007 and 2010 (image: João Bento).

To support its formal regulatory responsibilities, the City Council set up a department focused on implementing its architecture and urban design policy – Department 19. Their mission is to develop the Viennese cityscape in a contemporary way, fostering a culture of place-making and strengthening awareness of the designed living environment. Department 19 is split into four divisions:

- Urban development: working closely with the urban development department on zoning and land-use plans as well as on concept plans, giving expert advice on major projects and conducting studies on different urban design issues, for example on view corridors.
- Public space: working with the department for streets and infrastructure and giving expert advice on the impact of small interventions in the cityscape, such as kiosks and advertisement boards. This division also promotes citizen participation in the public-space design process and sometimes organises design competitions.

- Design review: working alongside the issuing of building permits to implement special provisions in the Viennese Building Code stipulating that buildings should fit into the cityscape. This division receives up to eight thousand requests per year, largely from private developers who have to submit detailed designs to secure a permission. For complex projects, or projects with a major impact on the cityscape, Department 19 may request a design competition or submit the project to a design advisory board.
- Public building: focusing on the design and delivery of Viennese public buildings, such as schools, kindergartens, office buildings and special buildings for other departments, such as the fire department. This is the largest division (around 30 staff, compared with around 7 in each of the other divisions), largely consisting of professional architects managing some two hundred projects at any time. Major projects are often managed through an open or two-stage design competition.

To conduct its work cutting across that of other departments requires that Department 19 maintains very good working relationships, including with the municipal social housing company (Wiener Wohnen) which it advises and which houses a quarter of the Viennese population in homes that are widely lauded for their quality (Licka and Rode 2014, and see Figure 3.22). Wiener Wohnen regularly promotes design competitions for new housing schemes and uses concept tendering through which the delivery of high-quality outcomes is built into the broader financial process of selling or leasing public land (see Box 22, p. 215).

To provide specific expert design advice to the City Council, an Advisory Board for Urban Planning and Urban Design has long been in existence, in various guises dating back to the Vienna Building Code of 1929. Today this is focused on reviewing zoning plans for the city and assessing, when requested, building projects likely to have a significant influence on the local cityscape. In practical terms this happens only for the most significant projects that are likely to be subject to public debate, with other projects reviewed in-house (within Department 19). While the process is discretionary and the opinions expressed are non-binding, they do tend to strongly influence political decision-making. Whether the Advisory Board process is used or not, it is nevertheless mandatory to obtain an expert opinion on zoning proposals and plans prior to a political decision.

Appointed by the Mayor of Vienna, the 12 members of the advisory board act on an honorary basis for three years and cover a range of

Figure 3.22 In Vienna 62 per cent of residents live in social housing, which has a reputation for the quality of its environments, space and amenities (Ball 2019), including here at the Alt-Erlaa Social Housing complex (image: Matthew Carmona).

expertise including architecture, civil engineering, spatial planning, historical monuments, property, urban ecology, social issues, and landscape. Meetings are not open to the public and members are expected to evaluate submitted designs from an independent position and without political influence, thus delivering important non-binding advice to complement the City's ongoing design review function (Bento and Laopoulou 2019).

Department 19 also collaborates with the Architecture Centre of Vienna and other partners to foster public awareness activities. These include exhibitions and publications, but also architecture tours around Vienna and educational programmes aimed at children and young people, with dedicated resources about the built environment prepared for use in Viennese schools. The educational programme 'What Creates Space?', for example, is a joint project of the City Council in cooperation with the Vienna Education Directorate and the Children and Youth Municipal Department.

The Architecture Centre of Vienna was founded by an initiative of the State and City of Vienna in 1993. Based in Vienna's museum quarter, the Centre is dedicated to showcase architecture and urban development in Austria. It offers a wide-ranging programme of events and exhibitions, amounting to some five hundred events a year including symposia, workshops, lectures, guided tours, and city expeditions to film series and hands-on engagement. It also provides a service for researchers and all those interested in architecture, and receives funding from the federal government, the city council and from private sponsors.

Comparing the landscapes

The three urban design governance landscapes set out above are just three of many thousands of such landscapes that could have been chosen, each representing particular cities, municipalities, or places in Europe. Even within Lisbon, the waterfront area has a different landscape to other parts of the city, while in London each of the 33 boroughs (including the City of London) has its own unique set of practices. Inevitably, because of the nature of the landscapes chosen – each for a whole large European capital city – the results are more complex and more layered than would be the case in a smaller settlement or largely rural area, for example. Yet the similarities also facilitate the drawing out of meaningful overarching conclusions from comparing the urban design governance landscapes.

A first clear observation is that all these cities are on the same journey, one in which design quality is on the agenda and being prioritised – in different ways and to different degrees. This was not always the case, indeed London and Lisbon were notoriously lax about such issues in the recent past, although since the 2000s each city has in their own way found a path towards building a culture of design quality. Sometimes this has come from the bottom-up, such as Lisbon's public space programme driven by the city council; sometimes from the top-down, for example London's mayoral system imposed by government from 2000 onwards in an attempt to address the complex governance issues of the city (including its design); and sometimes this is done in a more coordinated manner with central and local government seeming to work together, as represented by Austrian and Viennese *Baukultur* policy, each element building on and reinforcing the others.

Yet while the ambition may be similar – higher quality, more liveable and sustainable cities – because the cities are each starting from different places and are influenced by different governance traditions and structures, it is inevitable that they will be on different trajectories to reach their destinations. The urban design governance landscapes represented in Figures 3.6, 3.12 and 3.18 show this. London, the largest of the three cities (by some margin) is also the only one with a clear three-tier governance structure, and also demonstrates the broadest distribution of tools spread across both formal and informal categories, encompassing an increasingly strong reliance on informal tools. Here the city demonstrates an advantage that its size brings in the diversity and innovation of its urban design governance practices. However, there is also a hidden disadvantage. Thus, while design quality is clearly prioritised in some parts of the city (in some of its boroughs), this is far from true everywhere, and this leads to a lottery of provision that is not so apparent elsewhere.

Lisbon and Vienna are similar-sized cities (each about a third the size of London) and each have a two-tier governance structure, but while central government is dominant in Portugal it is not in Austria. This shows itself in a tendency for Lisbon to rely on the formal tools of urban design governance and the more basic forms of informal tool, namely information (albeit with an exemplary public spaces programme). Vienna, by contrast, has developed a sophisticated series of informal tools that work alongside and reinforce the formal tools of government.

Although each of the cities are using informal tools, some are more reliant on them than others, and this tends to reflect their stage in the overall urban design governance trajectory. What is clear is that where a strong national commitment exists to delivering design quality, this has a powerful impact in either establishing or boosting local ambition, with the ultimate aim of creating a system of layered competences (sometimes overlapping) that can consistently bear down on securing a culture of design quality. At the same time, delivery is almost entirely a local responsibility, and so local ambition is also key to building a sustained local commitment to design quality. The landscapes (Figures 3.6, 3.12 and 3.18) don't reveal if this is being achieved or not, but strongly indicate whether the tools are in place to make its achievement more or less likely.

From an examination of three urban design landscapes featuring a diversity of practices, the next chapter moves on to explore, more systematically, the various informal tools of urban design governance being used across Europe.

4

Understanding the informal tools

Drawing on learning from across the Urban Maestro project, this fourth chapter turns to explore each of the informal tools of urban design governance in turn. Beyond the European survey discussed in the previous chapter, the analysis draws from two sources, the systematic panorama of practices from across Europe gradually revealed during the course of the project, and a series of case studies that focused on particular experiences in greater depth. The chapter is divided into six subsections, each exploring a particular informal tool: analysis, information, persuasion, rating, support and exploration. The tools are illustrated with examples from the panorama and together reflect the diversity and often the cutting edge of European urban design governance tools and practices.

Building a panorama of European practices

Although the European survey of informal urban design governance practices discussed in Chapter 3 began the process of building a pan-European record of urban design governance practices, it relied on national-level institutions to identify informal urban design governance practices in their country. By itself this evidence offered a top-down view of the field that was sometimes limited because many practices are instigated and developed at city-wide or local scales. It was therefore vital to tap into the bottom-up knowledge of local actors in order to build a more comprehensive panorama of informal urban design governance practices. This involved two stages of work:

- Using the European survey as a starting point and then supplementing it through a snowballing process involving both on-line searches and pursuing leads suggested by in-person contacts, more than a hundred informal urban design governance practices were identified and reviewed. The majority were summarised in a series of published and searchable resources at https://urbanmaestro.org. The work was largely undertaken on the basis of published information leading to the posting, initially, of a fact sheet for each practice covering thirty countries. In addition to those identified by the team, an open call was made through the project website, and the suggested practices were added to the panorama if they met key criteria: informal, innovative and not already covered. While this work often relied on secondary sources, many of the practices were later discussed at project workshops (see Chapter 6) and verified through primary sources.

- Building on the panorama, and selecting tools that were both innovative and representative of different informal urban design governance practices, thirty in-depth case studies were undertaken. Some were researched and written by the research team on the basis of analysing secondary documentation backed by interviews with the key stakeholders involved. Others were commissioned as 'expert papers' from academics and professionals associated with particular practices (either through their research or practice). The intention was to gather greater insight into important practices and to feed that into the final element of the methodology, the workshops.

The discussion that follows analyses each informal tool of urban design governance before Chapter 5 relates them to financial mechanisms and Chapters 6 and 7 bring the tools together and connect them back to the larger urban governance context to discuss how tools are delivered through the diverse urban design governance landscapes found in Europe.

At this point it is worth noting that a few tools are more comprehensively studied and theorised at the European scale than others, notably architecture competitions and design reviews. These might be seen as the dominant informal urban design governance tools across Europe and it is therefore unsurprising that they have piqued greater academic interest. Key studies relating to these rating tools are discussed where appropriate in this chapter. Secondary sources of comparative information on other informal tools are largely non-existent.

Analysis tools

Analysis tools are the least interventionist of the informal tools, being largely concerned with building an evidence-base through which to understand the environment within which urban design governance is practised and the processes by which the built environment is shaped. Despite this, they can be powerful tools in their own right, helping to provide the raw material through which poor practices can be critiqued and best practices revealed, tools developed or abandoned, and around which arguments are built for change. They may also help governments to justify policy decisions by providing the raw material for more evidence-based public policymaking (Howlett et al. 2009). The information they provide should be public in order that the data can be used to underpin public-sector practices, and inform the decisions made by other actors.

Types of analysis tools

Three main types of analysis were identified across Europe:

- **Research**, focused on understanding design processes or particular design-based problems. Research is used as an evidence-base in order to focus attention on those practices, to devise solutions, including new policy responses, and to advocate for those approaches.
- **Monitoring** of initiatives, tools and policy objectives, particularly the measurement of the impacts from particular urban design governance tools, both prior to interventions and afterwards to evaluate their impact and to refine approaches.
- **Audits** of the state of the built environment, in order to understand the quality of the designed built environment and the challenges it presents. Such audits vary from the comprehensive evaluation of whole territories, to the measurement of particular local areas/neighbourhoods, to national audits of particular built typologies such as housing, schools, infrastructure and so forth.

Delivering analysis tools

Approaches to analysis vary across Europe, responding to the particular needs of project objectives and to the context within which the work is being conducted (in other words, who is doing the work, with what resources and to whom are they reporting). In some countries, forms of analysis are mandatory, for example as part of the preparation of spatial planning strategies such as the 2017 *State of Territory Report* conducted by the Romanian Government. The majority of governmental institutions and non-governmental organisations, however, use analysis tools on a discretionary basis at different times and for different purposes.

In some of the most sophisticated examples, dedicated teams are tasked with this form of analysis. The German Federal Foundation of Baukultur, for example, is responsible for managing and delivering the biennial *Baukultur* reports (see Box 1), an activity mainly conducted by an in-house team of four full-time employees but drawing in specialist expertise as and when required (Nagel et al. 2020). The German approach is unusual, both in its scale and in its conduct, given that the majority of analysis across Europe is conducted at a smaller scale and commissioned externally from consultancies or universities. This offers the opportunity to tap into concentrations of expertise in these locations, as well as to support innovative practices (such as the Flemish Bouwmeester's 'Bouwmeester Label' grant funding for small research projects that explore innovative and policy-relevant ideas), but at the expense of consistency in approach over time. Collaborative projects are also common.

Box 1   Assessing quality: Germany's biennial *Baukultur* reports (Germany)

The Federal Foundation of Baukultur is an independent entity whose purpose is to promote *Baukultur* (building culture) based on a belief that a high-quality built environment contributes substantially to quality of life in Germany (https://www.bundesstiftung-baukultur.de/en/). The Foundation's mission is to make the built environment a shared concern with four aims:

- To raise awareness of *Baukultur* among the public.
- To initiate a broad debate among building professionals on the quality of *Baukultur*.
- To encourage discussion on the subject of *Baukultur* among local authorities and state administrations.
- To promote the qualities of German *Baukultur* at an international level.

A primary tool of the foundation is its biennial *Baukultur* report, which is coordinated by the foundation on behalf of the German

---

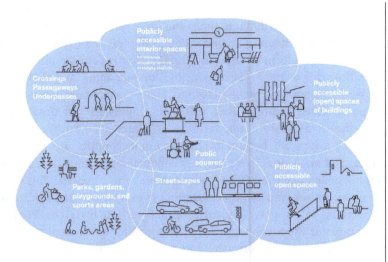

Figure 4.1 Scope of the 2020/21 *Baukultur* report (image: Federal Foundation of Baukultur 2021).

federal government as an official status report. The Federal Foundation of Baukultur is one of the few institutions in Germany that is entitled to submit a report to the Federal Cabinet and the Federal Parliament (the Bundestag and the Bundesrat) and this right of submittal gives the *Baukultur* reports a high status and ensures they are taken seriously by government.

Each report takes on a different focus. Earlier reports looked at housing and mixed neighbourhoods, small- and medium-sized urban areas, and, in 2020/21, public spaces (see Figure 4.1). The *Baukultur* reports are created with the involvement of numerous specialists, experts, associations, an advisory group, and the Foundation's own expert bodies (see Figure 4.2).

The report links the positions of the Baukultur Foundation with project examples from their numerous *Baukultur* workshops and arguments from expert discussions held in the run-up to report production. The report also includes statistical data, as well as the results of a municipal survey on planning practices and a population survey on the housing and living environment. The collected findings lead to concrete recommendations for action for all actors involved in planning and construction in Germany.

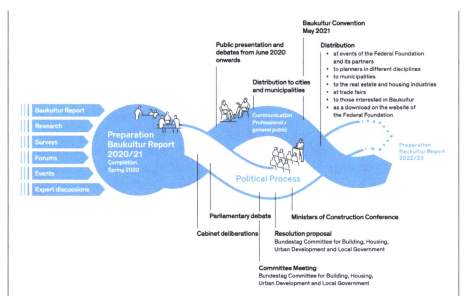

Figure 4.2 *Baukultur* report production process (image: Federal Foundation of Baukultur 2021).

Deployment of analysis tools?

Almost all respondents to the Europe-wide survey referred to the conduct or commissioning of research on design-related themes by central or local administrations or by arms-length or non-governmental bodies. Different types of 'state of the built environment' audits are also very widespread, often focused on particular types of development:

- Governmental organisations most often seek to build an evidence base about design processes in order to improve their knowledge and associated design governance processes. This work is done across spatial scales from the nation-state to city-wide and local governments. The Prague Institute of Planning and Development, for example, hosts an ongoing research programme providing empirical data for city council departments and other stakeholders, focused on the built fabric and public spaces of Prague.
- Arms-length governmental organisations (funded by government but with independent decision-making powers) use analysis tools not only to inform their own programmes but also to inform and influence governmental and private actors including, in the case of

the Design Commission for Wales (DCfW), the monitoring of design review. Some provide tools that others can use to conduct their own analysis, such as the Flemish Bouwmeester's 'Bouwmeester Scan', a tool available to local authorities in the region who want to map their spatial and policy strengths and weaknesses (https://www.vlaamsbouwmeester.be/nl/subsite/bouwmeester-scan).

- Non-governmental organisations also employ analysis tools to develop new knowledge and evidence about the built environment. Sometimes this is used to inform their members and/or assist them in their work, as is a key role of the Councils of Architecture, Urbanism and the Environment in France or the Danish Association of Architects (DAA). It can also provide the raw material for campaigning, as is the case in England where the Place Alliance's *Housing Design Audit for England*, launched in 2020, was used to build a stronger coalition around the case for design quality, building on the organisation's earlier publication, *Place Value and the Ladder of Place Quality*, which offered the raw evidence that stakeholders need to make the case for prioritising design quality (see Box 2).

Box 2   Campaigning for quality: Place Alliance (England, UK)

Established in 2014, Place Alliance is a non-profit network, hosted by UCL, that campaigns for place quality in England. The alliance is supported by more than a hundred organisations connected to the built environment (http://placealliance.org.uk/).

Through its body of work, Place Alliance supports evidence-based discussion at national and local levels. Its analysis initiatives utilise background research and evidence gathering (in collaboration with partners) that facilitate an evidence-based conversation and ultimately influence more informed policy and practice. These outputs and the research results they contain are presented in an accessible manner to related stakeholders, including to national policymakers, local authorities and professionals, as well as to lay audiences.

Research began with *Design Skills in English Local Authorities* (2017), a report that summarised the findings of a national survey of urban design skills/resources within local planning authorities nationally and how they had changed over the previous five years. The research, which identified a national crisis in urban design

---

capacity, led directly to government putting together a short-term funding package to address the issue, demonstrating the value of focused and directed evidence.

Since then, the research of Place Alliance has covered a diversity of topics: design review practices, the value of place quality, local politicians' attitudes to housing design, public perceptions of neighbourhood environments during the Covid lockdown, and the use and effectiveness of urban design governance tools. The highest-profile study – *A Housing Design Audit for England* (2020) – offered a systematic national audit of the design quality of the external residential environment (see Figure 4.3). The audit assessed 142 large-scale developments across England and provided enough data for comparisons to be made between regions and different approaches to the delivery of new housing. The project was an influential input into a sustained campaign nationally for a stronger priority to be given to design quality, a call progressively answered from 2020 onwards, thanks to significant changes in national policy on design (see Chapter 3).

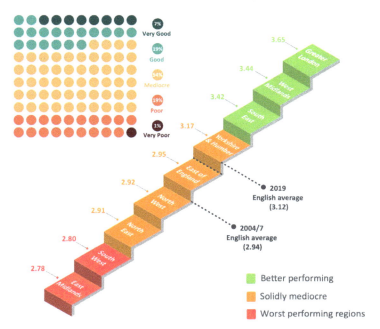

Figure 4.3   Housing design audit headline results, national and regional (image: Place Alliance).

Looking across the spectrum of analysis tools these activities transcend all stages of the urban design governance field of action – pre-development, development and post-development (see Figures 7.5a–c, pp. 279–81) – with evidence-gathering offering the potential to inform all approaches to the governance of design, and all regimes of implementation. Ultimately analysis can be a very political tool, allowing others to challenge policy, progress towards quality ambitions and to suggest alternative courses of action. The biennial *Baukultur* reports in Germany, for example, have an official status and are presented to parliament where they can be used to challenge governmental decision-making (see Box 1). Elsewhere the challenge is to ensure that the analysis is seen by the right audiences in order that it has an influence.

Experience of analysis tools

Above all, analysis tools feed urban design governance organisations with intelligence to aid decision-making, facilitate reporting on activities and policy directions based on evidence, and open up conversations with external parties. They can facilitate better communication on design and help to support stakeholders attempting to build the case for design quality, thus helping to foster a place-making culture. Ultimately, they can inform the use and effectiveness of all the other tools of urban design governance, but particularly the other informal quality-culture tools: information and persuasion.

Despite the benefits, analysis can be time-consuming and expensive and the benefits will rarely be seen quickly. For this reason, if conducted at all, analysis is often externalised or used only exceptionally when dedicated sources of funding allow. A parallel challenge is the inverse relationship that tends to hold between the speed at which research is produced and its rigour. Some institutions demonstrate the need to show their relevance to government through their contribution to topical debates, but a rush to produce analysis of complex multi-faceted built-environment concerns can either produce evidence that lacks depth or fails to adequately disseminate key messages in a suitably accessible manner.

Within government the use of analysis tools has become an everyday occurrence boosted by the rise of E-government and big data, which is informing many audits of the built environment using systems of urban indicators and statistical data. The use of richer qualitative data is less frequent. Biennial *Baukultur* reports, for example, started in Austria in 2006 and inspired the development of similar reports in Germany

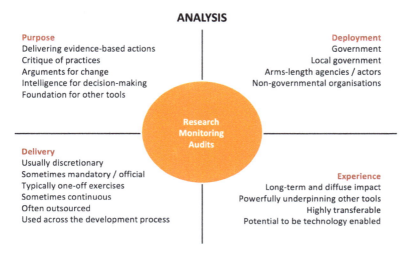

ANALYSIS

Purpose
Delivering evidence-based actions
Critique of practices
Arguments for change
Intelligence for decision-making
Foundation for other tools

Deployment
Government
Local government
Arms-length agencies / actors
Non-governmental organisations

Research
Monitoring
Audits

Delivery
Usually discretionary
Sometimes mandatory / official
Typically one-off exercises
Sometimes continuous
Often outsourced
Used across the development process

Experience
Long-term and diffuse impact
Powerfully underpinning other tools
Highly transferable
Potential to be technology enabled

Figure 4.4 Summarising analysis tools (image: Matthew Carmona).

in 2014, and in a simplified format in Switzerland in 2018. In this case transferability was assisted by the similarities in systems and of course language in these three German-speaking countries, thus facilitating the sharing of knowledge and experience. This demonstrates a regional spread of practices in Europe that is common across urban design governance tools. Generally, however, because analysis tools are not intrinsically tied to particular regulatory practices, most are highly transferable.

It was clear from the European survey that the most sophisticated governmental and non-/arms-length governmental organisations continually use these means to underpin their own practices through establishing an evidence-based approach to the design of the built environment. In these circumstances, evidence is the foundation on which other tools can be built (see Figure 4.4).

Information tools

Information tools are fundamentally about the dissemination of knowledge. Often this concerns good (or poor) design outcomes and processes, as well as related development practices, and why it matters. They help to raise awareness of design ambitions and know-how among stakeholders and to build interest (and capacity) within society at large. They are often closely related to analysis tools, building on research findings for example, but the knowledge underpinning such tools may also derive from the practice and experience of professionals as much as from systematic research. They are also used as the jumping-off point from which a drive to build a culture of quality is launched by establishing and articulating clear ambitions for change.

Types of information tools

Two main types of information were identified through the Urban Maestro panorama, the first being more passive than the second, which more actively takes learning to key audiences:

- **Knowledge-sharing** tools encompass practice guides and manuals, case studies and online resources of different sorts:
  - *Practice guides and manuals* are typically produced to disseminate the accumulated wisdom of particular groups or the insights garnered from research, and can be directed at filling gaps in knowledge, educating key players, offering specific technical information, disseminating evidence, or sometimes simply setting out a particular policy proposition. Often the advice is generic rather than specific to a particular place or project. The European survey revealed guides and manuals covering a very wide range of topics encompassing all aspects of architecture, urban design, heritage, landscape and sustainability, as well as a range of design process issues such as how to conduct a design competition.
  - *Case studies* of successful examples of architecture, urban design, landscape design, and so on can be used to inform and inspire development actors and even the general public, either through their collection into a library of exemplary cases or by publishing best-practice examples. Although they are still passive, cases studies are more directive in the sense that they identify specific 'best practice', and therefore go a stage further than the general principles contained in practice guides.
  - *Dedicated web portals* have been appearing across Europe to publish information about architecture, urban design, heritage, and so on. Some countries have developed online architecture and urban design databases to disseminate information on high-quality projects and to promote them nationally and even internationally, for example, the Finnish 'Architecture Navigator' curated by the national centre for

architecture, Archinfo Finland (https://finnisharchitecture.fi) (see Figure 4.5).

- **Active learning** involves the direct engagement of participants in a structured learning exercise. These involve basic and/or specialist training around aspects of the design of the built environment:
  - ○ *Specialist training* focuses on improving the capacity of professional stakeholders to deliver better design and are often technical or process-oriented in nature.
  - ○ *Basic education* encompasses educational programmes focused on laypersons or young people so that they can become knowledgeable and participant citizens in built-environment-related decision-making.

Figure 4.5 The Architecture Navigator provides information on contemporary and historic architecture across Finland, and allows searches by function, location, design team and other criteria; in this example, housing in Helsinki (images: Matthew Carmona).

Delivering information tools

The preparation and production of information tools varies according to the level of resources and expertise available in the institutions that promote them. Some are produced internally, others commissioned from external parties or developed on a collaborative basis with several partners.

The format and content of practice guides, manuals and case studies are adapted to the target audience, ranging from public officials to developers, designers, clients and the general public. For professionals, a more technical approach tends to be followed, whereas for lay audiences a more accessible approach is adopted. Architecture and Design Scotland, for example, developed the Inspiring Learning Spaces Toolkit in collaboration with the Scottish Futures Trust. The toolkit targets the key issues that will enhance learners' experience through the spatial organisation of learning environments and their management, all supported by leadership across the school community. Presented as a route map and supported by practical examples, questions and resources, the toolkit targets educationalists seeking to widen opportunities for learners in all schools by creatively rethinking the role of space (https://www.ads.org.uk/inspiring-learning-spaces-toolkit/).

Most of these types of resources are now provided electronically and often as a free download. Some institutions have also developed digital libraries of case studies championing high-quality architecture and urban design and disseminating best practice as part of their website resources. Examples are collected and elaborated externally or by staff within the commissioning organisations, who then upload them to online libraries that are thematically organised and searchable. Examples include the be.exemplary collection of sustainable urban projects put together by the Brussels Capital Region (http://beexemplary.brussels) and Nextroom, a well-known not-for-profit online platform for high-quality contemporary architecture focusing on Austria, but also covering neighbouring Slovenia, Slovakia, Hungary and Croatia (https://www.nextroom.at).

More active training and education tools are similarly distinguished by the audience that is being reached. The most conventional way of delivering specialist training tools is through Continuing Professional Development (CPD) programmes within architecture and urban design fields that range in level from introductory to in-depth and advanced. This may be delivered directly by the suppliers of the training using internal staff, or alternatively by invited experts, and typically entails a cost for the participants. Often these are one-off charges relating to a particular training session, but occasionally individual or corporate subscriptions are levied for a programme of events, a model used by Urban Design London (see Box 3). Ad hoc events, such as conferences, symposiums or congresses around particular themes are also common, for example organised by governmental organisations to disseminate new policy initiatives, and by professional networks to facilitate learning, networking and exchange among members.

Box 3   Enhancing professional knowledge: Urban Design London (England, UK)

Urban Design London (UDL) is a not-for-profit organisation established to assist built-environment professionals and decision-makers create well-designed spaces and places. It was set up in 2002 to offer training to relevant professionals from the public sector across London, but has since developed its range of services to include research, the production of guidance, and the conduct of design reviews. From 2021 it developed a national (England-wide) programme under the name Urban Design Learning (https://www.urbandesignlondon.com).

UDL is formally part of Transport for London but operates with oversight from its own board and advice from a network of 'wise friends'. It consists of a small team of seven and is largely independent from its host organisation.

UDL is in large part funded by subscriptions from the London Boroughs and other public-sector organisations such as the Greater London Authority, and several non-profits and private companies. Organisations pay a yearly fee to enable their staff to attend UDL events. UDL also benefits from a limited amount of private sponsorship, income from commissions, including work done for central government, some limited core funding from Transport for London, and income from one-off events such as its 2021 'Code school' (see Figure 4.6).

The largest part of UDL's work remains its training programme. This consists of a wide range of CPD-style events that cross the urban design remit, from technical training (such as designing cycling facilities) to process issues (for example dealing with the

---

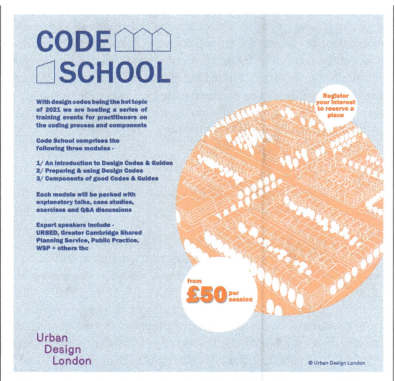

Figure 4.6 Urban Design London's 'Code school' supported a larger national drive to promote design coding as part of more design-focused housing development processes in England (image: Urban Design London).

planning system) to forward-looking trends such as how to achieve greener design. They range in level from introductory to in-depth and advanced. The programme of ad hoc events is accompanied by regular meetings for specific professional groups and networks, such as London's network of design review managers, local politicians, and young practitioners.

Educational programmes focused on lay and young audiences are usually short and introductory in nature. This type of initiative involves the preparation and provision of teaching materials and the organisation of events. This may be delivered directly by the institutions responsible, or indirectly, where resources are made available for others to use, for example educational resources for school pupils that focus on built-environment issues. The national campaign 'Panorama Nederlands' from the Dutch Board of Government Advisers provides a case in point. Here, an educational resource to be used by teachers with secondary school students focuses on the challenges and future spatial vision of the Netherlands. Teachers can order copies of this resource to work with students in class or use the digital materials available online (https:// www.collegevanrijksadviseurs.nl/projecten/panorama-nederland).

Deployment of information tools?

The focus of information tools can be at any stage of the urban design governance field of action (see Figures 7.5a–c, pp. 279–81). Yet while some guides may focus on very specific technical problems, such as integrating energy-saving technologies, very often the subject matter is more general and focused on raising ambitions at the start of the development process (or even, in the case of children's education, long before it). They are a tool typically deployed after the decision has been made to build a stronger culture of design quality and therefore to influence future (as yet unknown) development. A wide range of organisations are responsible:

- Governmental organisations are frequent users of knowledge-sharing tools, although far less frequently of more active learning forms. They publish guides and manuals on a regular basis covering different aspects of the built environment and a wide range of design topics. The Irish Department for Housing, Local Government and Heritage, for example, produces a wide range of urban design guides and practice circulars to disseminate current and exemplary practices in urban design, high-quality place-making and sustainable development, including the publication of best-practice case studies. Such practices are very common across Europe at national and local scales, and about half of governmental departments collect and publish case studies of successful examples of development to inspire, challenge and encourage decision-makers. Sometimes these are an end in themselves – published as an inventory (on- and off-line) – and sometimes they feed into other knowledge tools, such as practice guides. For example, the online Nextroom database for contemporary architecture continues to receive a grant from the Austrian Federal Chancellery to offer a wide range of documentation of outstanding projects and a long-term online archive.

- Non-governmental and arms-length-governmental organisations are more frequent promoters of active information tools, including them as part of regular events cycles and the services they provide. Almost all of the organisations of this type identified during the project seem to be involved in some kind of educational activities, with professional organisations focusing on professionals while cultural organisations focus on more general educational programmes, including for younger generations. Governments are also regular funders of these organisations, preferring to delegate this sort of specialist training provision to others rather than organise it themselves. Non-governmental and arms-length organisations are also frequent publishers of best-practice case studies through databases, publications and exhibitions. Many have extensive lists of publications, with the French Councils of Architecture, Urbanism and the Environment (CAUE), for example, collecting examples from across its network and making them available to all via its online portal organised in seven thematic sections: architecture, urbanism, environment, heritage, energy, landscape and biodiversity (https://www.fncaue.com/dossiers-thematiques/) (see Box 14, p. 173).

Often different forms of information are utilised together, with publications forming the basis for training. In the UK, for example, the government-funded the Design Network (a network of not-for-profit organisations) to provide training on design to local politicians around England who have a key decision-making role within the planning system. As part of this, a concise guide – *Councillors Companion for Design in Planning* – was produced to assist local politicians to evaluate good design.

An area of growth seems to be the reaching out to schools in order to get children to engage with the built environment, its impact and quality. For example, every year thousands of pupils and teachers take part in activities for schools at Sweden's National Centre for Architecture and Design (ArkDes). ArkDes prepares comprehensive school programmes covering a range of subjects allowing pupils to participate in topics from housing to colour and form in architecture. The ArkDes teachers inspire pupils by means of discussions, guided tours and practical tasks such as building models. In Finland the School of Architecture for Children and Youth (Arkki) is a non-profit organisation that offers a variety of architectural courses to young people and creates educational curricula for schools, museums and architecture clubs. It was set up specifically to promote educational activities to this audience as part of a unique national architectural policy programme, which has resulted in a wide range of new architectural resources and educational materials (Fröbe 2020) (see Box 4).

Box 4   Inspiring the next generation: Arkki School of Architecture for Children and Youth (Finland)

Arkki offers educational courses in architecture and design for students aged four to nineteen. They organise regular courses alongside large, more occasional events and workshops; produce educational materials; provide training for teachers and educators; and collaborate with schools and art institutions. Rather than focusing on architecture itself, Arkki's work focuses on developing capabilities to observe, evaluate, and reimagine the built environment, thus stimulating young people's minds.

Arkki was founded by three architects in Finland in 1993. It is a not-for-profit organisation that accepts financial aid, donations and bequests, as well as conducting fundraisers. Via its global arm, Arkki International, the organisation now has twenty centres across nine countries, including Greece, China, Cyprus, the Czech Republic, Turkey and Vietnam, where franchisees now operate local branches on the basis of the approaches and materials produced centrally (https://www.arkki.com/).

Arkki utilises a range of methods but emphasises 3D working models and 1:1 scale structures (see Figure 4.7). Their philosophy is that learning occurs through play and planned work on projects, hence their teaching methods revolve around allowing students to discover and learn on their own through active, personally guided and three-dimensional building. Different programmes are designed for child and parent groups (4–6 years), basic education (7–14 years) and advanced studies (14–19 years), each with age-appropriate projects to engage students' imaginations while introducing them to basic spatial concepts such as space, light, materials and structures.

Arkki's programme has been approved by the Finnish Ministry of Education and Culture as a creative extracurricular education programme, and on the strength of this the organisation puts significant effort into building partnerships and cooperation models

---

Figure 4.7 Using models to explore the built environment, Arkki Greece (image: Natalia Pantelidou).

both locally – with schools, nurseries and art institutes – and nationally, where it is represented on key education-related committees and cooperates with museums, city councils and the building industry at large

Experience of information tools

Information tools can focus on both the demand and supply sides of the development process. By providing new information and increasing the stock of knowledge on design through best-practice examples, manuals and guidance, as well as training of all sorts, information tools help practitioners in their day-to-day work. By doing so, they aim to create a favourable decision-making environment that appropriately prioritises design quality. Information tools also aspire to influence the general public by raising their understanding and design awareness through easy-reading documents and pedagogic material on different architecture and urban-design themes. Both play a role in the wider communication and campaigning activities that can help to persuade decision-makers of the importance of prioritising design quality; raise the aspirations, understanding and skills of professionals; and raise the expectations and demand for better design quality in society at large.

The benefits of information tools are often very diffuse and therefore gradual and difficult to measure. Nevertheless, these sorts of tools, particularly those directed at professionals, are some of the most popular in the urban design governance toolkit, with a close relationship to other quality-culture tools, namely analysis (which they help to disseminate) and persuasion (for which they can provide the raw materials). They also often have a direct relationship to quality-delivery tools that they help to explain and even systemise, including process guides to design competitions, design review, and other tools. They are cheap and relatively easy to produce, and via video-conference-based training programmes, published materials can be cost effective to disseminate to large audiences. Unfortunately, they also tend to be viewed as one-off initiatives that, once produced, may only be promoted for a short time before being left on the shelf to go out of date, rather than being promoted to new audiences.

Ultimately, the effectiveness of knowledge-sharing and active-learning tools (if measured by their impact) is likely to depend on their status, and in particular on the organisations involved in promoting them and the focus they have. No matter how worthy, practice guides and manuals typically remain only sources of discretionary guidance and inspiration, for example, *An Architecture Guide to the UN 17 Sustainable Development Goals*, produced by a collaboration of academic, professional and institutional partners in Denmark (see Box 5). Others are more directive, and even cross over into the formal category of urban design governance tools if their parameters become enforceable, for instance the sorts of public-realm manuals produced in Lisbon (see Chapter 3). Such sources of information also directly complement formal regulatory protocols by providing attractive, easy-to-read material directed across professional and lay audiences.

The sheer diversity of such tools and their quantity across Europe demonstrates that they are considered to be of value across the continent and are a tool that is readily transferable in type, if not necessarily in content. Collectively, these are the most widely used of informal urban design governance tools and are increasingly being delivered by more sophisticated online and interactive means, notably through internet portals and dedicated exhibition spaces. Whether this implies that they are effective, or just comparatively quick and easy to produce and operationalise, is an open question. There is clearly huge variation in practice across Europe, both in the quality of content and its articulation, but the basic notion that designers, developers, decision-makers and even the general public need better knowledge about what is and is not good design in different contexts seems to powerfully inform the production

---

Box 5   Guiding with a social purpose: *An Architecture Guide to the UN 17 Sustainable Development Goals* **(Denmark/international)**

An Architecture Guide to the UN 17 Sustainable Development Goals was published in two volumes in 2018. It illustrates, for each of the 17 United Nations Sustainable Development Goals (SDGs), possible approaches to address the considerable design challenges associated with the goals (see Figure 4.8). The aim is to make tangible how the built environment interacts with the SDGs, and to inspire architects and stakeholders involved in the built environment to engage with the challenges. The guide was created as a collaboration between the Royal Danish Academy's Institute of Architecture and Technology along with the Academy's Schools of Architecture, Design and Conservation, the Danish Association of Architects and the UIA Commission on the UN Sustainable Development Goals (https://uia2023cph.org/the-guides).

Both volumes are structured against the SDGs, with each briefly explained and then related to the implications for the built environment. A host of realised architectural or urban projects are presented, with each identifying the specific challenge and the particular site-specific solutions that were employed.

This guide is unique in that it creates a direct connection between an abstract charter at the transnational global level and examples drawn from specific, down-to-earth local practices. By displaying and highlighting possible methods for directly translating the SDGs into buildings and urban spaces, and by including projects from around the world, the guide is relevant to practitioners globally, with new editions now published in French, Japanese and Portuguese, as well as the original English.

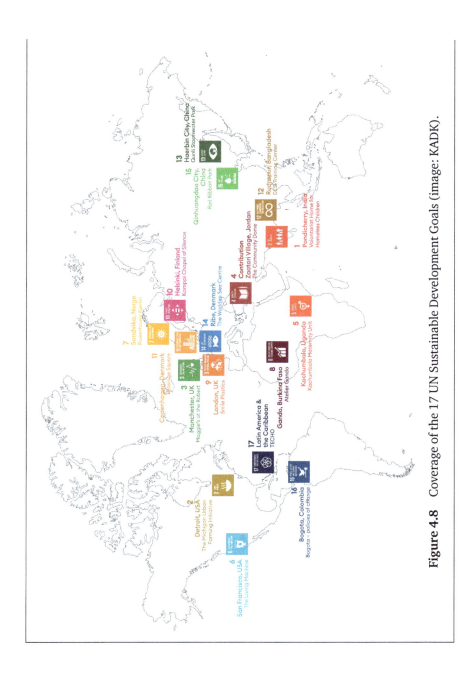

Figure 4.8 Coverage of the 17 UN Sustainable Development Goals (image: KADK).

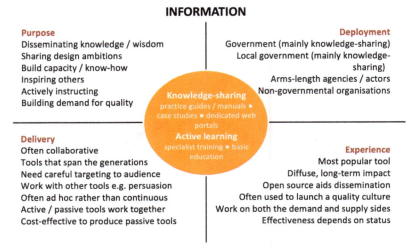

INFORMATION

Purpose
Disseminating knowledge / wisdom
Sharing design ambitions
Build capacity / know-how
Inspiring others
Actively instructing
Building demand for quality

Deployment
Government (mainly knowledge-sharing)
Local government (mainly knowledge-sharing)
Arms-length agencies / actors
Non-governmental organisations

Knowledge-sharing
practice guides / manuals •
case studies • dedicated web
portals
Active learning
specialist training • basic
education

Delivery
Often collaborative
Tools that span the generations
Need careful targeting to audience
Work with other tools e.g. persuasion
Often ad hoc rather than continuous
Active / passive tools work together
Cost-effective to produce passive tools

Experience
Most popular tool
Diffuse, long-term impact
Open source aids dissemination
Often used to launch a quality culture
Work on both the demand and supply sides
Effectiveness depends on status

Figure 4.9   Summarising information tools (image: Matthew Carmona).

of such tools. This is an area of activity that goes from strength to strength (see Figure 4.9).

Persuasion tools

As the name suggests, persuasion tools focus on persuading others about the merits of good design. They are more proactive than analysis and information tools because they actively take messages to key audiences such as politicians, investors, developers, professional groups and communities in order to engage them in a conversation. Their users aspire to raise awareness, motivate and mobilise public concern about the quality of places, influence practices and policies, change perceptions and practices in key areas, spread innovation, and directly advocate to critical audiences about the value of design for achieving better places. To do so, persuasion tools are often focused on particular defined audiences and typically involve partnership working, including collaboration across government and among a variety of organisations and groups.

Types of persuasion tools

Although approaches vary across the continent, the majority of governmental institutions and arms-length/non-governmental organisations utilise persuasion tools to promote good design. Two main types of tools were identified in the Urban Maestro panorama:

- **Promulgation tools**, such as design awards schemes or structured campaigns, focused on raising awareness and changing perceptions and practices in key areas:
  - *Design awards* vary across Europe, from high profile international prizes to local awards. They are focused on rewarding excellence in the design and/or development processes associated with completed schemes, and in so doing raise the profile of design quality and set new benchmarks for practice while also raising the profile of the organisations that establish them. There is a huge variety of awards promoted by state, regional and local governments, arms-length and non-governmental institutions (such as professional bodies, architecture centres and non-profit associations) and even by private firms. Their focus ranges from a specific typology, such as housing or commercial schemes, to professional achievement awards (for individuals or companies), to specific themes (including sustainable construction) or approaches to building (for instance, the use of brick), to awards for particular groups such as young designers, and for good design processes including commissioning practices. Awarded on a regular cycle, often annually or biennially, most design awards are explicitly promoted as part of wider awareness-raising campaigns, the goal being to reward best practice and innovation, but more importantly to raise the profile of design and to stimulate better practice within the sector (Biddulph et al. 2006).
  - *Campaigns* aim to raise awareness about aspects of design quality among those involved in commissioning and delivering buildings and developments as well as end-users and the general public. The intention is to change patterns of decision-making and raise demand for better design, with initiatives that range across three types of campaign: generic but often high-profile campaigns aimed at generally raising standards; specific campaigns featuring focused messaging on clearly defined development types or problems; and campaigns related to particular government policies or programmes.
  - *Events and festivals* celebrate a pre-existing design culture, whether based on heritage or contemporary design. Examples include the Madrid Architecture Week (see Box 6) and the Irish Engaging with Architecture Scheme, which finances cultural projects and initiatives such as exhibitions, events,

festivals and programmes, and is open to individuals, local authorities and organisations.

- **Influencing tools** aim to reach key decision-makers by taking the messages to them that design quality matters and is worthy of policy attention, investment, and of prioritising within public and private organisations, including developers. These tools include:
  - ○ *Direct advocacy*, from focused lobbying to larger meetings and events.
  - ○ *Alliance building*, through encouraging partnership between key groups of institutional actors or government departments in order to promote common practices that suitably prioritise and facilitate design quality.

Box 6   Engaging the community: Madrid Architecture Week (Spain)

Held for the eighteenth time in 2021, the Madrid Architecture Week is an annual event dedicated to the promotion of architecture and urbanism, including a diverse array of cultural activities, such as debates, exhibitions, architectural and urban planning itineraries, lectures and other open events (https://www.semanaarquitecturamadrid.com). The Madrid Architecture Week is organised by the Architects' Association of Madrid (COAM) through its Architectural Foundation, together with the City Council and the Community of Madrid (see Figure 4.10).

The Architecture Week is usually held in the first week of October and encompasses a diverse programme of events and activities in different institutions, including exhibitions, conferences, seminars and training courses. With new itineraries every year, one of the highlights of the event is the opening of buildings of recognised architectural value to guided tours for young and old people. The event also includes new collaborations: the 2021 Architecture Week featured Italy as the guest country, with participation from the Italian Embassy and Italian Institute of Culture.

The Architecture Week includes parallel activities, such as bestowing design awards that recognise the quality of recent architecture, good professional practices and exemplary initiatives

---

Figure 4.10 The annual Madrid Architecture Week involves a wide range of organisers (6), sponsors (9), media partners (5) and collaborators (56) to deliver the complex programme, including the Caixa Forum, Madrid (image: Matthew Carmona).

that have contributed to the dissemination of architecture; non-specialist training courses about the history and urban transformations Madrid has undergone; and the promotion of children's activities about architecture and heritage in various residential areas with the help of local neighbourhood associations.

Delivering persuasion tools

From the governance perspective, persuasion tools reflect the idea that the public sector should no longer be sitting back but should be actively and publicly making the case for good design, working through the network of organisations and groups that both influence outcomes and have a legitimate interest in delivering design quality. There are a wide range of institutions using these types of tool, leading to a huge diversity of practice across Europe. Persuasion tools have a strong connection with other urban design governance tools, and are rarely used in isolation. Stakeholders typically make use of various quality-culture tools in order to maximise outreach and impact, while the use and impact of quality-delivery tools are frequently disseminated through persuasion approaches.

These tools are more complex to deliver than other culture-quality tools, not least because they typically involve multiple parties and coordination (66 in the case of the 2021 Madrid Architecture Week), particularly when organised at the national level. Design awards, for example, tend to be promoted and organised by one institution, but often rely on wider collaborations to raise the profile of the award and support its organisation, and/or contribute financially. The French National Days of Architecture aim to raise awareness and stimulate architectural and urban design knowledge with a national event lasting three days and incorporating more than a thousand free events across the country, including meetings and debates, visits to architectural offices, visits to buildings and sites, urban walks, exhibitions, films, educational workshops, and so on. While the French Ministry of Culture is the overall coordinator, activities are delivered by institutional partners and their local members spread across the country, with several media partners involved to broadcast and disseminate the event.

Most of these tools are focused on the early part of the urban design governance process, helping to shape and influence the decision-making environment by raising awareness and arguing the case for good design. This is the case for most advocacy work, which is focused on encouraging actors to put in place the right sorts of resources, skills and processes to engage positively in design. Campaigns and events are also largely focused on the decision-making environment, on arguing the case for quality in order to get actors engaged and motivated around design, although their content and messages will focus on all dimensions of quality.

Alliances through partnerships and networks will ideally form early and will persevere, although different partnerships may focus on different stages of the place-shaping process. Finally, awards, which may sometimes focus on good process, more often on place quality and most frequently on project quality, will almost always be retrospective, looking back on a particular experience to make judgements about success. In doing this it is hoped that they will influence all stages of the design and development process (through the desire to win awards) and will also, through their impact, help to shape the decision-making environment in the future.

Deployment of persuasion tools?

Because they focus on convincing others about the merits of design quality, persuasion tools tend to concentrate on the early – pre-development – stages of the urban design governance field of action (see Figures 7.5a–c, pp. 279–81). The exception are design awards, which by their nature evaluate completed projects or processes – post-development – although they also then feed back into building a culture of design through celebrating success and inspiring others to emulate those practices. Persuasion tools are perhaps the most diverse tools as regards who is using them, with arms-length and non-governmental organisations being the most active in direct advocacy.

- **International bodies** promote a number of high-profile awards across Europe, making this the only tool consistently used at the international scale across the continent. The European Union Prize for Contemporary Architecture – the Mies van der Rohe Award – for example, includes an advisory committee drawn from 16 institutions in various countries, and the collaboration of 45 member organisations of the Architects' Council of Europe. Similarly, the European Prize for Urban Public Space offers a biennial award from the Centre de Cultura Contemporània de Barcelona (CCCB) in collaboration with five other European institutions, recognising the best works transforming public spaces in Europe (see Box 7).
- **National governments** use persuasion tools very widely, with most state territories having awards of some description, often organised as a partnership between government and other bodies. Governmental awards tend to promote best practice within particular policy fields, such as urban renewal, social housing, sustainable construction, or public procurement processes including the Golden Pyramid award, promoted by the Chief Government Architect of the Netherlands to recognise excellence in commissioning works of architecture, urban design, landscape architecture, infrastructure and physical planning. Less frequent are festivals and events arranged by governments, although an exception was the 2019 Italian Architectural Festival coordinated and funded by the Italian Government but implemented by several partners, including public and private institutions, cultural institutions, and foundations. Governments are also active in supporting arts-based architectural activities, such as the Portuguese Arts Agency's annual programme for the development of the arts, which includes architecture. By contrast, few government departments involve themselves directly in actively campaigning, preferring to delegate or establish partnerships with other actors for such explicitly promotional activities.
- **Local government** tends to mirror national government in its use of persuasion tools. Many regional authorities and larger

municipalities have appointed a city architect (or similar post) who, alongside other activities, is active in building a place-making culture through talks and interviews, promoting events, and hosting awards schemes. The City Architect of Riga is explicitly tasked with providing design leadership, cross-stakeholder advocacy and cultivating the conditions under which place-making is prioritised. Alongside other tasks the office maintains cross-professional engagement about ideas and projects that are significant to the community alongside popularising the best achievements in Latvian architecture. Some cities have also established their own architecture and urban information centres, which are very proactive at pushing for a diverse agenda of promotion and awareness (see Box 8). In the Netherlands, for example, there are around 35 local architecture centres, which collaborate through the umbrella 'Architectuur Lokaal' (https://arch-lokaal.nl). Taking a different approach, the Mayor of London, Sadiq Khan, appointed 50 Mayor's Design Advocates to work on the 'Good Growth by Design' programme, an architecture and spatial design strategy of the Great London Authority (see Chapter 3). While their work is varied, as the name suggests, a key element of their role is to advocate for design quality within and across London.

- Where established, **arms-length national and local champions of design** typically adopt persuasion tools as key parts of their delivery programmes, including exhibitions, events, and awards. Most of these organisations also conduct proactive intergovernmental or cross-stakeholder advocacy and partnership working to encourage a greater concern for design quality. Proactive intergovernmental or cross-stakeholder advocacy and partnership working was a notable feature where governments had appointed a state architect or similar body (such as an inter-ministerial commission or working group). As well as acting as a design champion across the public administration, helping to build in-house design capacity (or awareness) and drive organisational and culture change (Tiesdell 2011: 237), a common objective is to reach beyond those in government and elsewhere who are already convinced about the need to prioritise good design to those who are more sceptical. The French Inter-ministerial Mission for the Quality of Public Buildings, for example, promotes quality across the public-construction sector relating to new or refurbished buildings, infrastructure and open spaces.

- **Non-governmental organisations**, notably professional bodies, are active in this space, with awards schemes being particularly ubiquitous. A range of cultural institutions promote events and celebrations of good design, such as the annual Open House festivals across Europe, the biennial London Festival of Architecture or the Austrian Turn On Architecture Festival. These initiatives typically include a wide diversity of related activities, such as street installations, exhibitions, debates and conferences, guided walks and cycle rides, boat tours, parties, design workshops, short talks, and so on.

- **Independent networks and centres** increasingly exist to promote the cause of good design through proactive advocacy within and beyond their networks or localities. Networks exist both on a pan-European basis, such as the European Placemaking Network with its aim to bring together place-makers and share practice (https://placemaking-europe.eu), and within particular countries. The austerity cuts of the early 2010s in England, for example, led to the withdrawal of government from engaging in design and to the emergence of the Place Alliance with a remit to campaign for place quality, typically on the basis of research evidence (see Box 2, p. 120). Locally, architecture centres or institutes aim to disseminate knowledge about architecture and urban design, creating spaces for debate about the built environment. They develop a wide range of activities to achieve this, mediating expert and lay views, targeting different audiences, such as young generations (via school workshops, teaching materials and so on), professional designers (for instance via lectures and debates) and the wider public (via exhibitions, open house events, films and so forth). In France, the Network of Architecture Centres includes 33 centres delivering a wide range of cultural initiatives, such as exhibitions, debates, study visits, educational activities, workshops and publications. In Austria, the Architecture Foundation is an association of institutions that deal with the themes of architecture and building culture in Austria, with the goal of creating awareness of these issues.

Experience of persuasion tools

Instead of waiting for organisations and individuals to seek out knowledge, these tools take the knowledge to them, seeking to package key messages in a manner that engages attention and wins over hearts and minds about the importance of good design. Although governments are involved in these activities, increasingly they have also sought to set up and empower arms-length institutions to do the job while different non-governmental organisations and informal networks are using modern technologies to take a lead, helping to fill gaps left by government action.

Box 7   Rewarding excellence: European Prize for Urban Public Space (Europe)

The European Prize for Urban Public Space is a biennial award established in 2000 to recognise the best public-space projects in Europe (https://www.publicspace.org/the-prize). The prize upholds design principles based on an open, compact and inclusive city that supports the harmonious coexistence of citizens, a mix of uses, and sustainable mobility, while preserving the historical memory of places. It favours processes based on the fundamental participation of citizens in the design of shared spaces.

The prize is organised by the Centre de Cultura Contemporània de Barcelona in collaboration with five other European institutions: the Architecture Foundation (London), the Architekturzentrum Wien (Vienna), the Cité de l'Architecture et du Patrimoine (Paris), the Deutsches Architekturmuseum (Frankfurt) and the Museum of Architecture and Design (Ljubljana). The prize is also supported by a team of experts consisting of public-space specialists from around Europe. This guarantees a broad geographic scope and the quality of the works presented for the prize (see Figure 4.11).

Entries are open to works that have created, recovered or improved public space within the previous two years. The prize is jointly presented to both the authors (namely the designers) of the projects and to the city, public authority or other institution that sponsored or promoted it. While the prize does not rule out large-scale interventions, it is particularly encouraging of smaller, low-key and targeted works that play a part in improving the life of local citizens.

Figure 4.11 Winner, European Prize for Urban Public Space 2008, the Norwegian Opera House, Oslo (image: Matthew Carmona).

Box 8 The value of architecture centres: Paris Centre for Architecture and Urbanism (France)

The Paris Centre for Architecture and Urbanism is housed in the Pavillon de l'Arsenal in the 4th arrondissement of Paris (see Figure 4.12), funded by the City of Paris with contributions from a wide range of supporting partners, members and patrons. The building houses a series of temporary exhibitions (around 30 a year) relating to urbanisation and urban life in Paris, as well as permanent exhibits relating to the planning and development of Paris and how the city has evolved (https://www.pavillon-arsenal. com/en/).

The Pavillon is intended to be a centre for information and debate about the past and future of Paris, with a programme of constantly changing workshops, events, lectures and activities. In addition the building houses a documentation centre with thousands of books, magazines, newspapers and so on, all available to those with an interest in Parisian urbanism. The Centre also hosts a specialist bookshop and the FAIRE

Figure 4.12 The Pavillon de l'Arsenal, Paris (image: Matthew Carmona).

portal, an online accelerator of innovation on architectural projects and urban design (https://www.faireparis.com/en/). Physically it houses a 1:2000 scale model of the city plus a 37-square-metre digital interactive screen (see Figure 4.13).

The centre in Paris is one of many hundreds of architecture centres round Europe; in England they are often known as urban rooms (https://urbanroomsnetwork.wordpress.com). A comprehensive Europe-wide survey of such spaces was undertaken in 2003, identifying their role as encompassing education, participation, enabling and collaboration, although they rarely operated on a financially self-sustaining basis (Ford and Sawyers 2003: 68–70). The work concluded that 'the value of architecture centres lies not just in their passion for architecture but in their commitment to conveying that passion to the widest community. Theirs is a clear message: architecture is not simply for the professionals … giving people the opportunity to develop their interest and the confidence to participate in architecture. It is an absolutely crucial role' (Ford and Sawyers 2003: 6).

Figure 4.13 A digital screen is laid out on the floor of the Pavillon for visitors to interact with (image: Matthew Carmona).

Like other cultural-quality tools, assessing how effective persuasion tools are will never be straightforward. Advocating and raising awareness activities are usually an integrated part of a larger set of tools delivered across institutions and interlaced with different tools and initiatives. Though much activity will focus on key decision-makers, whether professional or political, a more gradual uplift in societal expectations is also possible by motivating and mobilising public opinion in support of high-quality environments.

Although cultural change is always likely to be a long-term objective, persuasion tools may also benefit the quality of developments in the short run by influencing decision-makers and investors to adopt design quality as part of their business model, as well as by persuading public actors and agencies to improve the quality of public developments (see Figure 4.14). Equally, the urban development process is characterised by a complex system of agencies and structures and by diverse actors, not all of whom have traditionally been concerned about long-term quality. This means that persuasion tools also need to be able to reach out and engage with landowners, development companies and real estate investors, as well as with politicians and the full range of built-environment professionals.

Figure 4.14 The economic collapse towards the end of the first decade of this century left city authorities in Dublin struggling to continue the city's regeneration of the decade before. The solution was found in a renewed appetite to forge collaborative alliances both within and beyond the city, so 'while the City Council has displayed leadership, it sees the role of facilitator as being critical in prompting collaboration and harnessing capacity' in order to continue the regeneration of the city with 'an urbanist's sensibility' (Gleeson 2015), for example here in Dublin's Docklands (image: Matthew Carmona).

If not, there is a risk of only speaking to the already converted about the benefits of good design.

Partnerships and networking with other organisations to build alliances for quality provide a powerful means to raise awareness and enable organisations to expand their reach and influence at minimal cost. A wide network of contacts and relationships with other organisations in government, industry, academia and voluntary and community sectors allows key messages to travel further and to maximise impact. For example, in 2020 the Place Alliance led five other organisations to campaign for the establishment of a Design Quality Unit for England, disseminating the message across industry and government and contributing, in 2022, to the creation of a new Office for Place (see Chapter 3). These tools are among those that transfer most easily between jurisdictions across Europe, with many cities having their own awards

PERSUASION

Purpose
Actively take messages to key audiences
Raise awareness, motivate, advocate
Spread innovation
Celebrate best practices
Inspire collaboration

Deployment
International bodies (awards)
Government (awareness-raising)
Local government
Arms-length agencies / actors
Non-governmental organisations
Independent networks

Promulgation
design awards • campaigns •
events and festivals
Influencing
advocacy • alliances

Delivery
Focus on key decision-makers
Typically used in combination
 with other tools
Reliant on willingness to collaborate
Largely look forward to culture change
Awards look back, recognising success

Experience
Popular and transferable
Reaching the unconvinced
Arms-length agencies increasingly
empowered to persuade
Networks, partnership and technology
allow organisations to expand their reach
Long-term and short-term impacts

Figure 4.15   Summarising persuasion tools (image: Matthew Carmona).

and awareness-raising events that, in turn, inspire other urban design governance activities (see Figure 4.15).

Rating tools

Rating tools are the first of the quality-delivery tools. Like the other tools in this meta-category they are more interventionist than the quality-culture tools, because instead of focusing on the broader culture within which decisions on design are made, they focus on particular projects, places or processes with the potential to shape actual outcomes. At the same time they will help to reinforce the general culture of quality. Rating tools allow judgements to be made about the quality of design in a systematic and structured manner, usually by parties (such as other professionals or community groups) external to, and therefore independent from, the particular design process being evaluated. They enable the public sector to systemise these judgements and make assessments about design quality in ways that are robust.

This can be done in two key ways. First, formative evaluations, feeding into and informing the design process, and second, summative, evaluating the design quality of already fully formed development propositions (albeit ones that will continue to evolve). In effect, these tools lead to judgements – good or bad – about design propositions, and by implication also pass judgements on the performance of the teams responsible for them. Because of this, their use can be controversial.

Types of rating tools

More than other categories of tool, the choice of which rating tools are used locally in Europe seems to depend on the previous culture, with tools such as design competitions, design review and the use of indicators often geographically defined. For example, competitions feature heavily in Francophone countries, indicators in Anglophone countries, while design review (in different forms) tends to be more widespread across northern Europe. The distinction between formative and summative defines the two main categories of these tools:

- **Formative evaluation** encompasses indicator (measurement) tools and informal design review (not conducted as part of a formal regulatory process), the results from which can feed directly into the generation and refinement of design solutions for development proposals:
  - *Indicator tools* seek to measure and represent aspects of performance – in this case design quality – in a manner that can be easily shared and understood. Examples such as the Design Quality Indicator (developed by the Construction Industry Council in the UK) establish a structure against which evaluation of design quality can be made, with ratings against the separate criteria made by experts or through structured conversations with stakeholders (https://www.dqi.org.uk). In this way they are developmental tools, designed to diagnose qualities, pass judgements and encourage collaboration. These tools do not seem to be widely used in Europe at the urban-design scale, although the small number of examples the survey revealed are well developed and tested. They have the potential to provide an assessment of the quality of buildings or places in a systematic and objective manner, although they also run the risk of oversimplifying complex sets of qualities (Carmona 2003).
  - *Design review* amounts to a peer review process for evaluating the design quality of proposed projects. Going by various names – quality review, place review, design surgeries, aesthetic control, design advisory boards, design commissions, building committees, project meetings, quality chambers, and spatial quality teams – the common thread is evaluation by an independent panel of experts unconnected to the schemes under review. Its immediate function is to improve the design

quality of individual development schemes by challenging development teams and offering constructive advice from a breadth and depth of experience that may not be available to the project team or within the municipality, including in more specialist areas such as inclusion, heritage, or sustainability. Design review should be seen as an improvement tool, focused on adding value to developments by helping to broaden discussions about projects, not least about the larger context within which developments happen.

- **Summative evaluation** tools include design competitions and certification schemes, which tend to evaluate schemes that are further advanced and (in the case of certification) perhaps even completed:

  - *Design competitions* are centrally concerned with encouraging better design solutions to defined urban problems, including encouraging innovation in design through pitting design/ development teams against each other. They are a long-established tool in Europe, dating, for example, back to 1899 in Poland when the first regulations for architectural competitions were formulated (Kowalczyk 2018: 196). They come in many forms (open, limited, invited, staged) and sizes (local, national, international), across two fundamental types: conceptual (ideas only) and project (relating to a tangible building project) (Lehrer 2011). Regardless of the type of approach, competitions focus on raising design standards through a competitive process that is rarely mandated, although there are exceptions to this. Long-standing French national legislation, for example, mandates a design competition for public buildings over a specified contract value (in 2020, €144,000 for state contracts and €221.00 for local authorities – Biau et al. 2020), while a 2017 Architecture Law in Lithuania places an obligation on public authorities to organise architectural competitions for structures that are important in terms of state and public interest, or as regards their architectural or urban impact.

  - *Certification schemes* involve awards to projects to denote that they have reached a particular quality threshold. As such they move a step further towards formalisation as they combine evaluation with an 'official' stamp of approval, although they do not proffer any formal consent or warrant. They are instead a verified benchmark or standard of quality, for example, for energy efficiency. Well know schemes, internationally, include BREEAM (Building Research Establishment Environmental Assessment Method) or LEED (Leadership in Energy and Environmental Design), each with their own criteria, evaluation frameworks, assessment panels and certification processes. These processes are often conducted after projects are completed, but can also occur on the basis of submitted drawings. Certification is increasingly being utilised across Europe, for example in Latvia and Slovenia where LEED and BREEAM are common, and in the Nordic countries where the Nordic Swan ecolabel is gaining traction, including for built-environment products (see Figure 4.16).

Delivering rating tools

The delivery of rating tools also falls neatly into two categories, although this time bringing indicators and certification – and separately design review and competitions – together. Indicators and certification tools tend to be developed as 'products' that are marketed commercially or given

Figure 4.16   Sustainability was a large part of the design of the Quartiere delle Albere's regeneration project by Renzo Piano in Trento, Italy. MuSe (the Science Museum) achieved a LEED Gold certification, and all of the residences and offices have a level B CasaClima classification, a local system used in the Autonomous Province of Bolzano. The scheme was among the winners of the 2013 CasaClima Awards (image: Matthew Carmona).

away by organisations with an interest in the field of design quality, whether national, industrial or international organisations. They can be used for a range of purposes, including awareness-raising, monitoring, decision-making, and benchmarking (Schultz et al. 2003: 331), and once created are adopted, used, and sometimes adapted locally.

The Place Standard is an indicator tool offering formative evaluation. It was developed as a partnership between the Scottish Government (Architecture and Place Division), NHS Health Scotland and Architecture and Design Scotland (see Box 9). The objective of the tool is to facilitate conversations about the physical elements and social aspects of the built environment, thus helping local stakeholders and communities to work together to evaluate the quality of places. As such it is not designed to be used centrally by one organisation but instead provides a common open-source tool for professionals and non-professionals alike

---

Box 9   Inspiring conversations: Place Standard (Scotland, UK)

Place Standard offers a framework for structuring conversations around places (https://www.placestandard.scot). It is based around 14 questions covering the physical aspects of a place (buildings, open spaces, transport) as well as the social aspects (for example, whether people feel they have a say in decision-making) (see Figure 4.17). Each is rated on a scale from 1–7.

Each question for participants is supplemented by secondary questions that highlight particular aspects for people to consider. All questions are phrased in such a way that they always refer to people's experience of the place with the result being a simple score based on a scale from 1–7, where 1 means there is a great deal to improve and 7 means that little needs to change. The scores of all fourteen themes are plotted in a spider diagram, which allows for an immediate visual representation of the perceived strengths and weaknesses of the places being analysed.

Although the Place Standard is a rating tool, it is designed not simply to analyse a site, but rather to bring people together, overcoming professional and non-professional boundaries to discuss the values and aspects of places against a structured framework. It provides a flexible model that can be adapted to different scales (see Figure 4.18) and methods of inquiry, and which has been used both within and outside Scotland.

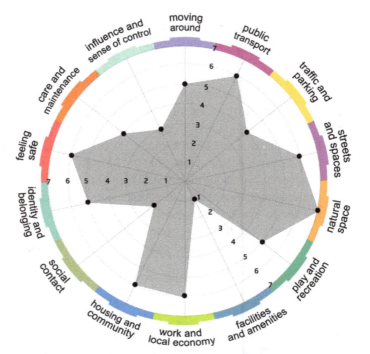

Figure 4.17 Example of Place Standard final spider diagram (image: www.placestandard.scot).

Figure 4.18 In preparing their City Plan for 2017–26 the City of Dundee used the Place Standard tool to deliver 504 online returns focused on understanding the qualities of the city that respondents valued or felt undermined their experience of place. Among the range of concerns this process revealed were issues of pedestrian accessibility and conflict with traffic (image: Matthew Carmona).

to use, with versions for children and young people in development. Building for Life, by contrast, is a certification tool providing summative evaluation. It was also developed by a consortium of partners and has gone through different versions over almost twenty years, with Building for a Healthy Life representing the most recent incarnation (http://www.builtforlifehomes.org). While anyone can evaluate projects using the principles, to receive a BfHL Commendation for projects requires a fee and independent assessment against the principles. Both tools are now run centrally by independent entities (a board in the case of Place Standard and a social enterprise for BfHL) that continue to develop and 'market' the tools.

Design review and design competitions, while more widely spread in their use across Europe, are both locally defined and delivered tools, and so exhibit a greater diversity of practices. While design review focuses on critiquing the work of single design/development teams, design competitions promote innovation by encouraging multiple teams to compete on the same design problem. Typically, an independent panel of experts is convened to evaluate the entries and ultimately select the winner, be that an idea (in the case of conceptual competitions) or a project solution.

Many competitions are one-off exercises, for example the 2019 Dutch Panorama Lokaal competition, a two-phase design ideas competition focused on residential neighbourhoods on the outskirts of cities and intended to attract multidisciplinary teams interested in working with local coalitions of municipalities, housing associations and other relevant parties. Others are part of ongoing programmes such as the open-call procedure utilised by the Flemish Government Architect, which in its twenty years covered 700 projects (Liefooghe and Van den Driessche 2019). The open call is free of charge for all public and semi-public organisations in Flanders, with schemes originating, in the main, from local authorities and Flemish government departments (see Box 13, p. 172).

A range of studies has examined the use of design competitions in Europe (Biau et al. 2020). One of the most comprehensive – *Competition Culture in Europe* – was conducted between 2017 and 2020 by Architectuur Lokaal (2021) who are based in the Netherlands. The overarching aim of the project was to break down barriers between all the diverse laws, rules and practices guiding the conduct of design competitions across Europe in order to allow greater access for design and development teams to competitions taking place beyond their national boundaries. A key output from the work was https://www.thefulcrum.eu.

Established in 2019, the website offers an international portal for architectural competitions and procurement assignments across all European countries. Among its resources is an *EU Competition Culture Dictionary,* defining key terms used to specify, and therefore define and run, design competitions across Europe in terms of how they are understood nationally (Architectuur Lokaal 2018). The research also revealed a range of problems faced by competitors, including:

- The diversity of practices across Europe, raising barriers to participation.
- Design competitions being used primarily as political instruments or marketing tools.
- The lack of fair compensation for those taking part.
- A failure to deliver schemes following competitions.
- The transparency and openness of jury selection procedures and their representation of society.

The research also identified widely varying perceptions over the strength of competition culture in the different countries investigated (see Figure 4.19). Reflecting these concerns alongside other, longer-established ones – notably that competitions are costly, risky, take a long time, and obviate dialogue between parties, including the public (Strebel and Silberberger 2017: 8; Kowalczyk 2018) – the project gave some insight into why this tool is favoured in some countries and not others (Architectuur Lokaal 2017).

Design review – in its various guises and names – seems to be a rapidly growing practice in Europe. In German-speaking countries, for example, design advisory boards now act as intermediaries between the interests of owners and the general public in many larger towns and cities, including in Innsbruck, where the design advisory board assesses the quality of projects submitted against specified criteria and offers advice to the city council that they can follow at their discretion.

Typically panels are appointed by municipalities and consist of independent design and related professionals, who conduct their work for the public sector and without charging those being reviewed. In England, commercial and not-for-profit organisations also provide design review services (alongside public-sector panels), competing in an open market both at national and local level to run panels for local authorities and to conduct reviews that carry a charge. The charge is typically paid by developers either to the provider of the review service or directly to the local authority that requested the review. This marketisation of urban

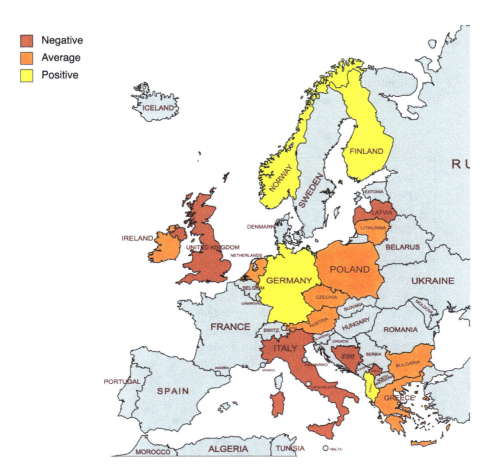

Figure 4.19 The competition culture in selected European countries in 2017 (image: after Architectuur Lokaal).

design governance is unique in Europe and, against early expectations, has resulted in a greater take-up of design review across England (Carmona 2018).

Around Europe, panels range in their focus, some focusing on specific projects and places and some on whole municipalities. They also vary in their size, administration, the numbers of projects they review, status, range of expertise, the discretion offered to project promoters to appear or not, and in the degree to which the advice is taken on board. In the Netherlands alone, Van Assen et al. (2018) notes that no two Q-teams are exactly alike (see Box 10), while Punter (2007: 195) concludes his international survey of design-review practices by noting that:

Each design review system will have its own priorities which will be strongly influenced by long-standing cultural conditions, the local politics of the development process, the perceived design failings of contemporary development, and particularly the sheer power of the market and the level of demand for accommodation.

Box 10   Delivering focused expertise: Spatial Quality Teams (Netherlands)

Spatial Quality Teams (Q-teams) provide advice about enhancing the spatial quality of buildings, streets, neighbourhoods, cities, landscapes and regions, and have been doing so for more than a hundred years in the Netherlands, with a recent survey revealing 139 teams spread across the country (see Figure 4.20 and https://q-factor.info/en/home/). Q-teams do not design projects but rather use various design governance tools to stimulate and preserve spatial quality. They are set up by local, provincial, or national authorities.

Figure 4.20   Distribution of Spatial Quality Teams (image: Sandra van Assen and José van Campen).

Q-teams are multidisciplinary teams of experts that provide independent advice on spatial developments and spatial policy. Assen et al. (2018) define two types of Q-teams: specific and generic. A specific Q-team operates within the framework of a specific planning or developmental area, within the physical boundaries of the spatial assignment, such as an urban development zone or an infrastructural or landscape development. Within this area, the team guides and assesses individual projects on their contribution to the quality of the whole and may last only for the duration of the assignment. A generic Q-team operates within given administrative boundaries (a municipality, a province or even a region) and has no defined end date (see Figure 4.21).

Q-teams provide knowledge and design capacity to authorities through formal and informal advisory practices developed by multidisciplinary teams of experts, typically at the early stages of planning and design processes. Although some focus on their design review function alone, others are charged with a more proactive role promoting and enabling spatial quality within a defined jurisdiction.

Deployment of rating tools?

Figure 4.21   The Q-team set up to review projects in the Almere new town was described by Van Ginneken (2008) as the 'conscience of the city centre', helping to guide the diverse projects that make up this new central area into a coherent place (image: Matthew Carmona).

Typically, jurisdictions either favour design review or design competitions, although in some countries, notably Belgium, both tools are used side by side. Likewise, in Zurich, developers can decide whether to submit for review to an advisory board or opt for a design competition, although they may be required to organise a competition for schemes if the advisory board rejects their scheme as substandard. In the UK, despite their formative potential, indicator tools are often seen – and used – as a less costly alternative for evaluating the merits of schemes.

Whichever are used, all rating tools focus on tangible projects and consequently on the development and post-development stages of the urban design governance field of action (see Figures 7.5a–c, pp. 279–81). They are used by a wide range of actors, although the dominant tools – design review and design competitions – are largely public sector oriented:

- Beyond certification tools that are marketed internationally, the best-known pan-European rating tool is Europan, the biennial international competition for architects under 40 years of age (see Box 11). The competition is organised by a foundation of the same name, but each participating country proposes their own set of sites, and national juries have the final say on decisions.

- While these tools are largely defined and used at the local level, national governments have had an important role establishing the policy frameworks into which they sit. For example, the French mandatory use of design competitions for all new public buildings above a defined value threshold has, since 1980, led to more than a thousand competitions a year, all overseen by a specific state agency, the Inter-Ministry Mission for Quality in Public Construction. Switzerland has a similar tradition, although competitions are organised locally, for example by the City Architect of Antwerp (Stadsbouwmeester) who organises design competitions utilising a two-stage process. In the Netherlands, a law of 1961 required all 355 municipalities to establish an aesthetic control committee. This formal system of design review has been complemented in more recent years by informal spatial quality teams covering a wide range of national and local projects and jurisdictions (see Box 10 above). Elsewhere regions (including the German Länder) and municipalities (for example in Austria) determine the correct provision, with national states also sometimes possessing their own urban design governance infrastructure. Switzerland's Federal Commission for the Protection of Nature and Cultural Heritage represents a case in point. In the UK, policy encourages and recommends the use of design review but local government determines whether to use it and how.

- Arms-length organisations have long had a role in delivering these tools. In the UK, the three devolved governments in Scotland, Wales and Northern Ireland have each set up organisations with a design-review remit, while the regional governments in Belgium all now have Bouwmeesters undertaking both competitions and design review. In the Brussels capital region, for example, projects above 5,000 square metres must include a design review undertaken by the Bouwmeester Maître Architecte (BMA), either a project meeting or larger quality chamber, and public procurement legislation requires that public-sector clients are required to have several candidates compete for any contract, in connection with which BMA routinely organises a competition. Finally, the 93 Councils of Architecture, Urbanism and the Environment in France have been mandated nationally to provide free design advice and guidance to public or private clients on design quality and participate in design competitions as well as in panels, akin to design review, in order to offer advice on projects (see Box 14, p. 173).

- Non-governmental organisations are less often involved, although in Denmark the Academy Council of the Royal Danish Academy of Fine Arts provides expert advice to municipal and state authorities when requested on architecture and spatial development projects. It can also, on its own initiative, obtain information on specific design interventions or art projects and make statements to state authorities and public institutions and to the public. Professional and learned bodies also have a role, including the Royal Institute of British Architects (RIBA) who, for a fee, either advise on the setting up of architecture competitions or run them on behalf of client organisations, who may have little or no experience and require an expert and independent organisation to take a lead. RIBA managed 11 such competitions in 2019 (https://www.architecture.com/awards-and-competitions-landing-page). Professional bodies in Estonia, Germany, the Netherlands, Portugal and Ireland offer similar services.

- Private and not-for-profit provision, notably of design review, only occurs in England, where an active market brings together a combination of in-house local-authority-run panels, externally run panels for local authorities, and ad hoc panels for hire. A small number of panels are also run by national agencies, such as the

National Infrastructure Commission. The system has not led to any obvious diminution in quality (often the reverse) although practices are very variable, with some parts of the country – including many of London's boroughs – using design review as a standard practice, while other parts of the country use it only occasionally or not at all (Carmona 2018). Private entities are also behind key certification and indicator tools in England, such as BREEAM and Building for a Healthy Life, while elsewhere in Europe they are more likely to be found backing design competitions (see Box 11).

Box 11   Raising standards competitively: Europan and Florenc (Europe/Czech Republic)

Europan is a biennial competition of ideas open to young professionals under 40 years with a university degree in architecture, urban design or related fields. It was first set up in 1988 and in 2021 completed its 16th round, with each round having its own overarching theme (https://www.europan-europe. eu/en/). The competition is simultaneously launched for potential development sites across Europe, with identical rules and judging methods for all. After registration on the Europan website, competitors are free to choose any of the available sites to obtain more information, and can submit their proposal online.

Europan is organised by a federation of the same name, consisting of national structures in participating countries and aided by cross-national scientific and technical committees. Each country proposes their own set of development sites and a corresponding brief and a national jury of experts preselects the most innovative projects per site (see Figure 4.22). A central Scientific Council then compares and analyses these projects at the European level and organises forums for debate between the site representatives and the jury members. National juries have the final say in decisions. Results are disseminated widely and Europan organisers assist winning teams with obtaining commissions for their projects by bringing together the designers, city representatives, and juries.

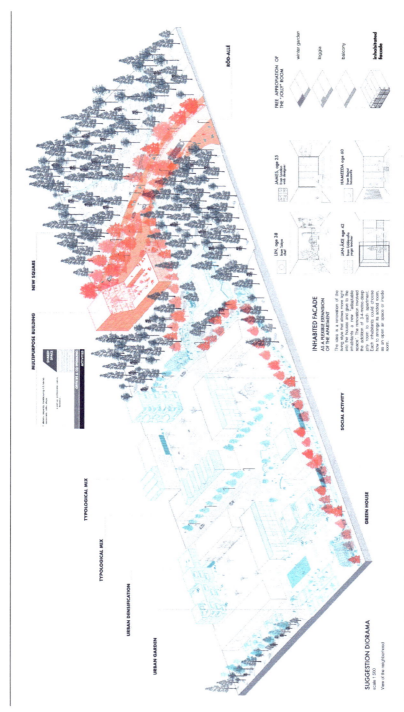

Figure 4.22 One of the winners of Europan 15, this scheme by an Italian team for the Uddevalla site in Sweden (image: Jalla!).

Europan serves a dual purpose: it provides a launching pad for young designers and offers them the opportunity to turn their ideas into real projects, while also offering cities and developers innovative solutions to local urban challenges and complex sites. At the local level, cities benefit from cross-national expert assistance to help them implement ideas and projects

More typical are professional competitions, either totally open, as was the case for the Florenc international design competition in Prague held in 2021, or limited in some way, for example the competition for the America's Cup Pavilion in Valencia (see Figure 2.5, p. 54). Although many competitions are sponsored by the public sector, the Florenc development site in Prague was owned by two private companies that funded the competition together. The huge significance of the site for the city (on the edge of the World Heritage Area) led to the involvement of the City of Prague in its organisation, the arrangement of which was agreed through a council resolution.

The competition was held in three phases – submission of portfolios (open), concept plan (five teams) and master plan (three teams), with the final master plans opened up to public comment before judging took place. The winner – Unit, Marco and Placemakers, and A69 – was announced in December 2021, with the city committed in advance to rapidly modify the 1999 city zoning plan to accommodate the proposals (see Figure 4.23).

Figure 4.23 Model of the prize-winning scheme for Florenc (image: Matthew Carmona).

Experience of rating tools

Tools that engage expert judgement directly in making those assessments – competitions and design review – are widely used and favoured across Europe. Those that filter opinions through a framework – indicators and certification – are less favoured, reflecting a fear that they can too easily become reductionist and fail to engage with the multi-faceted complexity of design. The potential of these latter tools to encourage engagement, structure discussions, and diagnose, monitor and clearly articulate qualities may not be well understood, although they seem to have a particular role to play in helping to systemise decision-making around the imperatives associated with climate change and the circular economy, both through the use of long-standing tools such as BREEAM and new tools such as Life Cycle Assessment, which is set to play a major role in Denmark, where CO^2 limits will be introduced on all new developments from 2023 (Carruth and Stokholm 2022). They also have the potential to be used alongside other tools of urban design governance, for example by reinforcing key persuasion messages or helping to engage communities in exploration. The Place Standard seems to have been most successful in bridging this gap in understanding, and is now used in 14 European countries and has been translated into Dutch, Greek, Norwegian and Turkish.

Design review and design competitions, in all their many forms, are generally considered effective and are often used as part of a sophisticated package of urban design governance tools, for example with hands-on support tools and alongside culture-quality tools. In Zurich, for example, design competitions have contributed to the improvement of the city's housing stock and have been important tools for promoting urban regeneration in peripheral and disused areas (Katsakou 2013), with design competitions mandated for housing cooperatives to access public land. Similarly, the Association of German Architects (BDA) supporting the establishment of design advisory boards across the country, has argued that they bring openness, transparency and quality into the building process, and help to ensure that 'more cities value their cityscape as a cultural asset' (Bund Deutscher Architekten 2011).

While design review is largely conducted behind the scenes, design competitions have the potential to be more public, helping to stimulate debate around key sites and projects. Design review, by contrast, adds design capacity in the public sector by providing a mechanism to bring in appropriate design skills as and when required. Both require political support to operate effectively but also a level of independence so that design decisions (offering advice or selecting winners) can focus on the best design outcomes and not on other factors.

Cost, however, is always a factor in the use of these tools, particularly in relation to competitions, which are largely funded publicly and (arguably) indirectly by design teams that are often properly compensated for the time taken to enter architectural competitions. Without compulsion in their use, the cost of running competitions can also count against them, as can uncertainties about what they might give rise to, for example, whether the winning schemes will be affordable and practical. In France, a decree approved in 1988 obliges French competition organisers to compensate the candidates to a minimum of 80 per cent of the value of the assignment carried out. Because of this, competitions are always restricted, usually to between three and five teams. In the Czech Republic the national Architecture and Building Culture Policy recommends the use of design competitions for publicly financed buildings, and in order to encourage municipalities to deliver this, has introduced a subsidy programme with half of the money given in prizes supported by the state up to €15,600 (see Box 12). The Urban Maestro workshops (see Chapter 6) suggested that limited or invited competitions reduce costs for the public sector while two-stage competitions reduce them for development/design teams.

Rating tools are designed to foreground design in a way that would not necessarily happen in conventional design/development processes. Inevitably this carries a cost, but it seems to be a cost increasingly prioritised by those who use them (see Figure 4.24).

Figure 4.24 Summarising rating tools (image: Matthew Carmona).

Support tools

Support tools are more hands-on than rating tools as they involve directly or indirectly assisting design and development teams and/or public-sector actors with particular projects or urban design governance processes. They enable the public sector to shape the decision-making environment of organisations, with a remit to directly influence or actually shape design outcomes and to influence the fundamental choices about development early in the development process. In this way governments can extend their reach to strategic delivery partners and to local actors in a manner that would otherwise be impossible. They can be direct, providing hands-on assistance, or indirect, for example through providing funding for others, but ultimately aim to influence processes and outcomes of design for the better. They do this through filling skills, capacity, and funding gaps in order to contribute to the larger urban design governance goals of the assisting organisation.

Types of support tools

Two main types of support tools can be identified depending on how the support is directed from those offering it to those in receipt of the support:

- **Funding** takes the form of direct financial support to delivery organisations, although this might also involve in-kind support, for example through the secondment of staff or the temporary loan of capacity to organisations. This sort of support can be used to fund either the core costs of delivery organisations, such as arms-length agencies or architecture centres, in order that they can organise and conduct their programme, or can cover the ring-fenced costs of delivering particular defined initiatives tied to defined quality objectives. These forms of support are indirect because the funding body is not delivering the programme being funded, but is instead supporting it financially and thereby handing over responsibility for others to deliver:
  - *Strategic grants* (grant-in-aid) are provided to a wide range of organisations offering different urban design governance services. The growing recognition of the importance of urban quality across Europe has, for example, led governments to set up and/or support arms-length agencies and centres with a design remit dedicated to driving the design-quality agenda nationally, regionally or at the city level. Examples include the

German Federal Foundation of Baukultur (see Box 1, p. 117), the Bouwmeesters in Belgium (see Box 13, p. 172), or the Paris Centre for Architecture and Urbanism (see Box 8, p. 145). The financial support is itself a tool – what Hood (1983) referred to as the application of state 'treasure' to a problem, in this case the delivery of better governance of design – that enables these bodies to operate and in turn to develop their own suite of tools to influence design quality.

  ○ *Programme (and procurement) grants* represent funding that is ring-fenced and time-limited for closely defined purposes, usually as a means to direct the efforts of delivery organisations to specific defined policy objectives or initiatives. For example, the Architecture Unit of the Fédération Wallonie-Bruxelles manages a specific budget to subsidise others to organise exhibitions, publications, seminars, conferences, debates, documentaries, and so forth, all of which raise the profile of architectural quality within the territory. Likewise, in the UK, government has funded a range of non-profit regional organisations within the nationally organised Design Network to deliver design training across England following the launch of a new *National Design Guide* in 2019.

- **Enabling** amounts to the provision of hands-on professional assistance or advice to design/development teams on particular projects, or when commissioning projects or preparing pieces of urban design guidance, policy or other tools, such as design competitions. Enabling is hands-on and direct, as it involves working directly with development actors engaging in the delivery of particular development projects or place-making strategies. A wide range of organisations provide enabling support to public and private clients – support that varies depending on the remit and resources of those organisations. It may include assistance on all strategic, management, operational and technical aspects of developments, from financial arrangements to bidding processes, recruitment, scheduling, drafting briefs and giving presentations, or mentoring and monitoring design work and local urban design governance activities.

Delivering support tools

The European survey showed that both forms of support are increasingly popular as governments at different scales set in place urban design governance infrastructures to provide leadership on design. Funding support from government to other stakeholders is widespread, and complicit in wide-ranging efforts to build a local design-quality culture and define and utilise other urban design governance tools. In turn, this echoes the exponential growth of new organisations across Europe in such roles (Sawyers et al. 2002: 7). For example, the provision of direct grant-in-aid to architecture centres around Europe has been leading to the production of a wide range of information and persuasion tools. Most of these organisations are totally or partially financed by the state, mainly through respective ministries of culture, state agencies or municipalities.

In some countries they operate within a public administration or as arms-length organisations, such as the Museum of Finnish Architecture, the Netherlands Architecture Institute or the Estonian Museum of Architecture, with funding in Estonia coming 85 per cent from state support (for rent, salaries, other expenses), 8 per cent earned income and 7 per cent from projects (exhibitions, publications, public programmes). Elsewhere they operate as not-for-profit organisations, private foundations, or on a mixed-funding model such as the Danish Architecture Centre (DAK) and the Irish Architecture Foundation (IAF), both of whom mix public and private funding to deliver their programmes. The specific arrangements for deploying financial support vary significantly depending on the local administrative and legislative context.

While public funding for these organisations will typically be tied to agreed performance objectives, there is also likely to be a lot of leeway in how those objectives are delivered and how budget might be moved between categories of expenditure and tools of delivery. By contrast, funding for defined initiatives is less flexible and rarely includes funding for the core costs of organisations such as their premises, administration, and so on, which then have to be paid for by other means. For funders it nevertheless has the advantage that it can be highly focused and can be redirected as circumstances and priorities change. The Czech national subsidy programme (see Box 12), for example, which supports architectural and urban competitions in the country, was refocused for its second round in order to favour smaller municipalities that had not previously benefited from the fund and that feature historically sensitive contexts where design quality is particularly critical.

Across Europe, many states, regions and cities have established a State Architect or Chief Government Architect to promote high-quality public buildings and public spaces. Typically supported by a small team, the aim is to intervene directly in the design of projects through the provision of hands-on professional enabling. Although the size and structure of these offices and their associated competencies vary, services

Box 12 Subsidising architectural and urban competitions (Czech Republic)

The Czech national subsidy programme for supporting architectural and urban competitions for the local procurement of design services related to public buildings, public spaces and planning documents aims to promote more frequent use of design competitions by municipalities. Competitions are regularly used in the larger cities of the Czech Republic, notably Prague and Brno (see Box 11 above) based on a belief that they foster higher-quality design. Smaller authorities, however, struggle to finance competitions, and the subsidy, coordinated by the Czech Ministry of Regional Development, aims to fill this gap.

The programme subsidises half the costs associated with competition prizes and awards up to a maximum of CZK 400,000 (€16,000) per competition. In 2019 a total of CZK 5 million was allocated for the scheme, with five projects eventually being funded, including competitions for the Cidlina recreation zone in Jičín, the Theatre park in Zlín, various projects associated with the centre of the village of Stredokluky and the Community centre in Říčanský mlýn (see Figure 4.25). Competitions funded in this way have to follow the competition rules of the Czech Chamber of

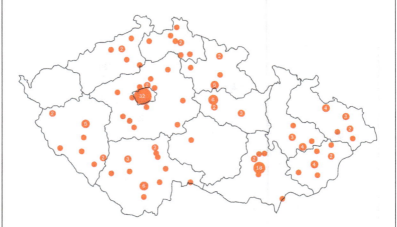

Figure 4.25 Completed projects based on design competitions in the Czech Republic between 1993 and 2019 (image: Tomáš Zdvihal).

Architects and Czech Chamber of Chartered Engineers and Technicians Engaged in Construction, while the competitions themselves can be organised by public administrations, private entities or not-for-profit organisations (Ministry of Regional Development 2021: 44–5).

The programme began in 2018 and the ministry originally planned to launch a call annually, although changes to political priorities have disrupted that ambition. Instead, based on analysis of the first year of the programme, the conditions for awards were redefined so that the funds spent are not concentrated on a select few municipalities but are spread throughout the country. In the future the selection process will favour municipalities that have not yet benefited from the programme, and notably smaller municipalities and areas with significant heritage value, where architectural quality is of particular significance.

usually include negotiating with or on behalf of other public stakeholders on design, providing advice to municipalities, and assisting governmental departments in processes of design. The Flemish Government Architect, for example, provides free support as an independent expert and adviser to the public sector, including to the Flemish government, provincial and local authorities, and associations with a public status (such as those related to the provision of social housing) (see Box 13). Architecture and Design Scotland (A&DS), similarly, offers a design support service that covers:

- Providing design support to local authorities and public bodies to help coordinate major built-environment investments.
- Helping stakeholders with diverse interests develop a shared brief for a project.
- Supporting public-sector clients in their approach to the market with the aim of helping them to attract the right partners or skills for the project.
- Developing guidance to promote better outcomes.
- Providing advice during the design development stage to help clients, design teams and planning authorities to recognise and prioritise the benefits for people.
- Sharing good practice between areas.

Box 13   The multiple roles of the Flemish State Architect (Flanders, Belgium)

The Vlaams Bouwmeester (Flemish Bouwmeester or State Architect) is an independent position appointed by the Flemish Government (https://www.vlaamsbouwmeester.be/). The incumbent Bouwmeester offers high-level expertise and knowledge across the fields of urban planning, architecture and landscape design in order to support coherent and potentially innovative approaches to design in Flanders. This involves seeking to develop a long-term spatial vision in consultation with the various administrations and external stakeholders, alongside the preparation and implementation of architectural policy. The ultimate goal is to deliver a high-quality living environment across Flanders.

Acting as an independent adviser, the Flemish State Architect is a bridge-builder who approaches projects from a cross-sectoral perspective and across policy arenas. One of their core tasks is to provide support and guidance to public officials on development projects and to contribute actively to the development of policy, advice and initiatives related to social challenges and their implications and possibilities in terms of high-quality design and construction. To achieve these goals, the Bouwmeester utilises several design tools, of which the most important is the open call – a competition process to help select designers for public contracts for local municipalities (see Figure 4.26). In 2022 the call reached its 43rd iteration, with three projects advertised: the call asked for submissions by teams with portfolios and a statement covering motivations, general expertise and an 'intention to collaborate'. This represents the first stage of the selection process.

The Bouwmeester also uses the Bouwmeester Scan and Bouwmeester Label (see analysis tools), conducts pilot projects and generally strives to raise awareness about topical issues, for example relating to shortcomings in Flemish regulations, while generally acting to champion architectural quality throughout the region. The work has a direct impact on public administration; improving design practices at the regional and local levels; influencing and fostering debate on the quality of new developments

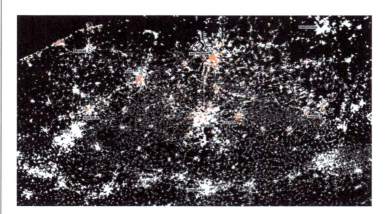

Figure 4.26 The location of twenty years of open call projects 1999–2019 (image: Liefooghe and Van den Driessche 2019).

in cities; shaping regional planning strategies; testing different approaches for incentivising quality; developing research, and so on.

At a lower level, these approaches are echoed in municipalities across Europe who have appointed city architects tasked with providing proactive advocacy and direct enabling of good design. At this level the 93 Councils of Architecture, Urbanism and the Environment in France provide arms-length enabling services, with free (government funded) design advice to both the public and private sectors across the county (see Box 14).

Box 14 Nationwide support network: Councils of Architecture, Urbanism and the Environment (CAUEs) (France)

CAUEs (in French, conseil d'architecture, d'urbanisme et de l'environnement) are one of the longest-established support tools in Europe, having been set up as part of the 1977 French Law on Architecture. Together they constitute a decentralised enabling service on the design of the built environment through a comprehensive network of non-governmental organisations spread across the country (https://www.fncaue.com/?page=home).

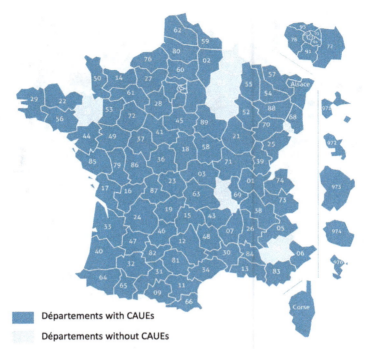

Départintes with CAUEs

Départements without CAUEs

Figure 4.27 Map of the 95 départements covered by CAUEs (https://www.fncaue.com/?page=home).

Administratively operating at the level of the French départements (95 out of 101 have one – see Figure 4.27), CAUEs are created on the initiative of local officials and are chaired by a local elected representative. They are invested with the public interest mission to advise, train, inform and raise awareness using a multiplicity of tools. Tools include free design advice to public and private clients, training for professionals and local authorities, schools educational programmes, and conducting awareness campaigns about the design quality of the built environment. Critical current preoccupations include the control of land consumption, the democratisation of architecture, and the management of natural and energy resources.

CAUEs are non-profit organisations, the main source of funds for which is a fixed percentage of the taxes on building permits charged by municipalities. In addition, they also receive funding from the services that they provide to public clients and from cultural events and activities that are often sponsored by external organisations (Bedrone 2011). The National Federation of CAUEs is an association that connects CAUEs and provides a forum for discussion and sharing of expertise, for example providing links to initiatives of individual CAUEs as well as to those of the different regional associations (see Figure 4.28). Externally it promotes the agenda and interests of CAUEs on the national stage.

Figure 4.28   The observatory of the architectural quality of housing, collected by the Île-de-France association, provides learning from regionally significant projects such as the Quartier Massena in Paris (image: Matthew Carmona).

Deployment of support tools?

Support via funding other organisations to deliver urban design governance objectives inevitably implies an interdependency, on the receiving organisation for funding and on the funding organisation on others to deliver. Typically the funding organisations are governmental, with funding requiring all the normal public-sector diligence and auditing to ensure the effective use of public money. Government actors dominate this category of urban design governance tools, which tend to be used across the urban design governance field of action – pre- to post-development:

- Governments, across different scales, are in large part funding urban design governance activities across Europe. Strategic grants are almost exclusively paid for by the public sector, as are most programme grants, with much more limited funding available from private sponsorship, donations to delivery organisations and earnings from commercial activities. Enabling, by contrast, typically occurs at greater distance from government by arms-length, non-governmental and not-for-profit organisations.

- By contrast, much spending of monies obtained through strategic grants is done by arms-length organisations set up to take forward national, regional and local design-quality agendas. For example, in Austria there is an architecture centre in each of the nine provincial capital cities, plus several cultural associations related to architecture and *Baukultur* that receive financial support from the federal, state and local level. In Portugal, the House of Architecture in Matosinhos was recently established with financial support from the City Council of Matosinhos and a wider group of partners. Support through enabling also tends to occur at this level, with arms-length actors using these approaches to reach out into local government and elsewhere to deliver the knowledge, skills and know-how to those at the delivery coalface. Architecture and Design Scotland, for example, offers a pre-design service for local authorities and social housing providers to ensure that place-making is at the heart of local housing strategies, the overall purpose being to build the right conditions for better design outcomes through the use of visioning to commission better places using design. At the city level, the City Architect of Antwerp gives advice to various service directorates on particular projects, project briefs or procurement processes, and supports the various external public daughter companies of the city concerned, among other matters, with schools and social housing.

- Programme grants are used by a more diverse range of organisations, including non-governmental, private and academic partners to deliver defined initiatives of the public sector, utilising (or delivering) a variety of tools, including training, guidance, research, design review, and enabling activities. In the Netherlands, Architectuur Lokaal is an independent foundation and centre of expertise and information devoted to solving spatial design problems. In the past a staff of ten has been supported by four ministries to give advice to both public and private clients reflecting their mission to act as a link between national policies and local practices. Today they are dependent on a mix of funding, with staff levels fluctuating accordingly.

Experience of support tools

Support tools allow the public sector to get more involved in a strategic manner in the delivery of design-quality agendas locally. This includes both shaping the work and the decision-making of key organisations, who themselves are influencing or actually shaping design outcomes, and influencing (early in the development process) the fundamental choices about development.

As with all informal tools of urban design governance, the impact of support tools will be limited by the financial commitment underpinning them. Most organisations responsible for promoting design quality within, at arms-length from, and outside government tend to be small, and while also often nimble and innovative, inevitably their capacity limits what can be achieved. In such a context these tools can help to expand capacity, for example though programme grants and enabling activities that bring in external expertise to work with urban design governance delivery organisations, such as the Panorama Lokaal initiative, which brings design teams to work with local communities in the Netherlands (see rating tools). Indeed, rather than having large numbers of experienced built-environment professionals within organisations providing expert knowledge directly, a model used instead in the UK by not-for-profit organisations such as the Design Council (or regional providers of design review services) has favoured keeping a flexible roster of external experts who can be called upon as and when enabling opportunities (and funding) allow (Carmona et al. 2016: 218–37).

By their nature, support tools operate in concert with the larger urban design governance toolkit, helping to deliver quality-culture and quality-delivery tools both through funding key organisations and focused urban design governance initiatives and through enabling activities such as the preparation of design briefs for competitions (see Figure 4.29). Supporting a decentralised network of organisations in this manner represents a powerful way of maximising impact and extending reach for the limited resources available to deliver a design-quality agenda – nationally, regionally or locally. The emergence of

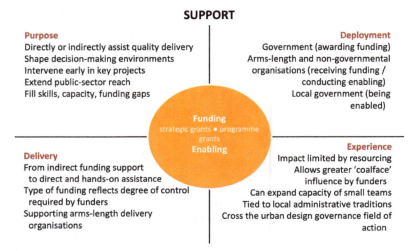

SUPPORT

Purpose
Directly or indirectly assist quality delivery
Shape decision-making environments
Intervene early in key projects
Extend public-sector reach
Fill skills, capacity, funding gaps

Deployment
Government (awarding funding)
Arms-length and non-governmental
organisations (receiving funding /
conducting enabling)
Local government (being
enabled)

Funding
strategic grants • programme
grants
Enabling

Delivery
From indirect funding support
   to direct and hands-on assistance
Type of funding reflects degree of control
   required by funders
Supporting arms-length delivery
   organisations

Experience
Impact limited by resourcing
Allows greater 'coalface'
influence by funders
Can expand capacity of small teams
Tied to local administrative traditions
Cross the urban design governance field of
action

Figure 4.29   Summarising support tools (image: Matthew Carmona).

arms-length organisations across Europe to drive forward this agenda has led to a pragmatic growth in the use of these tools, but they remain strongly tied to local administrative traditions and practices and to the availability of financial resources for their implementation.

Exploration tools

Exploration is the final type of informal quality-delivery tool. These approaches engage directly in the design process through mechanisms that investigate, test out and involve the community in particular design approaches. They are hands-on but exploratory in nature, either utilising temporary interventions or inputting into larger projects or place-shaping processes. Being exploratory in nature, they are also flexible and often innovative in the methodologies they employ. By actively involving third parties in the design process, they aspire to broaden and enrich the design/development process, influencing key decision-making relating to projects and places, often well in advance of formal regulatory processes or even development interest in particular locations.

Types of exploration tools

Although there is no rigid divide between approaches, and they can be used together, exploration tools can be classified in two main types depending on whether the focus of the tool is public or professional:

- **Proactive engagement** tools involve stakeholders and the community in particular projects or places, typically seeking their input, either prior to development or to encourage citizen input into the long-term management of urban assets:
  - *Design-led community participation* encompasses a diverse range of tools designed to involve communities directly in decision-making on the future of the built environment. By actively involving communities it is hoped to empower them while delivering better outcomes (more suited to local needs), encouraging positive communication between stakeholders and avoiding negative reactions to subsequent development propositions. Across Europe such processes are common but far from universal, encompassing forms of engagement ranging from the actual co-design of projects to various forms of action planning or design workshops/charrettes.
  - *Co-governance agreements* between local authorities and citizens for improving their surroundings or managing vacant and underused spaces and buildings are increasingly used and bring communities to the coalface as players in how places are actually shaped. While there is often a formal agreement (pact) underpinning such arrangements, there are also extended informal processes of collaboration between, for example, local councils, housing associations and residents sharing management responsibilities.
- **Professional investigation** tools investigate particular design challenges in order to identify and perhaps test out innovative solutions:
  - *Research by design* is used to explore design alternatives for key projects, places or problems. The tool encompasses a critical inquiry through design that may include speculative design, data collection and manipulation, visioning possible realities and alternatives, and even the physical construction of exemplar projects. Such approaches use the power of design to help stakeholders understand possibilities and therefore to inspire more informed discussions about the future potential of place. Across Europe, research by design is used by the public sector, notably city architects, to explore design alternatives in complex urban areas and for major development schemes before developers come forward with their own proposals.
  - *On-site experimentation* has become increasingly popular over recent decades, often encompassing forms of temporary

(tactical) urbanism in which interventions are made as a means to try out new arrangements, encourage engagement, or simply experiment with ideas over days, weeks or sometimes years. It can also involve the construction of exemplar projects, both for experimental purposes and to set standards for others to follow. Finally, at a larger scale, urban labs bring together a wide range of development actors to experiment with new forms of development/management using a variety of tools, including design workshops, public debates, artistic installations, social media engagement, and so on (Bulkeley et al. 2019).

Delivering exploration tools

The four tools in this category are diverse in their intentions and operation, and vary widely in their use across Europe. Design-led community participation, for example, can involve a one-off or short-lived exercise designed to focus input into a particular development process, or a sustained process over time. Scotland, for example, has utilised a charrettes fund, consisting of two strands – a Place Standard Conversations fund (see Box 9, p. 153) and a Community-Led Design fund – to support the delivery of participative design and place-based workshops. The fund was open to community groups, third-sector organisations and public authorities, with the Scottish Government contributing half the cost. These one-off and ad hoc events, often relating to the preparation of local Place Plans, contrast with the longer-term and more focused engagement used elsewhere.

In Nantes, for example, the interactive online platform Dialogue Citoyen facilitates ongoing conversations between local authorities and citizens about urban interventions and the future of unused spaces. In 2018 residents were invited to reconceptualise 15 unused places across the metropole, with resident suggestions later being grouped through technical specifications for each site and leading to an open competition for the sites and a public vote via the platform on the results. On the Île de Nantes – an area designated as an urban laboratory – local development company Samoa (Société d'Aménagement de la Métropole Ouest Atlantique) has been using a participatory process that brings together the developer, the Samoa urban planning team and future residents to define the use of key blocks within the master plan and to select a design team. Alongside educational workshops for young people on urban issues

(Archi'teliers), experimental modes of partnership and architectural competitions have been used.

Various forms of co-governance promote an even closer relationship between citizens and the places they help to manage. These have been particularly popular in Italy, where new legal tools are allowing various innovative neighbourhood agreements to enable local citizens' associations to assist in bringing under-used localities back into use. Sometimes described as the 'urban commons', they allow a form of collective sharing, management, production and ownership of critical urban resources, services and infrastructures (Antonelli et al. 2021). The Co-City project, for example, explored new approaches to the economic crisis of the 2010s and the reduction of public funds through the shared management of their urban commons by the City Council of Turin and active citizens. The project allowed new forms of citizen participation to be examined, focused on the regeneration of deprived neighbourhoods and abandoned buildings, all written into pacts of collaboration between the city's inhabitants and the city administration. The municipality of Reggio Emilia has implemented 160 such projects via 27 Citizen Agreements, involving a total of around 2,400 public and private stakeholders all spearheaded by a new Department of Competitiveness and Social Innovation with the explicit purpose of enabling a collaborative city model. Neighbourhood architects are appointed, one for each neighbourhood, as the go-between for the municipality and the public, with each process beginning with a neighbourhood lab. In Portugal, the BIP/ZIP programme brings together both community engagement and co-governance (see Box 15).

Box 15   Reshaping the public realm: Lisbon's BIP/ZIP programme (Portugal)

The BIP/ZIP programme supports small-scale, community-driven projects in Lisbon's deprived neighbourhoods, allowing bottom-up experimentation in the form of co-governance models, design solutions and cultural initiatives (http://bipzip.cm-lisboa.pt/). The programme is managed by Lisbon City Council.

Founded in 2011, the programme has aimed at implementing small, local interventions that promote the well-being of the whole community. These often focus on the city's Priority Intervention

---

Figure 4.30 The central but deprived neighbourhood of Mouraria has benefited from the Bip/Zip programme (image: Matthew Carmona).

Zones with responses designed to address defined social and urban challenges (see Figure 4.30) and ranging from physical interventions to new uses for public space and schemes designed to animate local citizens and get them engaged in their areas.

The programme is flexible in terms of partnerships and themes, with the promotion of citizenship, skills and entrepreneurship, inclusion, rehabilitation, and the improvement of life in neighbourhoods as key objectives. Its philosophy is based on the establishment of local partnerships, together with the parish and local associations, communities and non-governmental organisations, all contributing to the strengthening of social and territorial cohesion in the city.

BIP/ZIP has a strong participatory dimension, including participatory budgeting. A public tender is opened annually, with a maximum of €50,000 per project, all evaluated by an independent jury. Projects are deliberately small and quickly implemented, with a timespan of one year allowed for each project so that residents will see tangible results without getting bogged down in complex bureaucracy or decision-making.

Although professional investigation tools may involve citizen engagement in various forms, professional designers are usually firmly in the lead. In Belgium, research by design is a key tool of the Brussels Bouwmeester, used to help generate initial design guidelines for projects before they go into the formal regulatory processes of the municipality. Research by design processes also feed into policy preparation and help to shape key projects, with ideas often developed in collaboration with a range of different stakeholders. The Flemish Bouwmeester (see Box 13 above) runs Lab Space, a laboratory for complex spatial issues run in partnership with the Flemish administration responsible for spatial planning, and with other organisations as relevant. The lab offers design research and critical analysis on issues with a long-term socio-economic impact, for example on the metropolitan coastal landscape, the integration of renewable energy, the role of open space in and around Brussels, and the development potential of the Low Countries.

Moving off the page and onto sites, on-site experimentation ranges from one-off projects to ongoing programmes of work. At the larger end of this scale, urban labs typically bring together a wide range of development actors to focus on a particular area or topic, including universities, NGOs, local authorities, communities, and so on. Urban labs may last for a week, a month or in some cases several years, such as the three-year Praga Lab in Warsaw, which aims to reconnect local communities, NGOs and other actors to the redevelopment process in the Praga neighbourhood, using heritage as the link (see Box 18, p. 192).

Other cities have long-running programmes of on-site experimentation and engagement, often combining multiple projects at a small scale. These include Aarhus where the former Chief Architect notes: '1:1 scale temporary physical interventions have proved to be a useful engagement tool for gathering feedback and observations before settling on more permanent ways forward' (Willacy 2022: 31). Because they are small and inexpensive, such projects carry a low risk for politicians and allow innovation and experimentation that can be learnt from and swept away, or occasionally allowed to become permanent (see Figure 4.31).

Longer-established still are Germany's International Building Exhibitions (in German, Internationale Bauausstellungen, IBA), developed as living labs for planning and architecture (see Box 16), and a model that is now extended to other countries, including Austria, the Netherlands and Switzerland. IBAs always incorporate general aims of innovation and high standards of design focused on themes related to the

Figure 4.31 Temporary projects in Aarhus have ranged from new uses for abandoned shops to festivals, container cities, and the infinite bridge, here seen from above, which allows people to walk onto and over the sea. Originally a temporary structure, the bridge is now re-assembled each year between April and October as a meeting place for citizens (image: Aerodata International Surveys, CNES/Airbus, Aero Maxo Technologies Scankort Map data 2022).

geographical area in which they are situated. The Thüringen IBA, for example, which began in 2013 and is scheduled to run until 2023, focuses on urban and rural relationships, a particular issue in a region dominated by its rural hinterland, but which also characterises much of Europe. The IBA aims to recast the province as a place of progressive innovation and an experimental laboratory for the future. One example of this is the open factory concept, which is being used to convert old factory buildings into dynamic new spaces for creative studios, manufacturing workshops and community hubs, all together in the same place.

Besides urban labs, there has been an increase in the implementation of exploratory projects through the temporary occupation of vacant and abandoned areas. These can foster urban innovation and new ways of envisioning and living in the city. In addition, temporary occupations allow for experimentation with various activities that reveal the potential of unused spaces in order to attract new audiences as well as new cultural and economic actors. For example, the French National Railway Company (SNCF) is now widely using transitory operations to bring life to some of its huge portfolio of unused properties while testing out new uses and activities. In Zaragoza, the city council is promoting urban development

Box 16   Injecting innovation: IBA International Building Exhibitions (Germany)

Originally, International Building Exhibitions (IBAs) were conceived as a way of showcasing architectural achievements, the first being in Darmstadt in 1901. The format has changed from an architectural and urban exhibition to the promotion of integrated approaches to urban development. IBAs are led by local and regional authorities, and are time-limited programmes, usually taking place over a period of seven to ten years. They often address several themes, from housing prototypes and public-space interventions to engagement models and alternative educational initiatives (https://www.internationale-bauausstellungen.de).

IBAs seek to provide a vision for the future of urban areas (often an entire city) with visitors invited to participate in the process of researching and developing urban concepts. This means that today's building exhibitions become workshops spanning several years and aiming to influence a range of social, economic and cultural matters. Each IBA contains several significant and forward-looking concepts to inspire others and demonstrate innovation. They represent opportunities to explore models for new urban approaches and to gradually optimise the featured projects, all of which must go through an approval process. One of the main advantages of IBAs is their ability to overcome institutional barriers and establish practical cooperation on specific projects with a wide range of different players.

While there has been a constant development of IBAs in terms of their scale of operation, themes covered, organisational structure and number of actors involved, there are some common characteristics that can be traced through the years. IBAs tend to be independent organisations, usually in the form of a non-profit association linked to relevant public actors at the local, regional or state levels through protocols or institutional membership in order to secure a stable financial framework and cooperation. IBAs aim to combine bottom-up and top-down implementation strategies and are based on an informal process that can flex and adapt to local circumstances, and which attempts to enhance horizontal and vertical cooperation through shared work on projects.

Using an IBA format can strengthen planning perspectives and help overcome systemic barriers in the formal planning processes. IBAs have been behind a range of influential projects including in Berlin (1979–87; see Figure 4.32) and Escher Park (1989–99). Current IBAs include Parkstadt, Hamburg, Basel, Heidelberg, Vienna, Stuttgart and Thüringen. In addition to aesthetic and technological dimensions, these IBAs are incorporating complex social, economic and ecological issues into their work.

Figure 4.32 Berlin has hosted two IBAs thirty years apart, each exploring innovative urban typologies of their time as represented in the two images. The first (a), in 1957, explored new models for a future city in a context of the post-war divided city being rebuilt. The second (b), from 1979–87, explored new healing typologies with a focus on building new residential perimeter blocks (images: Matthew Carmona).

with an employment plan that engages the long-term unemployed in work cleaning abandoned empty plots of public and private land and utilising temporary public uses of these sites as squares, children's playgrounds, and community gardens, while clearing plots for their ultimate purpose, new housing. Likewise, the project *Les Grands Voisins* in Paris had a larger social purpose behind its temporary occupation of an abandoned hospital (see Box 17).

On-site experimentation also – more rarely – extends to the construction of exemplar projects. The Pilot Projects of the Flemish Bouwmeester, for example, are developed in collaboration with different

Box 17   Temporary occupation: Les Grands Voisins, Paris (France)

Les Grands Voisins is a project that encompassed the temporary occupation of the former Saint-Vincent-de-Paul hospital in the 14th arrondissement (district) of Paris while waiting for renovation works to start (https://lesgrandsvoisins.org). Owned by the municipality of Paris, the space was managed by three not-for-profit organisations – Aurore, Plateau Urban and Yes We Camp – who developed a wide range of activities with the aim of enhancing social inclusion and testing out new cooperative and supportive ways of living. Initially, from 2015 to 2017, this temporary occupation offered accommodation to 600 people in vulnerable situations and enabled 250 associations, start-ups, artisans and artists to use this unique environment. Following the success of the project, a second phase was launched to promote new forms of experimentation on the site and in the 14th arrondissement more generally.

The site was supervised by SPL Paris and Métropole Aménagement, the planning agency of the City of Paris, together with the project partners who had an annual operating budget of €2 million between them. In doing this, the City of Paris temporarily handed over the management of 10,000 square metres of buildings and 3,500 square metres of outdoor space to these organisations, which occupied the space with a mix of activities and functions. Their governance model was based on three thematic working groups and a committee for shared decisions as well as a general council. By 2020 (when the initiative closed) more than 2,000 people either lived and/or worked on the site, including in temporary homes for vulnerable persons. The site included meeting places for neighbours, workspaces for small businesses, associations, craftspeople, artists, and urban farmers, and services such as a social restaurant, a well-being centre, a cultural centre, and so on. It attracted over 600,000 visitors during its five-year span, largely to the 300-plus events hosted annually.

This project became one of the most successful examples of temporary occupation across Europe, featuring activities that emphasised community, the circular economy, and place-based solutions that prioritise diversity and creativity. It was captured in a documentary so that the learning could pass to new sites and other groups (see Figure 4.33).

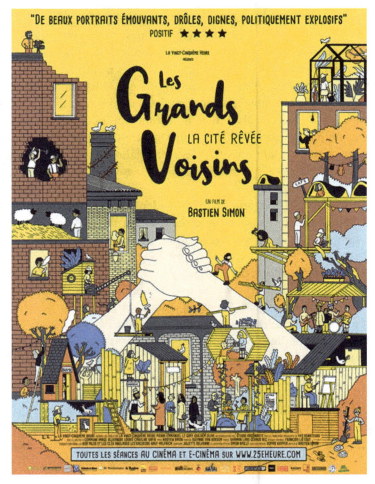

Figure 4.33 Poster for the documentary *Les grands Voisins: le cité rêvée* (great neighbours: the dream city) by Bastien Simon (image: Les Grands Voisins).

stakeholders and always have a social purpose. Themes have included care, responding to the aging population and the need for new models of healthcare provision, collective living aimed at rethinking trends in housing production in the context of densification, and 'Back in Circulation', a project that investigated how underutilised and polluted industrial estates could acquire a new meaning in Flanders. The 2021 theme focused on rehabilitating public spaces in housing areas, for which guidance outlining key concepts was issued – *Neighbourhoods with guts, neighbourhoods full of life* – to guide the process, with exemplar projects selected following an open call and a seven-stage process:

1. Protocol-based commitment between strategic partners.
2. Composition of the steering group.
3. Prior design research.
4. Scouting potential public and private partners with relevant projects reflecting the identified social ambition (via an open call).
5. Judging by steering group and selection of five pilot projects/ developers.
6. Composition of five project teams (designers and clients) and start of the design process.
7. Realisation phase (construction) and quality control by the project designers.

Each round was documented and promoted in order that lessons can be learned and innovations spread, making the whole process a form of research by design.

Deployment of exploration tools?

Exploration tools are typically site-specific, engaging citizens, design professionals and policymakers directly with particular projects and places. Relating them to the larger design governance field of action (see Figures 7.5a–c, pp. 279–81) reveals that they are primarily used early on, helping to shape early thinking about the project or place in question. Co-governance is the exception which, because it involves ongoing management, will likely continue throughout the lifetime of a project and beyond. These tools are deployed locally and therefore tend to be utilised by local (and sometimes regional) authorities, who have a more direct engagement with specific development processes.

- **National governments** rarely engage directly in exploratory tools, although do have a role in establishing the legislative regime within which citizen engagement occurs, either prior to or as part of the formal regulation of development. Much of this involves tokenistic consultation rather than fundamental participation in development proposals, with design-led community participation tending to be more discretionary in nature and therefore featuring in the informal category of urban design governance tools.

- Across Europe, **local government** is very active in promoting various forms of design-led participatory processes using design workshops, design charrettes, debates, and so on. For example, in Groningen, the Atelier (city architect) uses their own research by design to engage inhabitants in discussing various scenarios affecting the city, from the potential of public spaces to climate-proofing the city. Likewise, in Lisbon, the programme 'A Square in Every Neighbourhood' allows interested parties to identify what they would like to change in their neighbourhood by completing an online participation form or by attending a dedicated session for each locality leading to the generation of design propositions for local populations to discuss. The co-governance of urban assets is far less common but seems to be largely a phenomenon promoted by local government, with a particularly strong emphasis on these practices in Italy. Research by design and on-site experimentation are frequently used at this scale, with Bouwmeesters and city architects being some of the most frequent users. In Brussels, for example, the Brussels Bouwmeester Maître Architecte (BMA) uses research by design on projects that require a preliminary study to ensure that a range of options are properly considered. They help to ensure that the right questions are asked at the right time and can feed into other tools such as competition processes. One approach involves the 'zoom-out', where the BMA team takes a strategic view of a project to ensure that clients are aware of the wider context.

- **Private consultancies and non-governmental organisations** often act as facilitators to deliver proactive engagement tools. For example, in the UK, Glass-House Community Led Design is a national charity that supports communities, organisations and networks to work collaboratively on the design of buildings, open spaces, homes and neighbourhoods. Consultancies may be appointed by public authorities and others to conduct research by design and sometimes fund such studies themselves as promotional devices for their own services while contributing to larger public debates. One particularly active consultancy on this front is Farrells who have conducted many speculative projects helping, in particular, to guide strategic thinking on London, where they are based (https://farrells.com/publications/type/research). Non-governmental organisations are also active players in on-site experimentation, including the not-for-profit organisations set up to deliver each IBA living lab.

- As partners in stimulating the collective use, management, and ownership of urban assets, **communities** are central to the delivery of co-governance arrangements. Typically, this occurs through a range of non-governmental entities such as residents' associations, through which the role can be formalised.

Experience of exploration tools

Because exploration tools are proactive and focused on specific sites and places, they can reach out to non-professional actors in a manner that other tools cannot, potentially enriching design processes from development to final outcomes, with the potential to deliver a more inclusive and cohesive city. All these tools act as precursors to formal regulatory processes, bringing the power of creative design to inform more collaborative decision-making and inspiring more informed discussions about the future potential of place (Carmona 2021a: 485–92).

By engaging with a wide range of stakeholders and communities, including laypersons, professionals using these tools can come up against language, knowledge and vision barriers they may find frustrating if efforts are not made to overcome them. At the same time, mobilising community forces can bring influential voices, enthusiasm, and lay know-how to support initiatives through harnessing the economy of the commons. Meaningful results can also be achieved relatively inexpensively with urban living labs and temporary interventions often building on pent-up public and practitioner motivation to contribute to the improvement of their localities, and engaging bottom-up energies to do so. Several of the successful examples explored by Urban Maestro seemed to build on a combination of powerful political leadership and active community engagement (see Box 18).

In achieving this, exploration tools often use approaches in combination (see Figure 4.35). For example, design-led community participation activities will often use some form of knowledge-sharing and active-learning tools (see Information tools, p. 123) in order to

Box 18   Top-down and bottom-up in Warsaw (Poland)

Warsaw, like many large European cities, combines a concern with its past (a rich heritage) with a vision of the future, and in particular with making the city more liveable and sustainable. The City Architect of Warsaw is the director of the Architecture and Spatial Planning Office and takes a leading role in this, being responsible for spatial development policy across Warsaw. The office uses tools that transcend formal and informal categories, with the City Architect of Warsaw assuming the role of the city's design champion, explicitly tasked with providing urban design leadership, advocacy for design across stakeholders (public, private and political), and cultivating the conditions under which place-making can be prioritised in the city (https://architektura.um.warszawa.pl/baipp).

Key among her tools are the preparation and assessment of local municipal plans; monitoring of key projects under the City Revitalization Programme; conducting comprehensive public space transformation projects; operating the Urban and Architectural Commission; preparing and implementing architectural and urban design competitions and prizes; and handling matters related to the promotion of architecture within the city itself. Through these means the City Architect helps to set a context in which other actors with an interest in quality can thrive.

One such is the Praga Lab, which focuses on an area of Warsaw subject to processes of industrial decline, reinvention and gentrification, with significant new municipal investment in its revitalisation, now being met with private investment. Established in June 2019, run by the Warsaw branch of the Association of Polish Architects (OW SARP), and planned to run for three years, the lab aims to reconnect local communities, NGOs and other actors into the redevelopment process, using heritage as the hook (https://ohpraga.pl/?locale=en) (see Figure 4.34).

The lab's first step was to conduct research to understand public preferences relating to the area and to identify the stakeholders with whom cooperation should be established. With the research as a foundation, the lab moved on to construct a map as part of the online participatory platform aimed at revealing the different dimensions of local heritage. They launched a call to find

Figure 4.34 Praga district, Warsaw: creative interventions in a heritage context (image: Matthew Carmona).

artists and creative entrepreneurs whose work could be relevant to the Praga district and its heritage and conducted workshops to develop model solutions for the adaptive reuse of buildings. While the lab was time-limited, its experimental format was integrated into local governance (including up to the office of the City Architect) with the aim of ensuring that its findings would have a long-term impact, suggesting models that could be used elsewhere in Warsaw and beyond.

engage participants in the process. Likewise, research by design may take advantage of design competitions to explore different scenarios, stimulating new thinking about local places. These tools are used in an ever-growing range of cities across Europe, albeit that co-governance is still relatively rare. All are eminently transferable, perhaps explaining the growth in on-site experimentation across Europe in recent decades. At the larger scale, the recent spread of IBAs beyond Germany illustrates this, reflecting a desire to explore new urban scenarios as we move into the future.

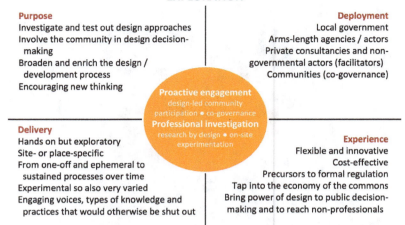

EXPLORATION

Purpose
Investigate and test out design approaches
Involve the community in design decision-making
Broaden and enrich the design / development process
Encouraging new thinking

Deployment
Local government
Arms-length agencies / actors
Private consultancies and non-governmental actors (facilitators)
Communities (co-governance)

Proactive engagement
design-led community participation • co-governance
Professional investigation
research by design • on-site experimentation

Delivery
Hands on but exploratory
Site- or place-specific
From one-off and ephemeral to sustained processes over time
Experimental so also very varied
Engaging voices, types of knowledge and practices that would otherwise be shut out

Experience
Flexible and innovative
Cost-effective
Precursors to formal regulation
Tap into the economy of the commons
Bring power of design to public decision-making and to reach non-professionals

Figure 4.35 Summarising exploration tools (image: Matthew Carmona).

5
The financial dimension

Urban design does not work in isolation. High-quality design solutions will be of little value if economic systems fail to allow for their implementation and long-term management in 'valued' uses. For this reason, urban design governance outcomes and processes are shaped by the availability of economic resources and the nature of financing instruments for projects. A key aspect of the Urban Maestro project was to investigate the role of finance in relation to the governance of urban design, and that is what this fifth chapter explores. It is strongly linked to Chapter 4 as the practices discussed also derive from the panorama of tools developed over the course of the project. Ultimately, this chapter makes the case that financial mechanisms and design tools need to work together, and high-quality sustainable development will only be deliverable through a better alignment of quality and economy objectives.

Finance and design

Writing in the first century BC, Vitruvius called for structures that exhibit firmness, commodity and delight. Ever since, these essential parameters have been taken as criteria of good design in a product design sense, and notably in architecture. Firmness (or stability) is where a design achieves the necessary technical criteria; commodity (or utility) is where it achieves the necessary functional criteria; and delight (or beauty) is where it has aesthetic appeal. However, a fourth criteria of 'economy' should also be added, not merely in a narrow financial sense of respecting budget constraints, but also in the sense of respecting and optimising precious resources (both economic and environmental). While environmental issues are increasingly integrated into European urban design governance frameworks from the pan-European scale downwards, economic concerns are not, or at least not so obviously.

In the context of the built environment, these economic resources come, primarily, in the form of financing – the act of providing funds (public or private) for development projects. Leinberger (2005: 24) argues: 'Learning how this system works, and how it may be influenced to accept different models, should be one of the top concerns of advocates of change', including those such as urban designers who need to manipulate it. This is because, as Ellin (1997) notes, 'form follows financing'.

There is no room to discuss all the nuances of development process and its economics as they relate to urban design here (see Carmona 2021a, Chapter 10 for a comprehensive discussion). Instead the focus in this chapter is on the specific interface between the tools of urban design governance and those of finance. Financial institutions, practices, regulations and constraints are intrinsic to any economic activity and operate at several interdependent scales, from the transnational to the very local (Adams and Tiesdell 2013: 183–6). Within the complex picture of modern finance, financial mechanisms with 'design strings' encompass the use of public and/or private financing instruments alongside and interconnected with one or more tools of urban design governance. This combination can ensure that economic resources are used in order to shape both development processes and design outcomes in a defined public interest.

This is quite separate (although may be linked) to the funding of urban design governance tools. While almost all tools of urban design governance will require funding in order to establish and operationalise them, far fewer will be linked explicitly to the financing of development.

The category of financial mechanisms used in development will encompass very different instruments. A traditional classification of financial mechanisms could be based on whether those are public or private instruments; it could also be based on the geographical scale; and for private instruments one could distinguish between equity and debt instruments, with bonds and loans being the typical instruments of debt financing.

Financial (and other economic) mechanisms that interface with design

Evidence shows that traditional financing instruments are unlikely to satisfy the pressing needs of sustainable urbanisation processes across the world. The Global Commission on Economy and Climate projected that under a low-carbon scenario, $93 trillion will need to be invested in infrastructure globally by 2030; an estimated 70 per cent of this infrastructure will relate to urban areas, with annual investments of $4 trillion, plus an additional $0.4 to $1.1 trillion to make these investments low-carbon and climate-resilient (Cities Climate Finance Leadership Alliance 2015). This implies annual investments exceeding 5 per cent of global GDP, and significantly exceeding the tax revenues of many nations. New revenue sources will need to be found to take on this challenge.

Looking at existing evidence through the lenses of the previous traditional funding frameworks, it can be argued that improvements are necessary at virtually every scale, often requiring greater coordination between public and private systems and across different scales. Conclusions from the UN Habitat III Conference (UN-Habitat 2016a) showed that public resources alone, including Official Development Assistance, will not be sufficient to implement the ambitious urban agenda. Private investment will be vital to augment the efforts of development finance and philanthropic funders, but these forms of finance typically carry a profit- rather than a public-interest motive and – seen in isolation – the most profitable avenue for investment may not be the optimum one as regards delivering design quality.

In reality there are many forms of private investor, just as there are many forms of developer. And just as there are varying motivations informing the operation of urban design governance, as discussed in Chapter 1, so investors and developers will have different combinations of motivation guiding their operations, many with a direct public interest – creating jobs, stimulating the economy, regenerating places, building a reputation, and so on. However, profit will almost always feature prominently in these lists, and sometimes exclusively so (see Figure 5.1). Public developers such as social housebuilders or transport agencies, likewise, may have motivations guiding their activities – such as housing the disadvantaged, maximising new home numbers, delivering functional infrastructure, and making the books balance – that don't necessarily emphasise the delivery of place quality or its long-term place value. The challenge is therefore to weight the system so that it is clearly in their interest to deliver quality. In other words, it becomes easier to make a profit or deliver more homes or infrastructure by designing it well. This can be achieved through formal regulation, but also through the sorts of informal means discussed in Chapter 4, namely those that stimulate demand for good quality, ultimately changing the culture so that it becomes unacceptable to deliver anything else.

Municipalities, in partnership with private and community actors committed to an area, can also utilise supply-side stimulation to stoke demand. The methods employed typically include encouraging or

Figure 5.1 Gated development in Gdynia, Poland, as an expression of development solely guided by the market/profit motive (image: Matthew Carmona).

subsidising flagship (catalytic) projects; subsidising development; area-based improvements; provision of infrastructure; investing in heritage retention; and/or developing design frameworks of various sorts. As development involves calculation of reward and risk, these actions are generally intended to reduce risk (to those making investments) and to provide a more secure investment environment while avoiding 'growth at any cost' or 'only for some' scenarios. In achieving this, better-quality design helps ensure that economic benefits are also spread more widely, while poor-quality design might reduce the speed at which impacts propagate through local economies (Carmona et al. 2001: 76–7; Brennan and Tomback 2013; La Rosa et al. 2017).

The public sector, consequently, is simultaneously stimulating/attracting investment, while also regulating the resulting development. One potential consequence of this is that design criteria may be relaxed or compromised to ensure investment happens, particularly in environments perceived to be disadvantaged and where reducing regulation is often seen as stimulus to growth (Van Doren 2005). However, investment in the public realm by municipalities and private actors alike can be rapidly undermined when regulatory processes permit substandard development schemes. This is often further complicated by

Figure 5.2 In this major new development in Helsinki, the roads infrastructure (bottom left), public transportation infrastructure (right) and private investment (top left) are all in place, but fail to integrate to create a place that is more than the sum of its parts (image: Matthew Carmona).

institutional fragmentation, whereby one municipal department (or an arms-length public agency) is concerned with stimulating development (such as an economic development or regeneration agency) and another is regulating it (such as the planning department/agency). This will be particularly so if policy and practices of various agencies are not adequately joined up, creating the opportunity for less scrupulous developers (those only in search of a quick profit) to exploit the gaps. The critical aspiration is to get joined-up thinking across the public sector, and preferably beyond (see Figure 5.2).

The finance toolbox

Funds for specific developments are typically raised through a combination of equity and debt finance. Debt involves loans, mortgages or bonds. Equity is cash, land, an existing building, foregone professional fees, shares and so forth, invested in the project. Lenders of debt finance have the right to be repaid with interest but do not normally have a legal interest in the project (except as security in event of default) nor any entitlement to share in development profits. Paid off after debt is serviced, equity is at much greater risk and, as a result, attracts much higher return expectations than debt does (Leinberger 2008). Lenders of equity finance participate in the risks and rewards of development, are entitled to share in development profits and have a legal interest in the project. Sometimes this interest can be very long-term and so is sometimes termed 'patient capital', so-called because the investor has the patience to invest in an asset or project with no expectation of turning a quick profit.

The public sector is both a lender and borrower of debt and equity finance. Access by municipalities to debt finance, for example, can be an important element of a broader strategy to plan and invest in urban infrastructure. Debt finance is not an additional source of revenue for municipalities; it simply converts future revenues into capital that is immediately available for investment by encumbering future revenues for debt service payments. Debt financing is therefore feasible only where municipalities can service their debt from revenues in a sustainable manner and where a robust regulatory framework for municipal borrowing is in place (Radcliffe et al. 2021). But while politicians may wish to see positive change quickly – and will raise money to facilitate that – government should also be the ultimate patient investor, given that the bounds of their responsibilities are fixed and they will always be there (a municipality, unlike a private developer, can't simply move somewhere else where projected returns look better).

There are various ways that national governments can shape local fiscal systems to make them more responsive to local needs. These include:

- Increasing local government autonomy over taxes, revenues, and expenditures.
- Supporting intergovernmental transfers of funds from higher levels of government for the general or specific use of localities.
- Authorising local governments to leverage fiscal tools like municipal borrowing and land value capture to raise funds locally to support economic development and infrastructure.
- Enabling localities to marshal resources that facilitate access to credit markets when they seek funds to support operations, maintenance, infrastructure financing, or service delivery to citizens.
- Enabling shared project execution through arrangements with private and other public-sector stakeholders, including the lending of equity to projects such as publicly owned land.

Mobilising local, national and/or international finance requires local authorities to approach urban development in a more integrated manner, bridging the gap between its financial, spatial and legal aspects. The power of integrated investment planning has been demonstrated in numerous examples across Europe (Squires et al. 2015) in order that capital investment needs (and associated borrowing) find the proper balance and duration, with the organisational financial capacity to service them. Arguably these processes need to be better analysed and understood so that they can be successfully adopted, and governments have been active in advising local government about how to do this, for example, in the UK the Local Government Association (2019) has published *Attracting Investment for Local Infrastructure: A guide for councils* in order to make them think more actively about alternative sources of funds.

In principle, any of the sources of finance already mentioned could be used for built-environment related purposes, and, again in principle, any could be linked to defined design-quality expectations. Whichever means is selected, there is the potential to use financial mechanisms alongside or as part of the urban design governance toolbox in such a way that 'good behaviour' is rewarded (namely the delivery of high-quality design) and 'poor behaviour' discouraged (poor-quality unsustainable development). Because these approaches involve finance, either the giving or receiving of finance by the state or private actors and its investment in the public realm, typically they are regulated and therefore lie within the formal side of the larger governance toolbox (see Figure 3.6, p. 83), many relating to dimensions of incentivisation. Financial resources can also support the production of tools of urban design governance within the informal support category, but in that context it is typically grant funding rather than development finance, and so has already been discussed in Chapter 4.

This linkage between design and finance (either positive or negative) will be apparent in most development projects, and certainly was in the development-related case studies by Urban Maestro, for example the large scale regenerations in Valencia, Oslo (see Box 19), Copenhagen and elsewhere. Falk (2011: 38) argues that the significant investments by the public sector in key locations across Europe – Lille, Amersfoort (and indeed across the Randstad), Karlsruhe, Freiburg (see Box 24), and Montpellier – and the huge private investment this additionally attracts, offer the ideal opportunity to attach design strings.

Peter Hall (2014: 295, 309) in his final, evocatively titled book *Good Cities, Better Lives: How Europe discovered the lost art of urbanism*, agreed. Taking an intellectual grand tour through Germany, Scandinavia, France

Box 19   Financing and guiding transformative investment in Oslo (Norway)

Since 2008 the city of Oslo has been implementing an ambitious Fjord city project. Bjørvika is a waterfront district in Oslo, undergoing redevelopment as part of this long-term transformation. The area's public spaces and physical infrastructure are being developed by the company Bjørvika Infrastruktur and will ultimately be handed over free of charge to the municipality of Oslo, which will become the property owner and take on responsibility for their maintenance. The quality of the public spaces is secured through a combination of various formal and informal tools that have built on the long-term vision starting as early as 1982.

The development was initiated by the municipality of Oslo in collaboration with state agencies and the national government and is governed as a collaboration between the council and Bjørvika Utvikling, which is owned by the private/public companies HAV Eiendom AS, Oslo S Utvikling AS and Entra ASA, alongside the private company Linstow AS (https://www.bjorvikautvikling. no/portfolio-item/information-in-english/). Together they own Bjørvika Infrastruktur.

The quality of the development delivered in Bjørvika is the result of a combination of tools and practices using a networked governance model that has delivered a holistic approach to place development, and the financial security necessary to produce quality urban design (see Figure 5.3). Bjørvika Infrastruktur raised finance to develop the public spaces and technical and physical infrastructure, whereas the Oslo municipality is responsible for the social infrastructure. A clause in the agreement stipulates that each square metre of sold property should yield a certain sum towards the provision of public space. A further clause prescribes that HAV Eiendom should provide a loan to Bjørvika Infrastruktur and that the public landowners can then develop housing and office buildings. This means that the municipality of Oslo does not take on any direct financial risk but is still in a position to dictate standards.

To achieve this, it has developed a range of informal tools, including a cultural programme, a design handbook and an

Figure 5.3 The buildings and public spaces of Bjørvika, in Oslo, reflect the public/private delivery model that gave the municipality an inside seat on all key decisions. Seen here are the distinctive 'barcode buildings' that featured in an early development phase (image: Matthew Carmona).

overarching environmental programme. These offer extensive guidelines and a set of indicators, allowing the developers and architects to interpret these principles and incorporate them into their projects. The planning authority has also utilised various tools to help inspire the developers and raise ambitions, including scenario-building workshops, debates and concept competitions.

and the Netherlands to European cities which, he argued, have got it right, he called for a 'locally based' model of finance that is responsive to local context, engages public and private actors in a shared endeavour and ultimately creates places in which people can thrive. This means irrevocably linking long-term investment strategies and a clear place-based vision for 'good cities and better lives', including finance decision-making that variously encourages the production and use of, or otherwise promotes the aspirations contained within, the informal (and sometimes the formal) tools of urban design governance.

Types of 'useful' finance mechanisms for design

It follows that to ensure financial mechanisms are used to deliver high-quality design, they need to be used in conjunction with the tools of urban design governance. Again, while any financial mechanism might, in theory, be used for that purpose, in practice some are far more commonly used than others. It is not the aim of this chapter to map all innovative development finance mechanisms, but instead to understand which approaches have the potential to engage directly with, and enhance, urban design outcomes and processes. Arguably effective financial mechanisms for use in combination with design aspirations fit within a larger set of economic approaches that encompass not only the manner in which finance is raised, transferred and applied, but also mechanisms that shape the economic equation that developers have to balance. This might include managing the regulatory process in order to streamline it and achieve faster permissions in exchange for better design, or offer tangible incentives if developers demonstrably invest in design quality themselves.

Drawing on these distinctions, and in order to investigate the link between finance and urban design governance, this stage of the Urban Maestro project began with a working classification (drawn from Carmona et al. 2016: 42–5) of possible finance mechanisms that have been known to be used in conjunction with urban design governance tools, or which have otherwise been used to help deliver defined urban design aspirations. The classification was used to identify possible practices from the European survey discussed in Chapter 3 and the subsequent panorama compiled and presented in Chapter 4. A selection of these were evaluated in greater depth through the project's case-study work and workshops, some of which are highlighted in the discussion and boxes contained in this chapter.

The working classification identified six mechanisms across two key categories:

- **Raising finance**, through subsidy and direct investment:
  - *Direct financing instruments* are used to help deliver urban quality and include loans or subsidies for well-designed development, direct public funding tied to defined quality thresholds, and various mechanisms for land-value capture.
  - *Direct public investment* in projects is used to reduce developer risks associated with the upfront investments in place quality through mechanisms such as area improvements, land transfer, infrastructure provision, and so on, but can also be used simply to give the public sector a seat at the table when key development decisions are being made.

- *Taxation supplements* can raise finance for direct investment in the places to which they relate. Typically, these are local in their application, with common mechanisms including Business Improvement Districts (BIDs), tax-increment financing, planning-gain (betterment) charges and development-impact fees.
- **Managing investment**, through process management, indirect economic stimulus and partnership working:
  - *Indirect financing instruments* are used to encourage the delivery of urban quality through mechanisms such as tax incentives (for instance reductions in local taxation or development taxes) and through zoning bonuses/enhanced development rights associated with certain types of scheme.
  - *Steering mechanisms* are designed to encourage good design through the direct involvement of the public sector in the development process, perhaps through the creation of public–private partnerships (PPPs) or the development of exemplar projects. They include the voluntary imposition by development consortia of guidance upon themselves, for example through a design code.
  - *Regulatory management* approaches are designed to reduce the formal regulatory burden in exchange for better design. This might include fast-tracking architect-designed schemes or streamlined regulation zones tied to following defined design parameters (Carmona 2020a).

The use of financial mechanisms in relation to design across Europe

As well as an overview of the use of informal urban design governance tools across Europe, the European survey explored how financial mechanisms can be used to encourage better design or to capture the benefits of better design. Almost all replies were given by national or regional government respondents and covered all six types of financial mechanism.

Within the raising-finance category, most financial incentive schemes were connected with heritage projects or the delivery of new housing. In both cases the finance was often dependent on meeting minimum levels of design quality, requiring that schemes are assessed in some way using a tool of urban design governance. Sometimes this simply required that a defined process had been followed, for example that a design review or design competition process had been conducted. Elsewhere it required that a defined quality threshold had been reached, with the requisite assessment made using a suitable rating tool.

The European survey also suggested that direct public investment is frequently used in Europe to (among other reasons) reduce the risks to the private sector associated with the upfront costs of delivering high-quality development. Respondents confirmed that for the public sector, the benefit comes in driving the sustainable development and regeneration of urban areas by funding awarded on a qualitative basis in which an assessment of design quality is often among the essential criteria for that investment, for example through commitments to meet design aspirations laid out in a practice guide or similar tool. Local (or even national – see Box 20) taxation supplements, by contrast, seem to be little used, although responses recognised that they have potential to be associated with the delivery of high-quality design. They are, however, discretionary in their use, and quality is just one of the many factors that might be encouraged in this way.

Box 20   0.05% for architecture: architectural stamp duty (Romania)

Timbrul de Arhitectură (literally, the 'Stamp of Architecture') is a stamp duty dedicated to the promotion of architecture and building culture in Romania. This unusual cultural fund is financed by tax levied at 0.05% of the investment value of any construction project once a building permit is requested. Consequently it amounts to a fixed percentage of the investment value of the construction taking place across the country, which is collected by local authorities and delivered to the two Romanian professional organisations of architects, the Order of Architects of Romania (OAR) and the Union of Architects of Romania (UAR) (https://oar.archi/en/timbrul-de-arhitectura/about-the-architectural-stamp-duty/).

The stamp duty is paid by the investor or owner together with the fee for the building permit for any construction where authorisation is required. When issuing this authorisation, local authorities must calculate the value of the investment and levy the

Figure 5.4 In recent years a major beneficiary of the Timbrul de Arhitecturã fund has been the Street Delivery festival in Bucharest, where for three days key central streets are closed to cars and opened to pedestrians and a series of activities designed to connect the public to artists, architects and artisans and to celebrate a street culture (image: Matthew Carmona).

appropriate charge. The recipients use the fund to finance a wide range of cultural activities of relevance to architecture, including events, debates, publications, exhibitions and so on (see Figure 5.4). In addition, the OAR has created a specific annual funding programme open to all creative professionals (not only architects), associations, organisations and publishers whose mission it is to promote architecture and building culture.

Ultimately, this stamp duty provides financial support for a diversified cultural programme, financed by an innovative funding scheme, aimed at disseminating knowledge among stakeholders and raising awareness about the value of design quality alongside its benefits to the general public. As the OAR states (Order of Architects of Romania 2019: 15), to encourage the 'democratisation of culture' in an architectural form and help deliver the *Baukultur* called for in the Davos Declaration (see Chapter 1).

Turning to mechanisms associated with managing investment processes, the most widely used mechanism within the category of indirect financing instruments seems to be the provision of tax incentives for the restoration of heritage buildings and to increase the energy performance of buildings. Zoning bonuses – a mechanism extensively used in North America to encourage the delivery of benefits such as new public spaces (Kayden 2005) – are, by contrast, infrequently used in Europe.

Steering tools were rarely identified by the national respondents to the survey, despite the well-documented role of the public sector in setting high standards of design in countless exemplar projects across the continent, from new neighbourhoods to public buildings and public-realm projects. There was also little recognition in the survey of the potential role of public–private partnerships in this area, perhaps reflecting an absence of knowledge at the national scale about such practices, rather than the absence of the practices themselves. Regulatory-management tools also seem to be rarely used in Europe, the exception being the UK where such mechanisms have been widely tried – although not always with design strings attached – and generally leading to worse-rather than better-quality development (Carmona 2020b).

The survey suggested that while all financial mechanisms are used in Europe, awareness of the potential to link financial approaches and design tools is low, suggesting in turn that the association is underexploited. The majority of respondents were unaware of any obvious linkages being made in their jurisdictions between design and finance.

Adding design strings

Despite the low level of awareness regarding the potential linkage between design and finance, further exploration of practices gathered during the Urban Maestro panorama, and explored in the workshops and case studies, demonstrated a clear potential to add design strings to the sorts of tools included in the working classification in order to reinforce design aspirations through financial mechanisms. These largely encompass tools in the direct financing instruments (see Box 21), direct public investment, indirect financing instruments (see Box 22), and steering mechanisms subcategories as compiled in table 5.1.

Table 5.1 Financial mechanisms and urban design governance tools compared (compiled by Matthew Carmona).

Initiative	Financial mechanism	Allied urban design governance tool(s)	Financial mechanism/urban design governance tool interaction
Raising finance			
Grenoble Public Space Programme: experimental processes for improving public spaces (France)	direct financing	incentive, exploration, information	The Grenoble-Alpes Metropole administration is promoting an experimental and design-led community participatory process for improving public spaces. To facilitate this, a guide for public spaces was developed, including an evaluation system via a participatory and incremental process that gradually scales up temporary interventions. Citizens define specific needs and bring this to the city administration, leading to a range of explorative projects over the course of three months. After an evaluation, each initiative may be expanded for one to three years. If successful, a final intervention will be carried out with a higher budget.
Mehr Als Wohnen: housing cooperative for a future generation (Switzerland)	direct public investment	incentive	The Swiss Housing Cooperatives are set up to secure high-quality living environments for their members. Swiss housing cooperatives are a distinctive form of affordable home ownership accounting for more than 5% of the entire country's housing. The Mehr Als Wohnen cooperative is financed by a variety of sources: members of the cooperative pay an equity deposit that is refunded (with interest) when they vacate their residence; the state grants special low-interest loans; and the co-op issues bonds and borrows through mortgages from banking institutions. The residents assist in the development of their areas by working together in teams, participating in workshops and voting for decisions. The expectation that flows from the public investment is for a high-quality development delivering long-term place value.

(Continued Table 5.1)

Initiative	Financial mechanism	Allied urban design governance tool(s)	Financial mechanism/urban design governance tool interaction
Citymaker Fund: matchmakers between place-makers and investors (Netherlands, see Box 21)	direct private financing, with direct public investment	incentive, support	Stadmakers Fonds recognises the difficulties that non-conventional place-making projects encounter with traditional sources of finance. The fund acts as a 'matchmaker' between place-makers and investors and is an initiative of STIPO and Stadkwadraat. In 2019 it received its first investment from the City of Utrecht of €1 million in the fund. Following this, the Citymaker Fund made its first investment in the province of Utrecht. A subsequent partnership with the Triodos Bank has exponentially increased the amount of capital available. The fund charges a low interest on loans, advises Citymakers and assists them with making a case for funding. All projects are evaluated on economic and social grounds.
Europan: ideas competition for young designers (Europe, see Box 11)	direct public investment	persuasion, exploration, support	First set up in 1988 and now run 15 times, this competition for young professionals under 40 years old utilises sites across Europe with 30% of projects being realised by the participating country authorities. Each Europan costs around 5–6 million euros, where 95% of the funding is offered by national and local level partners, with each country able to organise the competition and its ambitions on their own terms and according to their own budget.

By&Havn: model for holistic city development (Denmark, see Box 23)	direct financing (land value capture), direct public investment	incentive, support, information, persuasion, rating	By&Havn is jointly owned by the City of Copenhagen and the Danish state and operates on a commercial basis using land value capture, alongside other tools. By&Havn is responsible for the development of urban neighbourhoods, the establishment of roads and canals, parking garages, urban spaces and green areas. It sells building plots to various investors as well as to housing cooperatives and actively participates in urban living initiatives from the initial planning phases until the residents have finally moved in and the neighbourhoods have come to life. The revenue from its activities helps to fund major infrastructure projects in Copenhagen including the development of the metro as well as urban spaces, quays, jetties, parks and initiatives in the new urban neighbourhoods.
Managing investment			
Concept Tendering: funding mechanism that weights quality as well as price (Germany, Box 22)	indirect financing	incentive, rating	An alternative means for municipalities to lease their land. Instead of using a direct award or a bidding process (where price is the deciding factor), concept tendering brings to the fore the qualities and aspects of design/place by making them a key decision-making factor, equal to or even more important than price. Evaluation matrices are applied in an attempt to ensure transparency. The concept tendering procedure was first developed in the 1990s in Tübingen, and since then cities have been able to use a variety of different and diverse criteria, enabling them to compare the quality of submitted projects. Some of these criteria are assessed based on complex point matrices while others are assessed based on unweighted lists of factors.

(Continued Table 5.1)

Initiative	Financial mechanism	Allied urban design governance tool(s)	Financial mechanism/urban design governance tool interaction
Subsidies for architectural and urban competitions: encouraging the use of design competitions (Czech Republic, see Box 12)	steering mechanism	support, rating	The Architecture and Building Culture Policy that was implemented in the Czech Republic in 2015 defined the need to provide funding from the national public budget for local design competitions. The policy led to the shaping of a national subsidy programme. In 2019 the Ministry received eight bids from different municipalities, of which five succeeded and received financial support. The fund helps to overcome a reluctance to stage competitions because of the cost and administration time, which particularly reduces the enthusiasm for competitions in smaller municipalities despite their proven impact in improving development quality.
Oslo waterfront: regeneration, governing high-quality urban design (Norway, see Box 19)	steering mechanism (public–private partnership)	analysis, information, support	The development of the Bjørvika neighbourhood is a collaboration between the Oslo city council and Bjørvika Utvikling, which is jointly owned by private/ public and private companies. Quality is secured through a combination of various formal and informal tools. A clause in the agreement stipulates that each square metre of sold property should yield a defined sum towards the development of public space. A further clause prescribes how finance will be supplied to the project in a manner that avoids the municipality having to take on any direct financial risk. The coherence of the area is shaped through extensive guidelines and a set of indicators.

Be.exemplary: subsidies for exemplar architecture projects (Belgium)	steering mechanism (exemplary projects) support, information	The Brussels-Capital Region has conducted calls for projects to enhance and promote the construction or renovation of exemplary buildings. Their goal is to demonstrate that it is possible to achieve very good energy and environmental performance within a reasonable budget. Following three calls for project proposals between 2017 and 2019, 117 projects, both small and large, were selected amounting to 265,000m², and utilising €18.5 million of financial support. The exemplary nature of the projects is evaluated by a panel of experts and publicised on a specific website.
HafenCity: collaborative development of Hamburg's urban waterfront (Germany, see Box 27)	steering mechanism (public–private partnership), indirect financing incentive, rating, support	HafenCity is under the full ownership of the City of Hamburg and is being developed by HafenCity Hamburg GmbH (HCH), which oversees all activities as the city's manager of development, property owner and developer of public infrastructure based on public investment and revenues from the sale of land. HCH enforces a strictly competitive bidding process where the crucial factor for awarding the contract is the quality of the concepts submitted (weighted at 70%) and not the highest bid (30%). After ratification by the City Land Commission, the investor has to proceed with an architectural competition. For the developer the financing of the purchase price is postponed until after the building permit is granted, giving time to refine the design, secure finance and acquire potential users. Public and private sectors successfully cooperate in a way that shifts the core of the risk profile to benefit both city and investors.

Box 21 Investing in place-making: Citymaker Fund (Netherlands)

The Stadmakers Fonds (Citymaker Fund) sees 'place-making' as a major source for good, helping to make cities sustainable, inclusive and attractive (https://stadmakersfonds.nl). Despite their social impact, a healthy financial model is also necessary if initiatives are to be sustainable, but for new players in the field, it is hard to gain access to financing, particularly from traditional commercial sources that are not immediately interested in social returns. Stadmakers Fonds recognises the difficulties that non-conventional place-making projects encounter with securing finance. It therefore acts as a 'matchmaker' between place-makers and investors, with an emphasis on projects that contribute to creating a lively and inclusive city by investing in initiatives with a clear social as well as economic return.

The tool is an initiative of the multi-disciplinary urban consultancy STIPO and development finance specialists Stadkwadraat, and in 2019 received its first investment of €1 million from the province of Utrecht. Following this, the Citymaker Fund made its first investment in December 2019 in the city of Utrecht. A subsequent partnership with the environmentally and socially focused Triodos Bank has exponentially increased the amount of capital available for investment, with the aim of expanding the fund to other provinces and cities in order to grow it into a national and perhaps even a European fund.

The fund assists projects and individuals by either buying property or land, or by helping to finance the construction or renewal of buildings (see Figure 5.5). Their subordinated loans can be seen as equity rather than debt finance as they are fixed for ten years, giving traditional lenders the confidence they need to lend the remaining funds. The fund charges a low (below market) interest rate on loans (3–4.5 per cent) plus a management charge of 1 per cent (as opposed to 8–12 per cent from a traditional funding source). To mitigate the higher risk that the fund takes on through charging a low interest rate, the fund advises place-makers on developing their business model and assists them with making a case to the fund. This greater involvement gives a higher confidence in the investments being made. Initiatives under consideration

Figure 5.5 Vision for Het Hof van Cartesius (Utrecht), an early investment by the fund in a cooperative providing workspace for circular and green entrepreneurship. Starting in 2017 with two pavilions and 25 members, by 2021 eight had been completed, housing 110 members (image: Het Hof van Cartesius).

must meet STIPO's requirements against a range of social/design indicators, and those of Stadkwadraat on the business front. Only when both assessments are positive can projects move forward for funding.

Box 22   Balancing quality and price using concept tendering (Germany)

Concept tendering is a procedure used by an increasing number of German cities as an alternative means for municipalities to sell (or rather lease over the long-term) land that is in their direct sphere of influence (typically public land, although in some cases also partially private). Instead of using either a direct award, where conditions must be agreed upon with the buyer, or a bidding process, in which price is the deciding factor, concept tendering brings to the fore the qualities of the place and of the design by making them a key decision-making factor, equal to or even more

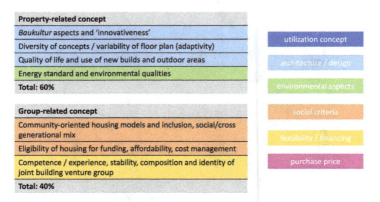

Property-related concept	
Baukultur aspects and 'innovativeness'	utilization concept
Diversity of concepts / variability of floor plan (adaptivity)	
Quality of life and use of new builds and outdoor areas	architecture / design
Energy standard and environmental qualities	environmental aspects
Total: 60%	

Group-related concept	
Community-oriented housing models and inclusion, social/cross generational mix	social criteria
Eligibility of housing for funding, affordability, cost management	feasibility / financing
Competence / experience, stability, composition and identity of joint building venture group	purchase price
Total: 40%	

Figure 5.6   Evaluation matrix used for the Olga plot joint venture, Stuttgart (image: after Temel 2020).

important than price. Evaluation matrices are applied in an attempt to ensure transparency (see Figure 5.6).

Concept tendering was first developed in the 1990s in Tübingen, in connection with the allocation of land to community housing projects. Using this process, cities may use a variety of different and diverse criteria, enabling them to compare the quality of the submitted projects. Some of these criteria are assessed based on complex point matrices (that is, the individual quality criteria and their relationship to one another are quantified), while others are assessed based on unweighted lists of factors. Concept tendering procedures are divided into two sections; the selection procedure and the options phase in which the architectural, legal and financial conditions are clarified. Only once both sides have agreed upon this process does the final change of ownership take place. Additionally, several concept tendering procedures also make use of a participant application phase prior to the actual selection or a simplified first procedure stage in order to reduce the number of projects that must be compared.

Concept tendering is a procedure that is being used more and more frequently across Germany, meaning that land is increasingly being awarded not to the highest bidder, but to high-quality projects. These projects are judged according to whether they contribute to the quality of the district under development, the form that they will take, and by what means they will be developed. As a result the innovation and creativity of project developers can be prioritised and a more cooperative planning process can be achieved, although as Temel (2020: 103) points out, 'What concept tendering is becomes clear when it is compared to an architectural competition: The aim of the latter is to find the best architecture for a plot of land, user or programme; the aim of the former is to find the best user and the best programme for a plot of land. Design is thus just one of a range of criteria being assessed, and exactly what weight that receives varies from process to process' (see Figure 5.7).

Figure 5.7   In the Olga plot concept-tendering exercise, design and environmental aspects received a 60% rating (image: Google map data 2022).

What was apparent from examining the cases included in table 5.1 above was a strong pre-existing desire to ensure either that specific developments would be of high quality, or that future (as yet undefined) developments would be. The various financial mechanisms were then used to ensure that quality, as an objective, was written into the operating system that would subsequently deliver those projects. This has a number of powerful effects:

- It 'locks in' quality, because in order to access the money and the development opportunity, a high-quality development becomes a prerequisite.

- It sets a high bar early in the development process, ensuring that the decision-making of all actors involved in the cases factor-in clear quality ambitions from the start.
- It expands the notion of value beyond a purely economic one to one that might be encompassed in the concept of place value (see Figure 1.2, p. 6), namely that projects should maximise economic, social, environmental and health benefits to be considered successful, and that the quality of place is fundamental to this.
- It utilises informal urban design governance tools as the means to establish the quality credentials of projects and ensure their subsequent delivery, and combines these with formal (and sometimes informal) finance mechanisms.

In this way the hypothesis that formal financial and informal urban design governance tools are potentially complementary is strongly supported by the evidence gathered during the Urban Maestro project. There is no direct financial incentive in the production of a design guide, for example, but the moment that public funding or permission to build development is made conditional on meeting its principles, a strong financial dimension becomes readily apparent. Most of the formal financial tools have an explicit incentive function; in essence they offer funds conditional on specific design attributes being delivered, where the definition of those design attributes are typically established in quality-culture tools and further defined and applied through quality-delivery tools.

Finance and design: chickens and eggs

A question of causation – a chicken-and-egg question – arises from these findings. Does the availability of finance incentivise the good design or does the promise of good design incentivise the finance? In most of the cases examined the two work together, with a key ambition to create better projects leading to a desire to develop approaches that will deliver on that ambition, approaches with clear finance and design components. Such processes, however, require a pre-existing ambition, and this is only likely to come if a pre-existing culture of design quality is in place. Equally, once up and running, the case studies show that the finance and design sides remain mutually reinforcing, with quality already delivered reinforcing the case for, and delivery of, more finance and more quality (see Figure 5.8).

Figure 5.8 The high design ambitions for Bo01 in Malmö were first established by the 2001 European Housing Exposition held in the city, with prototypes explored for the remainder of the Western Harbour area, which was designed as a carbon neutral mixed-use neighbourhood. Sixteen developers worked alongside the city drawing on 250 million Swedish Kroner to incentivise delivery of the highly sustainable ambitions established by the *Quality Programme*, a tool setting out standards and guidelines for sustainable urban design (Madureira 2014) (image: Matthew Carmona).

Of course, financial incentives will be only one of the many incentives created by urban design governance tools. A design competition, for example, may give a very small financial incentive but have a large reputational one, with long-term economic consequences for those who take part and are successful. There are also indirect financial impacts from the use of urban design governance tools. For example, a tool that supports the delivery of good design through facilitating the provision of design expertise to either a public authority or a development partner, even if it does not give money directly, is de facto a form of financial incentive because the assistance provided translates into lower costs and in time may deliver higher revenues from projects. Many of the quality-delivery tools, particularly those associated with support and exploration, will have indirect economic consequences.

There are also many real estate actors (public and private) that are already motivated to produce high-quality development for combinations of economic, social and environmental reasons. They may not need a financial incentive to do so, but engaging with the tools of urban design governance can potentially provide them with means to turn those aspirations into reality, and to inculcate that vision in other parties. This reflects the notion that much development occurs within a system of networked governance in which motivations are complex and intertwined and will not always be straightforward, or always stem from expected sources. Two key tools with particular relevance to such complex governance environments – land value capture (LVC) and public–private partnerships (PPPs) – were picked up again in the final stages of the Urban Maestro project and are discussed further in Chapter 6.

While combining financial mechanisms with informal urban design governance tools appears to be very effective at delivering high-quality sustainable developments – in particular the combination of finance availability with design strings (see Figure 5.9) – this does not mean that such a linkage is always necessary, nor necessary in perpetuity. Because informal tools create a culture within which design is prioritised, over time the need to incentivise design quality through other formal and financial means may fall away, leaving actors that are intrinsically motivated to deliver high-quality design and who will continue to do so given that the expectation is established. In such circumstances urban design governance may revert to the use of informal tools in isolation as a means to continue nudging all actors to do even better and to prevent any backsliding if other factors, notably the economic context, change (Corr and Plagnol 2018).

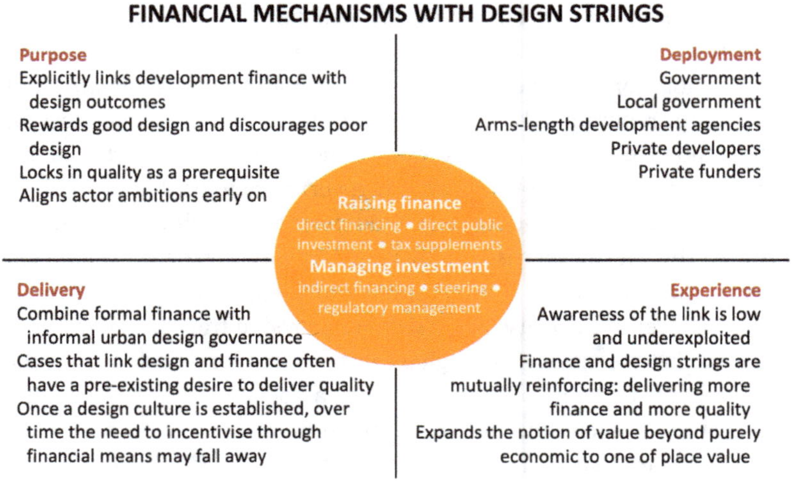

FINANCIAL MECHANISMS WITH DESIGN STRINGS

Purpose
Explicitly links development finance with
  design outcomes
Rewards good design and discourages poor
  design
Locks in quality as a prerequisite
Aligns actor ambitions early on

Deployment
Government
Local government
Arms-length development agencies
Private developers
Private funders

Raising finance
direct financing • direct public
investment • tax supplements
Managing investment
indirect financing • steering •
regulatory management

Delivery
Combine formal finance with
  informal urban design governance
Cases that link design and finance often
  have a pre-existing desire to deliver quality
Once a design culture is established, over
  time the need to incentivise through
  financial means may fall away

Experience
Awareness of the link is low
  and underexploited
Finance and design strings are
mutually reinforcing: delivering more
  finance and more quality
Expands the notion of value beyond purely
  economic to one of place value

Figure 5.9 Summarising financial mechanisms (image: Matthew Carmona).

6
Interrogating the tools

This penultimate chapter of the book focuses specifically on learning from across the range of workshops and other events that sat at the core of the Urban Maestro methodology. Over two years these events brought together practitioners, policymakers and students from across Europe to explore in greater depth the range of urban design governance tools revealed by the project and as discussed in the two previous chapters. The aim was both to interrogate the practices and, more importantly, to consider the collective lessons that might be drawn from their use. The results of these discussions are summarised in twenty propositions under six headings that are used to structure the chapter. Finally, we address the vital question of how practices travel, or how transferable are practices of urban design governance across a continent where the governance of the built environment is both diverse and complex.

Knowledge transfer (in both directions)

From the start, Urban Maestro was envisaged as a learning and knowledge transfer project, rather than as conventional research. The workshops that occurred throughout the project (see Figure 2.9, p. 64) were a critical part of this, providing a two-way learning process: imparting knowledge from the project team to participants and in the other direction from participants to the project team.

This two-year interaction began at the Urban Maestro launch meeting (hereafter LM) held in Brussels in February 2019, and was followed by workshops one and two, which took place in Valencia (June 2019) and Porto (February 2020) respectively. Both workshops attracted a mixed audience of practitioners, academics, policymakers and others to talk about urban design governance practices both in the host cities and elsewhere. They were structured around a series of formal presentations and breakout groups. Workshops three and four took place after the coronavirus pandemic had taken hold across Europe (respectively in June and November 2020) and were therefore hosted online, again with featured speakers and practices, and time for collective reflection. These workshops were also structured around formal presentations and discussion, with workshop three featuring online breakout sessions.

Workshops were between one and one-and-a-half days in length, and each concluded with a closed meeting of the project advisory group as a means to reflect on the workshop discussions and begin the process of extracting key findings. Urban Maestro also hosted a dedicated session at the World Urban Forum 10 in Abu Dhabi in February 2020 (hereafter WUF) and conducted a masterclass (hereafter MC) for students and academics over three weeks in September 2020. A final policy dialogue (hereafter PD) occurred in March 2021, when provisional lessons from the project were presented and feedback garnered from a large and diverse online audience of 250 practitioners, policymakers and academics. At both the WUF and during the final PD, the concepts and practices explored by Urban Maestro were shared with practitioners and policymakers from the global South. This chapter, therefore, also includes some references to practice and problematics of urban design governance from beyond Europe.

Each event (collectively referred to in this book as 'workshops', and individually hereafter as WS1, 2 and so on) was carefully curated around a theme and a complementary set of practices so that the individual practices featured at each event could be subjected to rigorous analysis while reflecting on the conceptual framing provided by the research team (see Figures 2.8, p. 61, and 3.4, p. 79). All the Urban Maestro workshops were recorded and systematically written up in a sequence of event reports. These reports provide the primary source materials on which this chapter is based and can be accessed at https://urbanmaestro.org/events/. The event that gave rise to the points discussed in this chapter is noted in brackets at the end of the relevant passage or paragraph.

The intention in this chapter is not to focus on particular urban design governance practices in-depth, but instead to look across the range of Urban Maestro workshops to reveal key cross-cutting themes, critiques and insights that were revealed by the discussions between approximately seven hundred participants over the eight events. The analysis is divided into six sections examining:

1. The culture and commitment to design quality
2. Building the toolkit for urban design governance
3. The governance of urban design governance
4. The power and people of urban design governance

5. The economics of urban design governance
6. How practices travel

Each section is further divided into a series of propositions that are supported by the evidence gathered during the workshops. These twenty propositions are brought together to conclude the chapter. Throughout Chapter 6, findings from the workshops are referenced back to where they derived from through the use of the acronyms shown in brackets in Table 6.1.

The culture and commitment to design quality

A first set of propositions focus on the drive across many cities, regions and countries in Europe to build a culture of place quality underpinned by a focus on design.

There are widely shared aspirations to build a local culture of quality

The focus of Urban Maestro was on 'New governance strategies for urban design'. Urban governance and urban design are both contested concepts and the subject of much debate about what constitutes good governance and good design, with the term 'urban design', in particular, being understood very differently in different parts of Europe (see Chapter 1). Against this backdrop it was surprising that few questioned the scope or legitimacy of either concern during the workshops, and therefore of the practices under discussion.

While individual experiences and practices used different terminology and had different foci, collectively underpinning them were two broad beliefs:

- First, that the benefits associated with improving the quality of urban places are manifold, extending across economic, social, environmental and health policy spheres. Consequently, there is a need to expand our understanding of design beyond narrow aesthetic considerations to these broader 'place value' remits.
- Second, design 'quality' does not happen by accident, by itself or under the auspices of the free market acting in isolation. Instead, there is an important role for the state in helping to shape the decision-making environment within which buildings, spaces and places are themselves shaped.

Table 6.1 Urban Maestro workshops (table: Urban Maestro).

Workshop	Theme	Practices	Approx. attendees
Launch meeting (LM)	Launching Urban Maestro	No specific practices	35
Workshop one (WS1)	Soft power and urban design governance	*Baukultur* initiatives of the Swiss Federal Office of Culture / tools of the Budapest city architect / Caserne Mellinet project in Nantes / design review in London / tools of BMA Brussels / Valencia waterfront regeneration / diffusion of Vancouverism	50
Workshop two (WS2)	Informal tools for a better-designed environment	Place Standard, Scotland / International Building Exhibition (IBA), Heidelberg / Swiss Cooperative housing, Zurich / Les Grands Voisins, Paris / Panorama Lokaal, Netherlands / tools of the Warsaw city architect / Grenoble Public Space programme / BIP-ZIP programme, Lisbon	65
Workshop three (WS3)	Innovative development tools: competitions, urban development strategies, review tools	Europan / Czech national subsidies for architecture competitions / concept tendering, Germany / Stadmakers Fonds, Utrecht / Bevel development project Luxembourg / Samoa île de Nantes, Nantes / Q-teams, the Netherlands / design advisory boards, Austria / Design for London	175
Workshop four (WS4)	The finance/design interface in urban design governance	Milan REFLOW project / land value capture in Copenhagen and Freiburg / Oslo waterfront regeneration / La Marina da Valencia / the Miss Miyagi model, Leuven / By&Havn, Copenhagen / Community Land Trusts, Brussels	125

World Urban Forum 10 (**WUF**)	Urban design governance in the global South	evolving public space in South Africa / the Green Kigali experience, Rwanda / the Medellín model, Colombia / sustainable development goals (SDG) project assessment tool in Asian cities	50
Masterclass (**MC**)	Testing urban design governance	International Building Exhibition (IBA), Thüringen / Room for the River, Netherlands / Petit Île / Citygate II, Brussels / Co-city Torino, Turin	120
Policy Dialogue (**PD**)	Provisional findings discussion and interrogation	diverse practices drawing from across the Urban Maestro panorama	250

The workshops confirmed that such beliefs apply both to how we design and integrate new neighbourhoods, infrastructure and interventions in urban areas, but also to how we handle the existing urban fabric.

This notion of extending what might, in the past, have been viewed as a narrower and more traditional view of design is encompassed in key concepts that underpinned many of the practices reviewed across the workshops, including circularity, urban metabolism, health, the 15 minute city, *habitabilité* and *Baukultur*. For example, *Baukultur* advances a holistic approach to the built environment encompassing all human activity that changes the built environment at all scales from spatial design to architectural detail and across areas both old and new; and embraces not just the tangible built environment but also all the processes that collectively shape it (WS1) (Conference of Ministers of Culture 2018; Carmona 2014a).

Beyond Europe, these broader notions of the value of high-quality urban design and the importance of its proactive pursuit through good governance have been increasingly reflected on the international stage, including explicitly through the 2015 reformulation of the United Nation's Sustainable Development Goals (SDGs) (see Box 5, p. 134). Goal 11 (sustainable cities and communities) explicitly covers such concerns, while other goals implicitly address them, for example those relating to climate action, gender equality, and good health and well-being (WS1). The Urban Maestro workshops revealed that while it is not important to have fixed common definitions of what design quality means (as this will inevitably vary across contexts), it is vital to promote the idea that quality is important (WS2), and that urban design governance concepts can be applied from the largest spatial scales of strategic projects such as the Room for the River project in the Netherlands (focusing on the redesign of Dutch river environments and their future management) (MC) to the smallest scale of individual public spaces (for instance BIP/ZIP in Lisbon – see Box 15, p. 181). This notion of building a culture of quality is widely shared across Europe and Urban Maestro confirmed that the continent has much best practice to share (WS2).

Building a culture of quality is a long-term project requiring sustained commitment and influence over the key levers of delivery, while persuading others to join

Fundamental change can only occur if investment processes are maintained over long periods of time, requiring attention across different spatial scales, from small-scale everyday interventions to large scale strategic projects. Underpinning these scales are careful strategic planning, smart infrastructure investment, and ongoing investment in the public realm, exemplified in cities such as Copenhagen (see Box 23) and Freiburg (see Box 24) where quality-led investment both in new and existing areas has been sustained for decades (WS4).

Box 23   Sustained commitment to quality: By&Havn, Copenhagen

Copenhagen is a city with a long-term commitment to its public realm, as exemplified through the work and influence of Jan Gehl and the long-term movement of the city away from domination by cars to a place in which walking, cycling and public transportation are the norm. This philosophy has also been built into the work of By&Havn, a publicly owned development and operating company that focuses on the creation of coherent, well-functioning and sustainable urban neighbourhoods in Copenhagen, particularly in and around its harbour districts (https://byoghavn.dk). By&Havn uses a diverse array of tools to do this, including innovative competition briefs, funding schemes, and Land Value Capture.

The company is jointly owned by the City of Copenhagen (55 per cent) and the Danish State (45 per cent) and operates on a commercial basis. This form of ownership gives By&Havn a long-term perspective and ensures that the developments taking place in the city are strategic, sustainable and future-oriented.

By&Havn is primarily responsible for the development of urban neighbourhoods, the establishment of roads and canals, parking garages, urban spaces and green areas. It sells building plots to various investors as well as to housing cooperatives and actively participates in urban living initiatives from the initial planning phases until the residents have finally moved in and neighbourhoods have come to life. Their business strategy for 2020–23 has focused their efforts on the creation of sustainable neighbourhoods, with a particular emphasis on following the UN's 17 sustainable development goals. These new development areas must contribute to climate- and energy-friendly solutions and to the continued positive evolution of the city and port's economy, as well as meeting platinum standard in the DGNB (global certificate for

---

sustainability) certification system. Buildings are certified to the DGNB gold standard.

By&Havn is also responsible for the Port of Copenhagen. The port consists of a commercial harbour with a container and cruise terminal operated by Copenhagen-Malmö Port AB, as well as a living recreational harbour with public bathing and leisure opportunities, tour boats and other recreational activities (see Figure 6.1). The revenue from its activities goes towards common goods such as paying for major infrastructure projects in Copenhagen, including development of the metro, urban spaces, quays, bridges, jetties, parks and initiatives in the new urban neighbourhoods.

Figure 6.1 Today Copenhagen's waterfront is a haven for walking, relaxation, contemplation and exercise (of all sorts), providing the city with an animated blue lung (image: Matthew Carmona).

A long-term approach can help cities ride development waves and crises of all sorts and remain confident about delivery. Taking a quality-led approach from the start of key projects and sustaining it throughout can help to reduce risk and provide confidence for investors – including government – while building place value. This implies both the provision of upfront infrastructure and a clear vision for the places being shaped. A key lever is control of land: maintaining a controlling interest in public land can help public authorities to ride a rising wave of value and increasingly push for greater quality using a combination of soft and hard powers (see Box 23). The alternative is to sell land and leave the market to deliver with only relatively crude regulation to hold the design-quality line (WS4).

Examples of delivering high-quality design outcomes where the key differentiating factor was the state's control of the land were repeatedly presented and discussed in the workshops. In effect these were situations where the public sector was in the controlling seat, or at least had a seat at the table as visions for places were generated. How that position is then utilised to secure public benefits brings the potential of soft powers to the fore, notably through the vital tool of persuasion, including convincing real estate partners and public authorities to invest in (longer-term) public goods by demonstrating the reality of patient capital (see Chapter 5) leading to enhanced public and private returns (WS4).

Political commitment, with flexibility, is key

While commitment to building a quality culture is broad, sometimes this is absent or can be flaky in the context of other priorities or when political leadership changes. The innovative Czech programme for providing national subsidies for the running of local architectural and urban design competitions has suffered in this way, with shifting national priorities leading to a turning on, then off and then on again of the funding tap for this initiative (see Box 12, p. 170). In that case, reliance on a single source of national departmental funding for the initiative has led to its vulnerability, and discussions have considered how to diversify the funding to create a more comprehensive and significant system for supporting competitions in the future. However, in this field, where small steps are often more feasible than larger ones, efforts have concentrated first on trying to ensure this small subsidy remains in place and then building from there (WS2).

Given the slow pace of urban transformation, where present, greater political continuity in the application of public policy has paid dividends, leading to continuity (in ideas rather than leadership) beyond the standard duration of political terms. Political leaders seem more likely to build on the work of their predecessors in cities where there is a consensual urban and political culture, such as in Vienna (see Chapter 3) or, beyond Europe, in Medellín. Rather than spending time re-inventing formal plans and associated regulations from one administration to the next, in such places soft powers seem to allow a more evolutionary process focused on quality (WUF).

But not all regimes make the use of such powers easy to deploy. It was noted, for example, that in Rotterdam the mayor does not have formal powers to shape the built environment and consequently there is an incentive to use informal tools. In this case the political authority of the office gives legitimacy to the informal tools and makes them work more effectively. By contrast, in Budapest the tradition is for a very formalised mode of urban governance. Bringing forward informal processes such as experimental temporary interventions are therefore particularly challenging under the Hungarian public procurement framework (WS1).

In the global South, the opposite can be the case. In Kigali, for example, the flexibility that informal tools allow because of the soft forms of power they rely upon has been important in overcoming the limitations of more formal (hard power) mechanisms. Engagement with the community to promote regular voluntary collective works – so-called community days – are one such example, allowing inhabitants to take an active role in the design and construction of interventions from which they will directly benefit (WUF). A world away, the Samoa Île de Nantes developments (see Chapter 4) have relied upon a strong political vision for setting the level of ambition that both public and private actors will need to reach, but the master plan that this vision gives rise to is also flexible enough to allow for incremental delivery and experimental interventions, often underpinned by co-design processes across the island (see Figure 6.2) (WS3).

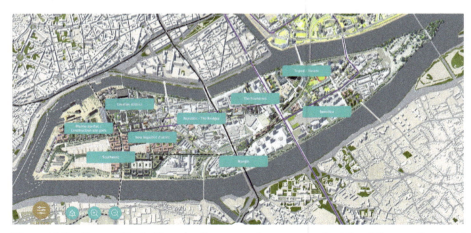

Figure 6.2 Samoa île de Nantes, diverse projects across the island (image: https://www.iledenantes.com; https://www.samoa-nantes.fr/).

This way of working requires a different mindset from the public sector, and the nurturing of what Charles Landry (among others) has called a 'creative bureaucracy' to facilitate these processes (https://charleslandry.com/themes/creative-bureaucracy/). In Grenoble, the format of testing innovative citizen-led public-space projects (see Figure 5.5, p. 215) has also meant a stretching of the 'business as usual' roles of civil servants, who subsequently had to adapt to the requirements of a new experimental format. An evaluation of the Grenoble experience, conducted in parallel with the project, showed that some aspects of the work were great successes and some failures. It revealed a wider truism, that more flexible and temporary modes of working carry risks and require a willingness to sometimes fail in order to learn and succeed over the long-run (PD).

Building the toolkit for urban design governance

The second set of propositions looks at the urban design governance tools being used across Europe and in particular at the role of informal tools within that mix.

From design culture to design delivery, and from design delivery to design culture, the two are mutually reinforcing

While the focus of the Urban Maestro project was on tracking, understanding and sharing how European aspirations for a better-quality built environment are being delivered through the active interventions of public authorities in the governance of design, from the start the focus was on the informal tools of urban design governance that derive from the use of the soft powers of the state, typically beyond the constraints of regulatory systems. As was said by one respondent at the launch of Urban Maestro: 'All stupid buildings have got a building permission. If we want a better built environment, we need other tools' (LM). The need, it seems, is for more intelligent tools that can inform decision-making and lead to better decisions, rather than limiting processes to the formally defined possibilities set out in legislation.

The workshops revealed a widespread acceptance of the power of informal tools and associated soft powers to shape agendas, from the international stage, such as UN-Habitat's (2015) *Global Public Space Toolkit*, to the local stage, notably the countless guides, systems of design competition, review and support used across Europe. Early on, the Urban

Maestro project conceptualised a division in the category of informal tools between those designed primarily to build a culture of good design, and those focused more on shaping the delivery of individual projects (see Figure 3.3, p. 76). While such a division will never be absolute – delivery tools can help to reinforce the culture, and culture tools underpin the delivery – a broad acceptance was apparent through the workshops that both roles are necessary in order to respond to and embrace the complexity of European urban development and the range of actors involved in or impacted by it. The advice proffered by the Bouwmeester Maître Architecte in Brussels provides a case-in-point. This goes much further than simply articulating legal regulations; instead it strives to influence the environment within which quality is negotiated at the beginning of projects (https://bma.brussels/en/). As with any form of soft power, it is never absolute but serves to convince others in a variety of informal ways (WS2).

The Urban Maestro masterclass concluded by asking: which should come first, quality culture or quality-delivery tools? The remainder of the workshops suggested that as they are mutually reinforcing the question sets up a false dichotomy – they work together and need each other to be truly effective (MC). As the OMC (Open Method of Coordination) Group of EU Member State Experts (2021: 103) notes, for design quality to truly embed within the wider culture requires that the public sector embarks on a journey in which design quality ultimately becomes part of the strategic direction of jurisdictions, 'celebrated by both the public and private sector' (see Figure 6.3).

Creative (even visionary) not bureaucratic tools are required to deliver place quality

Informal tools tended to push professionals and indeed administrations into new ways of working, for example placing architects within the realm of mediators, and local authorities as promoters of visions or as their implementors (WS1). As was observed in workshop 2, it is important to offer a 'perspective in which people can dream' as it mobilises positive forces and can help to contribute to a greater alignment of stakeholders' otherwise uncoordinated interventions. In part this relates to the potential for informal tools of urban design governance to help to underpin, establish, articulate, promote and deliver place-based visions, beyond those that the market would deliver working in isolation (WS2).

Design competitions are a good example of this, as tools able to generate debate and innovative ideas for high-profile prestige projects as

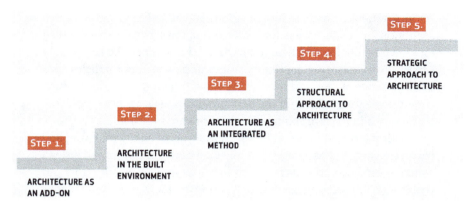

Figure 6.3 The ladder of architectural culture in which quality moves through five steps: step one, architecture and design is not part of the everyday public conversation, practices or priorities; step two, architecture is valued but seen as simply part of a final form-giving, 'styling' stage of the development process; step three, architecture is integrated into all stages of the multi-disciplinary development process; step four, architecture is integrated more deeply across governance scales with design professionals inputting directly into policymaking across a wide range of sectors; step five, knowledge of architecture and design fundamentally informs planning, forecasting, procurement and the full range of development practices that the public sector engages with or influences – design quality is widely aspired to and celebrated (image: OMC 2021).

well as for ordinary places and common design problems in which the outputs may be generalisable lessons for sites beyond those that are subject to the competition, for example the Panorama Lokaal scheme used in the Netherlands (see Chapter 4). In this respect, competitions as a design governance tool should not be just about defining winners and losers (although that is necessary to encourage involvement) but can be part of a learning culture in which innovative solutions for different problems can inform ongoing practice. So, while competitions need infrastructure and resourcing to make them work, the outcomes may be less important than the process if that process helps to build the long-term quality culture (WS2).

Turning to public-space projects and the case of Pretoria discussed at the WUF, the municipality has sometimes hesitated between a general laissez-faire and the adoption of strict control measures, both proving relatively ineffective. At the initiative of a local community or the private sector, in a few cases the public authority has looked directly to these local actors to establish an urban-design vision and build a broad and collective aspiration for quality. When done, this can cut through sometimes stifling top-down regulation and help to fill the gap between public and private expectations, ensuring continuity of urban development policies over longer periods of time and over different public administrations. In such circumstances the need is for the hard powers of the state not to stifle the bottom-up initiatives of communities and private stakeholders (WUF).

Other forms of informal tool such as forms of audit, guidance, and persuasion may be less focused on individual sites or localities and instead aimed at establishing a narrative for localities around which actors can coalesce (WS2). Copenhagen's strong narrative of success in reshaping its public realm for pedestrians and cyclists builds on tried and tested approaches that in turn build on a consensus around a clear vision of what sort of city Copenhagen should be; one also understood and favoured by investors (WS4). Elsewhere, design quality is too often still viewed as a luxury rather than a necessity and remains in search of a new narrative encompassed in the search for equity, vitality and sustainability (LM).

In this regard, the workshops demonstrated how storytelling plays an important role in urban design governance, although transfer of the ideas contained within such narratives is not always easy (WS2). Those responsible for Switzerland's *Baukultur* initiatives, for example, face the challenge of how to transfer this new national priority into action at the level of the country's cantons (see Figure 6.4). Cantonal administrations, it seems, do not always accept such centrally imposed initiatives and/or can be too rigid and bureaucratic in how they implement them (WS1).

In such cases soft powers are limited by the willingness of state authorities to embrace their message, although the recent experience of the Covid-19 pandemic may have greatly extended that number. The period has shown how in times of crisis, the use of informal tools may be the more practical and perhaps the only available option given the time and complexity required to adopt formal regulations in the face of acute pressures. The use of temporary public-space guidance and temporary public-realm interventions have been widespread across Europe during the pandemic (see Figure 6.5) and demonstrate the potential power and effectiveness of such informal tools (WS1).

Informal informs and formal formalises: formal and informal urban design governance work together

One of the strongest messages from the workshops was the complementary nature of formal and informal tools and the need for them to

Figure 6.4 In Geneva, the need to build new housing to tackle an affordability crisis has led to major expansion plans, including here in the huge Acacias Bâtie redevelopment area. This has been accompanied by a realisation that major growth needs to be underpinned by a consistent emphasis on high-quality *Baukultur*, something that has not always been the case in the past (image: Matthew Carmona).

be used together, perhaps at different stages in a project's evolution and to meet different objectives. Informal tools, for example, seem particularly effective on a number of fronts, including:

- Helping to build a culture of quality.
- Underpinning formal processes with evidence and experience.
- Facilitating more creative/visionary thinking in early development phases.
- Engaging groups or individuals who would otherwise be turned off by formal processes. (WS1)

At the delivery phase, by contrast, formal tools are needed to provide the ultimate guarantee of the public interest through the implementation of regulations with legal authority (WS1). The use of formal instruments (land use controls, taxation, and so on) also underpin the use of informal tools, making them viable as governance approaches. For example,

Figure 6.5 Temporary pandemic-inspired public-realm interventions became commonplace in 2020/21 such as in Greenwich, London (a), allowing more space for pedestrians to pass each other safely, and in Dublin (b), where feet painted on the ground every 2 metres offered a visual reminder of the safe distance to queue (image: Matthew Carmona).

maintaining control through hard-power regulations on the proportion of dwellings available for Airbnb in touristic locations such as Porto is central to preserving the character and identity of such places, which can then be enhanced through informal tools and public investment (WS2) (see Figure 6.6). Success comes from aligning formal and informal processes towards the same ultimate objectives.

In practice, there is no strict barrier between soft and hard power in urban design governance but instead they are often used together, for example design review processes feeding into formal development consent regimes (WS1). London provides a case in point. By requiring design review for certain large-scale proposals, the London Plan has had a very significant influence on driving a greater take-up of the practice across the city. By 2021 there were 30 active panels, with research suggesting the model was proving very effective in encouraging more design review with no diminution of standards (see Chapter 3). The panel advice is not binding and the process is discretionary, with less than 1 per cent of planning applications currently reviewed in London, but when conducted, design review helps to develop and refine design proposals prior to their formal consideration by development management (WS3).

There is also a continuity of approaches from more formal to less formal. These include formal processes that have a discretionary

Figure 6.6 Porto's Praça de Lisboa now contains a new high-level park (above retail and parking) in the centre of an area formerly in decline. The site was subject to two competitions organised respectively by the municipality and by a citizens' collective who launched the 'No rules, great spot' competition to encourage debate about the future of the space. The final scheme was carefully controlled, being immediately adjacent to the boundary of the UNESCO World Heritage site, yet establishes an innovative green space within which relaxed informal activities occur with users shaping the space daily to their own ends (image: Matthew Carmona).

dimension (as in the London case) and which may be more akin to informal tools than to strict regulatory variants, as well as tools in which informal mechanisms are fully embedded in the formal mechanism (WS1). In Germany, the concept tendering procedure utilised to deliver greater public value during the public disposal of land offers an example (see Box 22, p. 215). The process is divided into two stages, first the selection procedure, and second the options phase in which the architectural, legal and financial conditions are clarified. This second stage has the potential for informal tools to be used alongside the formal mechanism of concept tendering in order to guide decision-making. The financial incentive to do this is generated by the potential to purchase land below full market value. This in turn offers the 'opportunity space' to deliver higher-quality development and a more considered design process (WS3).

The most sophisticated approaches use tools in combination and in multiple ways

Urban design governance tools are rarely used in isolation, with the most sophisticated jurisdictions utilising a combination of tools, including formal and informal approaches and both quality-delivery and quality-culture tools. The Bouwmeester Maître Architecte in Brussels, for example, utilises four primary tools:

- Design competitions are the dominant tool, with a two-stage process and the transparent publication of jury reports to assist both the public sector and private developers make better design decisions.
- Quality chambers deliver design review in a systematic manner for key sites, with review compulsory in Brussels (since 2019) for any projects with a coverage exceeding 5,000 square metres.
- Research by design (an explorative design process) helps to generate initial design guidelines for projects before they go into the formal regulatory processes of the municipality.
- Diverse communication channels promote and raise awareness about the importance of architectural and urban design quality in Brussels (WS2).

In Riga, the City Architect's office is tasked to give design advice to stakeholders involved in the planning process. This advice is complementary to, but independent of, the mandatory regulatory processes and is provided through an advisory-board mechanism comprising the city architect and a board of 16 professional experts, mostly from NGOs. Supplementing this, the office organises an annual architecture award in Riga; an annual conference on design quality (open to all); and is regularly involved in research projects, both those seeking a better understanding of development practices and of research by design aimed at feeding directly into the development process (WS3).

These and other successful cases of integrated urban transformation make use of a powerful combination of formal and informal approaches to urban design governance. Beyond Europe, in Kigali, neither formal nor informal approaches were proving very effective until they were combined. According to one observer they could 'not do top-down, nor do bottom-up' when attempting to transform the city's poorest housing areas. Instead, by creating mechanisms of urban design governance that mixed soft (bottom-up) community engagement and participation approaches, backed up (when necessary) by hard regulatory approaches, they were far more able to deal with the physical, social and economic complexities of the situations being faced (WUF).

Even individual tools can be used in multiple ways for multiple purposes. Competitions, for example, are used primarily to select a designer for projects and for gathering different creative ideas for significant projects, sites or design challenges, but the third workshop revealed that they can also be used to:

1. identify new design talent, in a market that tends to favour tried and tested teams;
2. stimulate a public debate on sites and projects (see Figure 6.6 above);
3. garner involvement in helping to define particular projects or address defined problems;
4. help build a culture of good design – locally, nationally or internationally;
5. stimulate a pedagogic role, allowing those involved to learn and evolve;
6. conduct research by design; and
7. input into more transparent processes for the development/sale of key sites based on maximising public value rather than financial return (WS3).

Informal is more flexible and reactive to local and immediate needs

The irruption of the Covid-19 global pandemic into the research period also helped to demonstrate the value of soft urban design governance in emergency situations. It is well accepted that crises of various forms can lead to innovation in governance approaches and to new links and networks among different actors (citizens, public administrations and so on). When facing crisis situations, agility and adaptiveness are great assets, and favour the use of soft powers. The widespread adoption of tactical urbanism solutions across Europe to deal with the impact of the pandemic on public space proved to be particularly effective (see Figure 6.5 above), demonstrating a responsiveness to short-term changing needs that harder regulatory approaches were unable to respond to (WS3).

Explorative co-creation processes fall into this category and can be more effective than top-down models in meeting immediate local needs and opportunities (WS3). The Grands Voisins project, in Paris (see Box 17, p. 187), provides a good example that was never conceived in terms of a set of pre-determined outcomes but instead as a process that was constantly changing and was therefore always flexible: responding to the urgent needs of the locality through a time-limited collaboration of landowners, investors, businesses and residents (WS2). Such processes can facilitate experimentation and enable the building of a long-term vision in a more collaborative manner, much as they can at larger spatial scales as well (see Figure 6.7).

Figure 6.7   At the largest scale – planning for whole cities – informal approaches are being favoured by cities such as Birmingham, Malmö and Hamburg as means to explore complexity and risk and competing visions for change while promoting dialogue among citizens and other actors over future directions. This is the role of plans such as Birmingham's *Big City Plan* (published in 2011), which are designed to be propositional and flexible rather than restrictive and regulatory (Barth 2015). While the *Big City Plan* sits alongside a formal development plan that guides the city's development management decision-making, it remains an ambitious vision document, containing both high-level principles and concrete plans for local transformations, such as to the city's principal station – New Street – and its surroundings (now realised). In 2021 work began on rolling the *Big City Plan* forward to 2040 (image: Matthew Carmona).

The governance of urban design governance

Next came a set of propositions concerned with the structural and administrative contexts into which urban design governance is situated.

Public-sector-led urban design governance is the rock on which place quality is built, but is not the whole story

While regimes of urban design governance will largely be shaped by the public sector, the very notion of 'governance' implies that the state is not the only actor involved in the process and may not even be the initiator of initiatives. This may be particularly the case in emerging economies and developing countries, as discussions at the WUF revealed, in large part because of the reduced reliance on the state to deliver local environmental-quality solutions, matched by a greater reliance on community-level bottom-up initiatives. Elsewhere in the global South, in places where coherent public-interest-focused administration is available, the state can provide a strong vision that harnesses other stakeholders. In both circumstances, the use of informal tools of urban design governance utilising the soft powers of the state can offer a greater flexibility leading to greater local buy-in over time. Examples in South Africa, Rwanda and Colombia showed that such tools provide the means to create and deliver more coherent urban-quality visions that aren't stifled by an overreliance on hard regulations, and that can facilitate positive initiative from wherever it comes – communities, politicians, the private sector, and universities (WUF).

In Europe, the most obvious examples of this sort of bottom-up design governance came in the various temporary-use schemes explored by Urban Maestro. Given their localised and tangible nature, these represented powerful instruments to mobilise community forces and demonstrate the value of specific design solutions. Where used, they often reinforce neighbourhood cohesion and can help to garner greater commitment to necessary development, even in areas resistant to change. At the same time, temporary interventions – whether top-down or bottom-up – can lead to local conflicts if their limits and operation are not sufficiently defined from the start, namely with regard to their duration, ongoing governance arrangements, objectives, and so on, or if they are not sufficiently supported by local political leadership (see Figure 6.8). There is also the danger that they may fail to inspire meaningful change or to become institutionalised, with participants at the PD arguing that

Figure 6.8 The Marble Arch Mound (a), installed in an attempt to lure shoppers back to the West End of London following the pandemic, was poorly executed, doubled in cost (to £6 million) and was poorly received by visitors following a failure by Westminster City Council to manage the project properly and a rush to open the mound before it was ready. By contrast, the Carlsberg City development in Copenhagen employed a range of temporary diverting public-space strategies to help create a 'brand' on the city's former Carlsberg brewery site, following the financial crisis of 2008 when private development came to a halt. These, including the Rope Forest (b), quickly disappeared when the market recovered, leading to a public debate over the value of such temporary projects (images: Matthew Carmona).

for schemes to move from experimentation to transformative impact requires:

- Trial and error – not expecting to get it right first time.
- Proper costing and procurement of temporary interventions to control cost and quality.
- Gradual improvements – with schemes building one upon another.
- Proper analysis and feedback from users to inform ongoing programmes.
- Better governance of temporary interventions with a focus on the user-centred experience.
- Engaging users of all ages, including children and the elderly.
- Excellent communication to, and cooperation with, all public and private stakeholders (PD).

Other organisations can also play important roles in helping to instigate, underpin (with their knowledge and networks), and deliver urban design governance. This way of working came to the fore in the UK following the austerity-led withdrawal of the state in the 2010s. Applied university research (such as that of the Place Alliance – see Box 2, p. 120) and the move of the private and not-for-profit sector into the delivery of design review in England (see the London case, Chapter 3) both provide examples, although ultimately their impact would not have been so decisive unless the state was a) receptive to such external inputs and b) willing, in the case of design review, to actively encourage a diversity of providers in policy (WS2). In the Caserne Mellinet project in Nantes, an architectural practice took the lead in the public consultation process concerning the future repurposing of this old military base, providing a further example of a public authority externalising what some would regard as a core function of urban design governance (WS1).

The right structures and the right people are both necessary to champion design quality and shape the most effective urban design governance

Together, the Urban Maestro workshops reinforced the vital importance of local leadership determined both by structure (the organisations, capabilities and policies in place to deliver design quality) and agency (the individuals engaged in the process and their abilities to act independently), although the diversity of arrangements across the continent lead to different mixes of influence.

The case of design review in England represented a case of fundamentally changing the structure within which design quality considerations were being evaluated, breaking the traditional understanding of urban design governance as a state-led activity and, as a political choice, inviting market players to fill the gap. The UK government also published policy that created a space for this market in design review to develop and mature by requiring local authorities to have design review arrangements in place. By bringing in a new set of actors and a model to finance them (private developers paying) the change has reinvigorated the practice, including encouraging many more local authorities to set up design review panels, while the panels themselves consist of varying combinations of independent professional experts (WS1).

Elsewhere, key individuals have been appointed to drive forward practice, including city architects, bouwmeesters, design champions, and the like. These positions influence the quality of architecture and city development through varying levels of independence, ranging from what Tiesdell (2011) classifies as 'design advisers' (advising others who may or may not take the advice) to 'change agents' (with a clear leadership role). Some are part of government while others are arms-length positions from government, although all are ultimately accountable to their political masters. Their roles sometimes have a direct link into formal regulatory functions such as plan-making, but often rely on soft stimulating, convincing and advising powers – powers born of the authority that such positions confer, and the respect that they motivate others to give to the individual who holds the role (WS1).

Bento and Laopoulou (2019: 93) explore such positions in their report on the role of state architect teams. They note:

> Assuming the role of maestros, state design champions steer and motivate the diverse public actors to raise design standards and seek the most innovative and effective ways of creating better built outcomes … state design champions have the potential to improve intersectoral coordination and interchange between the different stakeholders promoting a more inclusive policy making process.

In this sense state design champions are having a positive impact on overall design governance processes, 'providing direction and leading to a more efficient and orchestrated administration'. At the same time, they argue, it is important not to reduce spatial design leadership to a single person or an organisation, as ultimately places are shaped through the inputs of a wide range of actors, as a collective endeavour. They conclude that governments should appoint a public actor as design champion to lead a culture change in relation to the built environment and help establish a consistently favourable climate for design quality.

In the first Urban Maestro workshop, the Brussels Bouwmeester Maître Architecte commented that the power of the expert (design champion) only comes through finding and maintaining political capital, and that this requires five ways of working:

- Be a tightrope walker – being prepared to criticise public authorities when necessary, but not to the point where you are seen as 'the perpetual opposition voice'.
- Build coalitions – creating alliances with the private sector, civil society, other local authorities and international organisations.
- Be a creative bureaucrat – by empowering local administrations to be more independent and to get relevant actors out of their silos.

- Be transparent – gain support and build trust by letting the public see the internal logic behind decisions.
- Choose your battles – don't make enemies all the time but be critical enough to have a meaningful opinion on important spatial decisions.

In this, the role of the Bouwmeester (defined in legislation), the back-up provided by his team, and their relation to the range of organisations and processes engaged in decision-making are all key – in academic terms, 'structure' and 'agency' working together (WS1).

There is a potential dark side to informal urban design governance

Although the workshops revealed an overwhelmingly positive picture of the potential of soft urban design governance, there was also a recognition that potential downsides were possible if these forms of influence were used for less altruistic purposes, particularly given the absence of the sorts of checks and balances associated with more formal processes. The use of soft powers offers no guarantee of an ethical approach to urban development.

The spectre of gentrification – or the displacement of lower-income residents and businesses by incomers – regularly surfaced in workshop discussions, with concerns expressed that urban design-quality improvements would attract new investment, but at the expense of established communities (WS2). Others argued that gentrification is inevitable as part of the economic restructuring of cities and that design quality is a symptom of such processes rather than its cause. As such, it is gentrification that needs to be 'inoculated against', rather than development quality discouraged (WS4), as happens so effectively in Vienna (see Chapter 3) and typically more intermittently elsewhere (see Figure 6.9)

Few believed, for example, that the solution to the dilemma was to leave disadvantaged communities living in substandard environments. Increasing problems of gentrification in Copenhagen have been met with the inclusion of a safeguard that 25 per cent of new housing should be affordable (WS4), while initiatives such as Zurich's Cooperative Housing system and the Community Land Trust in Brussels were advanced as examples of retaining property for social housing in areas subject to transformation (WS2). Like formal tools of urban design governance, funding can have 'design strings' attached to ensure design quality is delivered alongside social sustainability (WS2).

A further potential dark side of informal urban design governance was identified at the WUF workshop, relating to the potential for

Figure 6.9 Changing the image of social housing through small-scale environmental intervention, San Basilio quarter, Rome (image: Matthew Carmona).

non-regulated (informal) forms of governance to be more susceptible to corruption and a lack of transparency, particularly in the global South. Although corruption in any form of governance is always a threat, the potential for soft-power approaches to also engage bottom-up community interests may provide the antidote, thanks to an increased engagement from citizens than typifies many formal governance approaches (WUF). At the same time, soft-power relations can be difficult to grasp, and while relations on paper between actors may appear transparent, in real-life the interaction and power-play between actors is often more complex. As the Urban Maestro Masterclass suggested, there can easily be a gap between 'how it works' and 'how it is supposed to work' (MC).

The power and people of urban design governance

The fourth group of propositions focused on the stakeholders engaged in, and affected by, urban design governance, and on the balances of power between them.

Informal tools offer great potential for inclusive and engaging decision-making on design

Another tension that played out across the workshops was the balance between input to decision-making from the top (political and administrative) versus the bottom (from or within local communities). The first workshop, held during European Placemaking Week in Valencia, brought a particular emphasis on themes of co-creation and participatory and citizen-led processes, reinforcing the notion that, though the public sector might be the ultimate arbiter of urban design governance regimes, citizens, private companies and the third sector all have critical roles to play in feeding into, sometimes contesting, and generally helping to deliver on quality ambitions (WS1).

Discussion highlighted the need to put citizens' voices at the centre of design governance processes, whether through traditional participative mechanisms, via new technologies, or through more active and engaging co-design and co-implementation arrangements (WS1). On all these fronts there is potential for innovation to secure a greater involvement of communities across the operation of many informal tools. In relation to design competitions, for example, how competition briefs are defined, the nature of juries and their deliberations, how discussions and results are disseminated, and whether the general public can vote or otherwise express an opinion on a project, all provide means to democratise the process. In Brussels, public authorities have been wary of involving the public too much in development-related decision-making, and in order to address this gap the Brussels Bouwmeester Maître Architecte has been experimenting with including community participation in competition juries, thus securing a civil-society voice from the start of design-related decision-making.

Turning to design review, despite a widespread concern that the focus on professional expertise too often fails to reflect a community voice, instances were highlighted where that was not the case. Q-teams in the Netherlands have the potential to include one or more 'non-expert' citizens, while some design advisory boards in Austria, for example in Salzburg, are open to the public at all stages of deliberation (WS3). Mainstream design-review practice, however, is dominated by professional voices, which raises issues about the value of different forms of knowledge – professional versus lay knowledge – and the weight that should be attached to each. Related to this are questions of transparency and equal opportunities to get involved in design governance processes; both as regards the ability to take part (for instance to be selected for a panel) and to have access to ongoing decision-making (WS3).

There is also a question of resources, as opening up processes can make them more costly and lengthy to administer, potentially less effective, and can raise untenable expectations. On the flipside they can help to deliver more locally acceptable schemes and can assist in building trust between local communities and public administrations, both as a result of the process and as a precondition for successful implementation (MC).

On this front, the younger participants engaged in the masterclass were bullish about the need to involve communities early and in a more fundamental manner, and optimistic about the role of new technologies such as crowdsourcing and social media platforms to facilitate this. Processes with citizen engagement at their heart rather than as an add-on have the potential to turn on its head the way some of the formal and informal tools of urban design governance are used, facilitating a more iterative and ongoing conversation about urban change (MC). Citizens' assemblies, for instance, are being trialled as a means to secure an ongoing conversation about place (WS4), including Madrid's City Observatory, which was given formal status in 2019 (OECD 2020).

Power and power imbalances shape processes and outcomes, but design governance processes can shift thinking

A key question implicit in this discussion is: where does decision-making power lie? The evidence presented in the workshops suggested that not only do patterns of power and influence vary from country to country and city to city, but also across and within the tools of urban design governance. Nevertheless, because soft-power tools are more flexible and less directive, they have the potential to distribute power more equitably, although power imbalances (notably between development interests and communities) will typically remain.

There is a wider concern that civil society is not always engaged in design governance processes, which tend to engage professionals, dominated by architects. Architects themselves complain, however, that informal tools can unduly impinge on their role, requiring their involvement, for example, in competitions, panels, juries and other forms of evaluation for which their time is poorly compensated, and which therefore fail to appropriately value their expertise (WS3).

Ultimately, any tool is limited by how willing stakeholders are to engage with it and by where real decision-making power lies, whether at the level of the actors involved at the coalface or as expressed by one contributor to the masterclass, 'higher up the food chain of government' and/or among private development interests (MC). Design review provides a case in point, as a tool limited by the authority and credibility of the panel. The authority of design review is determined, for example, by how its recommendations are used and notably by whether municipalities take notice of them when granting development consents. Similarly, its credibility will be determined by who is on the panel, whether their opinion is valued by those receiving the advice and by the expertise (lay or professional) that they bring to the process (WS3).

Of course any informal tool is only one mechanism within a wider urban design governance landscape, and will not work in isolation. Nevertheless, when such tools work well, they are able to shift opinions by showing developers and public servants possibilities that they may not have previously envisaged. The right design idea at the right time can cut through uneven power relationships and challenge preconceived ways of thinking (WS3), although there is also always a role for disruptive, oppositional or subversive thinking in order to challenge the status quo and, in some circumstances, deliver more innovative and/or inclusive solutions (MC), such as those at Samoa île de Nantes (see Figure 6.2 above) or to respond rapidly to urgent needs (see Figure 6.10).

Figure 6.10   This hastily constructed sign and the planters denote this as a pedestrian street, instigated in Malmö following the wave of vehicles-as-weapons-of-terror attacks that hit Europe from 2016 onwards (image: Matthew Carmona).

The quality of the conversation is important to enriching understanding and mutual learning

Rather than focusing on immediate results, some informal urban design governance practices emphasise the importance of stimulating debate about the quality of the living environment. This approach can reinforce the brokerage, mediation, engagement and persuasion roles within urban design governance, opening the development process up for a new kind of leadership based on better mutual understanding. The Place Standard tool, for example, was developed to help inspire constructive conversations between different actors, bringing people together across professional and non-professional boundaries (see Box 9, p. 153) (WS2).

The language used by professionals when talking about architecture, urban planning and development processes is a vital part of this, either inspiring a common understanding by using common everyday vocabulary and avoiding jargon, or conversely driving a wedge between professionals and citizens (WS2). To facilitate the former, the Place Standard uses simplified language and clear questions for guiding a discussion that can be easily transferred to any context.

Beyond engaging communities, the discussion in successive workshops revealed the importance of aligning stakeholders – public, private and community – behind a clear set of quality priorities, with processes that allow learning to flow in all directions (MC). Successful examples seem to have created a positive coalition of partners to back an approach, with a common understanding of objectives underpinned by mutual trust, enabling partners to embark on processes even if the final outcomes are not known from the beginning. In other words, trust can enable space to be left for improvisation, innovation, and adjustment through time. Good examples of this are the International Building Exhibitions (IBAs – see Box 16, p. 185), pioneered in Germany, which use a quadruple approach involving businesses, research and education, public administration, and civil society to deliver complex, often experimental, development processes with shared learning at their heart (WS2).

The economics of urban design governance

The penultimate group of propositions looks at the major secondary focus of Urban Maestro, namely how urban design governance intercedes with finance, potentially reinforcing the delivery of high-quality design.

There are design/finance and soft power/finance divides, but also a great potential to bridge these gaps

The workshops repeatedly demonstrated that in most cases there is a professional disconnection between the worlds of design and finance (or specifically the economics of development). Although discussions revealed the potential for the innovative use of development funding to create schemes with positive spillovers and synergies, few presenters could fully unpack the economic rationale and business models associated with specific tools (WS2).

Across Europe, the disciplines of real estate development and architecture/urban design fit within their own schools of thought, which interact but rarely truly connect. An obvious conclusion is that urbanists need better training, as their understanding of real estate dynamics is often poor, and without such an understanding it is difficult to engage real estate interests by bringing 'asset values' as well as 'potential values' to fully bear on positively shaping places. The reverse is also true, that real estate actors – including those working in the public sector – need better means of accounting for place value (and not just economic value). In Cambridge a carefully organised programme of study tours and visits was enlisted to turn around perceptions and encourage a greater consensus between politicians, planners and key development actors in the city (see Figure 6.11). It is now one of relatively few places in the UK in which a two-way learning culture has been nurtured so that lessons from earlier projects can be continually revisited and new approaches refined (WS4).

A further disconnection was also apparent in the obvious gap between the use of the informal tools of urban design governance and the finances of development. Thus, modes of financial incentivisation can be found primarily in the formal toolbox of development (perhaps because of the need for formalised transparency in the use of public funds) while informal/soft-power incentives tend not to be explicitly financial.

As discussed in Chapter 5, there is an important distinction to be made between funding and finance. Although public funding such as the Czech subsidies programme for design competitions (see Box 12, p. 170), and some private funding, including for design review in England, is provided to support local practices of urban design governance, these forms of funding are not directly focused on the financing of development (WS3). They would, however, impact indirectly, for example through encouraging better-designed outcomes with a different set of economic dynamics, although these forces are poorly understood.

Figure 6.11 From the late 1990s onwards, Cambridge had structures and tools in place to deliver a much-needed planned expansion of the city. One such tool is the informal Quality Charter for Growth, which was drawn up following study tours to exemplar developments elsewhere in the UK and around Europe. The Charter focuses on the four 'C's of Community, Connectivity, Climate and Character, which have become the template against which new projects, such as here at Trumpington Meadows, are evaluated by the Cambridgeshire Quality Review Panel (image: Matthew Carmona).

The potential clearly exists, however, to explicitly link design aspirations and the economics of development, using informal tools to encourage what was described in Chapter 5 as good behaviour (good design) and discourage bad (poor design). Indeed, the workshops explored forms of information (for example the Swiss *Baukultur* policy), rating (such as Place Standard), support (for instance Dutch Q-teams), and exploration (say, the temporary public realm improvements in Budapest), each of which indirectly impacted on development value and financing through changing the culture, expectations and environment for investment to one in which design was prioritised. This will have long-term impacts on both the monetary and intrinsic value of the places so affected.

This is a relatively under-explored topic in the academic literature, and the workshops identified a need for a better understanding of how financial mechanisms are used as part of wider design governance approaches and of the specific impacts they have on the ground (WS1). Nevertheless, a working hypothesis can be proposed that informal tools are effective at creating a good culture of design and at gently nudging proposals towards better outcomes, and that finance can explicitly support these functions alongside any incentivisation through formal governance mechanisms (WS2).

Formal financial mechanisms can incentivise design quality, but they need design strings attached

Beyond the impact of the more intangible informal tools, the workshops discussed a number of formal financial mechanisms with the potential to attach design strings, in other words, which can be used to lever design quality on the promise of i) finance, ii) land, or iii) public investment (WS3). An example of each follows.

City makers funds such as Stadmakers Fonds (see Box 21, p. 214) are formal financing mechanisms that tend to be more focused on quality, given that place-based innovation is written into their objectives. Such funds act as matchmakers between socially motivated developers and investors but are still rare in Europe, tending to be associated with places that already have a tradition of social enterprises/development. While many questions remain about the replicability of such initiatives in other contexts and scales, and about their financial viability in different economic contexts, they seem to possess the potential for the effective use of direct financial incentives to deliver enhanced design outcomes (WS3).

Concept tendering (see Box 22, p. 215) is a form of competition used in Germany with a focus on overall site development rather than specifically on design. By transferring public land at a discount price, it provides an explicit financial incentive for the private developer to deliver concepts with defined social attributes. This formal mechanism can be used to encourage good design through including design as a quality factor to be considered when evaluating 'concepts'. However, it does not always follow that this is the case, as local priorities vary and design quality may be usurped by other factors (WS3).

Examples in Kigali showed that in a context of limited public resources, informal tools and soft powers can help to encourage investment and become a bridge to bottom-up initiatives. At the same time, the case of Medellín indicated how a coherent and sustained use of public investment in the city's infrastructure can create the right incentives for private actors to also invest. In Medellín, its economic model allows for funds generated by public utilities companies to be reinvested into its long-term urban transformation (WUF).

Land value capture and PPPs have the greatest immediate potential to link finance with the delivery of superior design

Two particular financial mechanisms, from respectively, the 'raising finance' and 'managing investment' categories of the working classification discussed in Chapter 5, were selected for in-depth analysis in the fourth workshop. Mechanisms of land value capture (LVC) and public–private partnerships (PPPs) (or Public–Private–People Partnerships) were chosen based on the potential revealed in earlier workshop discussions and accompanying case-study analysis (PD). In particular, LVC has the potential to capture private resources and direct them towards public urban improvements, while PPPs can coordinate public and private resources towards delivering a shared vision for urban quality.

Over the last decade both mechanisms have been strongly supported by the United Nations, the World Bank and by other agencies, as important answers to the typical funding gap for delivering urban infrastructure (United Nations 2017; UN-Habitat 2016b), although in reality these mechanisms take on profoundly different characteristics in different territories (WS4). LVC and PPP do not generate urban quality themselves, but when properly designed and combined with (formal and informal) tools of urban design governance, they can assist in achieving desirable outcomes by empowering stakeholders that are not motivated solely by the profit motive. Their use can also lead to the involvement of stakeholders motivated to produce better and more inclusive design outcomes, as was the case in Freiburg (see Box 24), Copenhagen (see Box 23 above) and Oslo (see Box 19, p. 202).

In each of these cases, careful strategic planning and design, formal mechanisms of land assembly and associated value capture, and a positive partnership between the state and private interests (PPPs) created the conditions for high-quality outcomes born of what Falk (2011) has coined the ABC of Ambition (combining top-down and bottom-up aspirations), Brokerage and balance between competing interests, and Continuity over time (WS4). It also necessitated that public authorities were seen as trusted partners, requiring, in turn, financial competency born of the ability to be clear and realistic on feasible returns, avoiding disappointing private investors, and carefully choosing projects that are sustainable on all fronts, including economic (PD).

Box 24   Capturing value in Freiburg

As property values are created by rising prosperity, accessibility, and changes to the planning status of land, Land Value Capture begins from the principle that the community should enjoy a share of this. There are various ways in which government can capture a share of rising land values: forms of taxation including death duties, capital gains taxation and property taxes; negotiated developer contributions on sites (a complex and time-consuming, albeit responsive, process); infrastructure levies applied to the anticipated value of completed developments; betterment taxes tied specifically to the land value increase as a consequence of a change in its planning status; tax increment finance, with public authorities raising bonds on the basis of expected increases in property taxes; and finally Land Value Capture, where the public sector utilises landownership directly to take a share in developments. There are numerous examples of Land Value Capture mechanisms around the world, and the OECD is in the process of producing a 'global compendium' to record these (https://www.oecd.org/cfe/cities/land-value-capture.htm).

Germany offers some of the best mechanisms for Land Value Capture as enshrined in federal planning law, which allows for speedy public assembly of under-used land, but also enables the municipality to recover the costs of land preparation. *Unlegung* is a process for readjustment in which the municipality retains land equal to the increase in value subject to a cap of 30 per cent on greenfield land and 10 per cent on inner city land. The municipality pools the land and resells serviced sites to either the previous owners or to small-scale developers, unless the landowner is able to undertake the agreed plan themselves and within a certain timeframe (Falk 2020).

Such a system enabled the City of Freiburg im Breisgau to develop the exemplary urban extensions of Vauban (see Figure 6.12) and Rieselfeld on the edges of the built-up area. These well-known cases of sustainable urbanisation are linked by extensions to the city's tramways and include extensive greenery and community facilities such as shops and schools. Sites for housing were made available to building groups, *Baugruppen* (130 in total), which enabled a much greater diversity of designs and a more rapid rate of development to be achieved than relying on private developers.

Figure 6.12 Vauban, a sustainable urban neighbourhood (image: Matthew Carmona).

Though these developments are complex, the rules or codes in the Building Plan set out for Vauban are largely listed on a single sheet of paper contained within the relevant B-Plan (*Bebauungsplan*), with the design principles retrospectively set out in *The Freiburg Charter for Sustainable Development* (Academy of Urbanism 2012). The charter includes key process-related features of the projects, encompassing a consistent commitment to sustainable design quality for 40 years; a commitment to cooperation and partnership, including bringing industrial and university partners to the table; developing a culture of engagement and communications with the city's citizens; and utilising tools such as design competitions and expert panels to retain a focus on quality through to delivery.

As long as land prices allow for financial returns that are viable, there is huge potential for social and environmentally motivated development outcomes, but if financial or regulatory incentives do not push in that direction then standard real estate products may prevail (see Figure 1.3). Constraining capital gain, for example by taxing short-term land speculation, may contribute to pushing investors to focus on longer-term objectives and financial returns, while incentives towards corporate social responsibility might be considered when encouraging quality and social outcomes from real estate activities, with knock-on benefits in terms of building places that will continue to deliver a good return over the long run (WS4).

Convincing real estate partners to invest in (longer-term) public goods such as high-quality public space requires demonstrating the reality of its return. While some intrinsically understand this, persuading others requires creating space for using the soft powers of discussion and negotiation, or alternatively bypassing traditional real estate markets altogether in favour of encouraging more socially motivated (local, small, individual) investors who are looking for projects with more moderate returns but good societal added value. The investments made by Stadmakers Fonds in Utrecht (see Box 21, p. 214) and elsewhere, and the work of Miss Miyagi (a socially focused design/development house based in Leuven) offered good examples, although whether such niche models can be generalised and developed at scale remains unknown (WS4).

Design governance carries a cost that is typically (although not exclusively or always) borne by the public sector

Irrespective of their long-term benefits, all design governance tools carry a cost. While some tools, such as International Building Exhibitions (IBAs – see Box 16, p. 185) rely heavily on the existence of long-term state-led financial support that may be difficult to mobilise in all contexts, other cases showed that meaningful results can be achieved with relatively inexpensive measures, for example the training programmes offered by Urban Design London average out at just £37 per training place (see Box 3, p. 127) (WS2).

Some worry that costs are not always fairly shared. Professional associations, for example, have complained that architectural competitions needlessly exacerbate competition among design studios, leading to an excessive drainage of resources as design teams are not properly recompensed. They call for stricter guidelines on the rules and conditions for architectural competitions, preferably at a pan-European level. The Architect's Council of Europe (2016: 1) argue that architectural competitions are 'the perfect source for innovative, economic and sustainable solutions' but advance nine rules for conducting them to ensure that they remain so, covering: equality of opportunity for all participants; transparency of procedure; independence of the jury; thoroughly preparing the brief; anonymity of participants; adequate prize money and remuneration; copyright issues properly addressed; a mechanism for dispute resolution; and, ideally, the participation of citizens (PD). Discussions at the workshop suggested that, overwhelmingly, this positive view of the value of competitions was the dominant one, with participants rationalising that:

- Open competitions are not mandatory to participate in.
- Competitions provide an opportunity for young designers to project their design thinking at a wider scale, and some competitions (such as Europan; see Box 11, p. 162) are specifically focused on achieving that.
- Competitions foreground design creativity and focus attention on design quality.
- Even if participants do not win, the visibility that competitions can give can be beneficial (WS3).

The use of two-phased competitions, in which the first phase requires only a minimal investment in time and the second phase is restricted to a limited number of the best candidates, was seen by many as striking a fair balance between the need for offering opportunities to emerging talents and for avoiding an unproductive waste of resources (WS3). Others felt that the requirement to demonstrate prior experience represented an important barrier to young or emerging studios, generally requiring the association of such practices with more experienced firms in order to take part (PD).

Competitions (like other tools) also carry a significant cost for their promoters (in the Czech Republic seen as 2–2.5 per cent of development costs – WS3), perhaps explaining the divergence in their use across different countries. In Europe, competitions are typically financed by public funds (and by the free or below-market rates of entrants). In contrast to practices further afield (see Figure 6.13), in Europe mechanisms to extract the costs of competitions from development value do not seem to exist. Instead, in order to promote their use, two forms of initiatives have been utilised by cities, regions and countries:

1. Offering direct subsidies for the costs of competitions (Czech Republic).
2. Providing indirect subsidies through the provision of technical, legal or administrative assistance to prepare the competition brief, selecting eligible candidates and juries, provision of legal or administrative assistance, and conducting deliberations (for instance Cellule Archi, Wallonia – the equivalent to Bouwmeesters elsewhere in Belgium); or through promoting specific competition formats (such as Panorama Lokaal in the Netherlands – see rating tools) (WS3).

In England, the direct payment by developers for design review provides a rare example of the beneficiary-pays principle in operation (see Chapter 3).

Figure 6.13 Today, the City of Sydney (the central area of the Australian metropolis) runs a unique formal competitions process for large-scale developments. Developers agreeing to take their developments through this competitions process can benefit from an additional 10% floor area or height bonus and – in the case of a fully open competition – a 50% reduction in the Heritage Floor Space requirement (the need to purchase transferable development rights from heritage buildings). Through their exhaustive study of the process, Freestone et al. (2019: 311) conclude that it offers an effective means of prioritising design quality, delivers generally better-designed outcomes, and 'enable[s] the public interest to be prioritised if not guaranteed in more creative, cooperative and productive ways' (image: Matthew Carmona).

How practices travel

The final set of propositions focuses on the diffusion of urban design governance practices between jurisdictions and across contexts. A sizeable literature focuses on the diffusion of policy-relevant ideas and practices, including: the dispersal of grand theories of urban governance (Pierre 2014); more concrete forms and practices of regulation (Ladi and Tsarouhas 2017); innovations in technology (Parkes et al. 2013); and innovations in the tools available to policymakers (Tait and Jensen 2007). Rogers (1995: 35) notes that diffusion, in this sense, 'is the process by which an innovation is communicated through certain channels over time among the members of a social system'.

As argued in Chapter 1, urban design ideas have a long history of travelling in this way, with the French Beaux-Arts tradition, the British garden cities movement and European Modernism in its various guises all exported around the world in the last century, only to return somewhat later in modified forms including suburban sprawl, internationalism and new urbanism. Thompson-Fawcett (2003: 268) observes the highly social nature of diffusion, and that movements like these diffuse, first, through personal interaction, and later, by gathering momentum as networks of communication are established, 'networks that are social, professional, para-professional and international'. Tait and Jensen (2007) emphasise the key 'translation' process as part of this, so that ideas or tools that might seem to be neatly packaged into a 'black box' for unpacking elsewhere, in fact need interpreting and modifying in relation to the new context in which they are being applied.

In relation to urban design, Loew (2012: 333) sees the rapid travel of practices as inevitable given today's globalisation of ideas in architecture and urban design. Thanks to the internet, social media, the ease of international travel for consultants, and (now) video conferencing, ideas travel faster than ever before, including positive trends such as the twenty-first-century models of sustainable urbanism in which Europe has been leading the way (Rapoport 2013) and which Rysler (2019: 20) even claims are 'common throughout Europe'. Tenders and architecture competitions are also routinely advertised internationally, while many larger firms have multiple offices spread across Europe and around the globe; again, speeding up the exchange of ideas and their spread. Yet while practices of urban design – for better or for worse – travel increasingly quickly, this does not necessarily extend to the *governance* of urban design, where the legal, regulatory and administrative contexts vary so profoundly (see Chapter 2) and continue to add layers of complexity and obstruction before any black box can be unpacked.

Softer tools diffuse better across complex and varied contexts

The Urban Maestro project revealed a huge diversity of urban design governance practices across Europe, but also very little systematic sharing of tools beyond high-level architectural policies and more recently the notion of *Baukultur*. The geographical variation of such practices is fundamentally shaped by diverse governance contexts locally, and while the workshops revealed an obvious strong desire to learn from each other and share experiences, the sheer complexity of practices that vary at country, regional, city and even local municipality level remains a barrier, as does the need for some clearer organising concepts to cut through the complexity, and a new language of urban design governance.

Yet while variations in legal and administrative contexts make the transfer of hard-power tools and approaches particularly challenging, this does not apply to softer forms of tools, whose non-statutory nature requires only resources, initiative and ambition to operate them. It follows that softer urban design governance tools are more transferable.

The challenges were illustrated in the very first workshop through the non-European experience of Vancouver. This example showed that transferring a particular design solution, even as a broad decontextualised concept, may not succeed if there is no transfer of the underlying urban design governance arrangements and aspirations. The Vancouver model (like the Medellín one in the global South) has travelled globally and became part of a larger theoretical discussion on urban policy, which demonstrates how policy and ideas don't transfer seamlessly from place to place but alter and adjust, sometimes successfully and sometimes not. Toronto attempted specifically to import what had been dubbed 'Vancouverism' but despite many similar factors (national context, developers, and so on) many of the ideas were only transferred superficially (see Figure 6.14). The image (or style) was there to link to Vancouver but the underlying governance practices were lacking in key aspects – not least the lesser determination of municipal authorities in Toronto to deliver high-quality outcomes – leading to the developer behaving differently and ultimately delivering lower-quality results (White and Punter 2017).

Figure 6.14 Vancouver and Toronto condominium blocks compared (image: Matthew Carmona).

The experience draws attention to the dangers of simplifying knowledge when trying to learn from other places (WS1). Discussion at successive workshops suggested:

- There are many – and good – reasons to borrow ideas from elsewhere, as other places can inspire, motivate, and challenge us to think differently.
- First, however, there is a need to identify what localities are already doing well (and what not), recognising the challenges of importing models wholesale from elsewhere, and the need instead to adapt any tool to the local context.
- In so doing it is possible to learn a lot from misses as well as successes: 'reflecting back on our own practices and failures'.
- Differences may range from subtle to very profound, bearing in mind that local design cultures also differ, and that underlying hidden factors, rather than particular practices, might be responsible for the differences in outcomes that are seen.

Nevertheless, Europe does have experiences of the successful transfer of soft urban design governance approaches. These extend to whole systems, such as the 'Copenhagen model', which was widely referred to in the workshops as a model where concerted attention to the public realm has helped to transform the city's fortunes, lessons not lost on other European cities. Similarly, the idea of Bouwmeesters began in the Netherlands and spread and expanded to Belgium. Alternatively, single tools might be the focus of successful transfer. The Place Standard tool originated in Scotland but has since been adapted and used across Europe, including in Slovenia, Denmark, Latvia, Lithuania, and the Netherlands, while the model of International Building Exhibitions (IBAs) has now been adopted outside of Germany, in France and Switzerland (WS2). Other tools and practices are now routinely shared online, including by the Urban Maestro project, and on an ongoing basis by Placemaking Europe (see Chapter 1).

Varied design and governance cultures mean that some tools travel well and others less so; the key is to choose the mix that is right for local circumstances

So far there has been little cross-European learning beyond ad hoc projects focused on particular defined practices such as design competitions (see rating tools). Despite this, some tools have been adopted across Europe and are widely considered effective. The use of design guidance of various descriptions exemplifies this (see Chapter 4: Information tools, p. 123), as most of the organisations responsible for delivering urban design governance services that contributed to the workshops had produced guidance of one form or another as a means to encourage and/or disseminate better design practices (WS3).

Under different names (see Chapter 4: Rating tools, p. 149), design review is also widely adopted and considered effective at delivering better design outcomes across Europe. In this position panels have increasingly moved away from a focus on aesthetic considerations to a broader concern with delivering wider urban benefits. When it operates well, design review acts as a means to challenge and shift thinking, both of developers and of public authorities. Panels operate within a wide variety of contrasting governance and policy frameworks, but all share the need for a strong political mandate to give panels legitimacy (WS3).

Other tools, notably design competitions, are strongly favoured in some locations but deliberately eschewed in others. In some countries, including Austria, Denmark and Switzerland, design competitions are widely used for bigger building projects commissioned by governmental bodies (national, regional or local) and for important development propositions (see Figure 6.15). In France, the legal obligation to host competitions for contracts above a defined threshold value is well established. In others, competitions are rarely used, notably in the UK where they are associated with cost overruns and heightened risk, despite the architectural competitions service provided by the Royal Institute of British Architects (see Chapter 4) (WS3).

Despite the absence of systematic European learning, initiatives discussed in Chapter 1 – notably the Davos Declaration and the New European Bauhaus – demonstrate a determination to prioritise built-environment quality across the continent, transfer best practices and spread learning. None have been more active in this than Switzerland, not only at the pan-European scale – leading the Davos initiative – but also nationally. In the final Urban Maestro Policy Dialogue, this vital national diffusion role was emphasised to encourage policy coherence and integration on design, empower regional and local administrations, share knowledge and foster innovative solutions, and instigate or support collective learning processes. In Switzerland, for example, while there are many informal tools available, they have been difficult to access for many of the smaller cantons, and so the national level has been pursuing its own post-Davos agenda designed to encourage the development of local

Figure 6.15 In 2005, an invited international competition was won by consultants West8 for the design of the reclaimed area above the then-proposed new tunnel for the M30 ring road around Madrid (the tunnel is below the pedestrian/cycleway on the far bank in this image). As well as a new strategic landscape, the proposals envisaged a family of smaller projects including squares, boulevards and parks, and a family of new bridges to connect up the urban districts along the new Madrid Rio (image: Matthew Carmona).

practices (https://www.bak.admin.ch/bak/en/home/baukultur/service/kontakte-und-organigramme.html) (PD). The New European Bauhaus has the potential to echo this at the pan-European scale.

Twenty propositions

The numerous presentations and diverse discussions across the eight organised events of Urban Maestro combined to form a robust and rigorous testing bed for the ideas underpinning the project, encompassed in the notion of soft urban design governance. Inevitably some tools were examined more closely than others, and discussions often resulted in many more questions than answers. Generally, however, the concepts encompassed in the analytical framework (see Figure 2.8, p. 61) and typology of urban design governance tools (see Figure 3.4, p. 79) were well understood and found to be widely applicable, with the research showing that Europe has been as innovative in its thinking on the governance of urban design as it has been on the delivery of projects with heightened place value. In this regard the continent has a positive story to tell.

Collectively the results can be summarised in twenty propositions under the six headings that structured this chapter:

- **The culture and commitment to design quality**

    1. There are widely shared aspirations to build a local culture of quality.
    2. Building a culture of quality is a long-term project requiring sustained commitment and influence over the key levers of delivery, while persuading others to join.
    3. Political commitment, with flexibility, is key.

- **Building the toolkit for urban design governance**

    4. From design culture to design delivery, and from design delivery to design culture, the two are mutually reinforcing.
    5. Creative (even visionary) not bureaucratic tools are required to deliver place quality.
    6. Informal informs and formal formalises: formal and informal urban design governance work together.
    7. The most sophisticated approaches use tools in combination and in multiple ways.
    8. Informal is more flexible and reactive to local and immediate needs.

- **The governance of urban design governance**

    9. Public-sector-led urban design governance is the rock on which place quality is built, but is not the whole story.
    10. The right structures and the right people are both necessary to champion design quality and shape the most effective urban design governance.
    11. There is a potential dark side to informal urban design governance.

- **The power and people of urban design governance**

    12. Informal tools offer great potential for inclusive and engaging decision-making on design.

13. Power and power imbalances shape processes and outcomes, but design governance processes can shift thinking.

14. The quality of the conversation is important to enrich understanding and mutual learning.

• **The economics of urban design governance**

15. There are design/finance and soft power/finance divides, but also a great potential to bridge these gaps.

16. Formal financial mechanisms can incentivise design quality, but they need design strings attached.

17. Land value capture and PPPs have the greatest immediate potential to link finance with the delivery of superior design.

18. Design governance carries a cost that is typically (although not exclusively or always) borne by the public sector.

• **How practices travel**

19. Softer tools diffuse better across complex and varied contexts than hard ones.

20. Varied design and governance cultures mean that some tools travel well and others less so; the key is to choose the mix that is right for local circumstances.

While the last proposition confirms that all the tools of urban design governance are not appropriate everywhere, the effectiveness of informal tools as a set of practices came through strongly across all the workshops, not just for building a culture for design but also for delivering real projects on the ground, often enriched by the engagement of diverse interests, including communities (WS1). As one contributor commented: 'Governments that are serious about quality reach for the informal toolbox', across all levels of state intervention: national, regional and local (PD).

Soft-power and hard-power tools are not the same. Soft-power tools require us to think differently about urban problems. Instead of 'requiring' action, such powers are about 'nudging' stakeholders in the right direction through influencing, convincing and even seducing them into action. This can limit their impact, as they do not determine the final actions taken, but if used well, they can change long-term cultures and practices and, thereby, have a far greater impact. Because of this, they need to be used alongside, and not instead of, hard-power tools and, when used effectively, they eventually may change how often and in what circumstances regulations and other tools are utilised (WS2).

More research is required to examine how tools vary between contexts. A particular challenge lies in how to measure success – what targets, indicators and measures of improvement are appropriate, and how they should be built into the operation of tools locally (MC). But as the workshops and Urban Maestro generally showed, there is a diverse urban design governance toolbox, and tools work best when they are not operating in isolation but instead as part of a larger system that mobilises a range of informal (soft power) and formal (hard power) instruments to address urban challenges (WS3). This also encompasses expertise in the financial aspects of development, and how hard financial incentives can be tied to the soft strings of urban design governance to deliver high-quality urban design and place value for all.

7

Landscapes, tools and fundamentals for delivery

The final chapter brings the book to a close with a series of clear and succinct conclusions that draw from across the range of investigations and associated discussions explored in the book. The chapter discusses the various landscapes of urban design governance found across Europe and how the tools deployed within these landscapes can be used together – including with financial mechanisms. It concludes that whatever the local circumstances and tools ultimately chosen to engage with design quality, governments – both national and local – should begin by reviewing six fundamental factors, the six 'C's of culture, capacity, coordination, collaboration, commitment and continuity. These are all required, and underpin many of the best practices brought together in the book.

Bringing tools together within diverse urban design governance landscapes

One of the key insights from Urban Maestro has been that tools of urban design governance work most effectively when used together. Used together, 'formal' and 'informal', 'culture-quality' and 'design-delivery' tools, and 'urban design governance tools' and 'financial mechanisms' can all reinforce quality aspirations and deliver enhanced outcomes. But this does not occur by chance. Instead it occurs within an urban design governance landscape that reflects the wider governance dynamics within a territory and the power relationships between different actors (see Figure 2.7, p. 59).

The types of urban design governance landscape

Examining practices across Europe, six broad types of urban design governance landscape can be identified within which individual tools are defined, combined and put into practice. The types reflect commonalities across countries born of a shared culture, history, legal system and traditions of administration and urban governance (Rysler 2014; 2019), as well as the simple fact of proximity and/or shared language. They reinforce the point made in Chapter 4 that some tools are favoured in some countries but not in others.

Type 1: Top-down directive

Some countries with a long engagement in prioritising design quality have utilised national legislation to establish clear expectations for local government. France is the most obvious of these, with national government playing a key role in supporting design competitions and establishing a system of local enabling (through the CAUEs) and architectural centres across the country. The Netherlands has set similar national minimum expectations for design review around which local practices develop and expand, for example the spread of Q-teams, architecture centres, city architects, and aesthetic control committees, all feeding sophisticated practices at the municipal level.

Type 2: Top-down discretionary + bottom-up

The UK also has a top-down tradition of government setting the context within which urban design governance occurs, although based on flexible national policy that is interpreted at the local level. This is most obvious in England where national policy has swung widely over the years (from supportive to agnostic and even, at times, oppositional to the governance of design) and where, as a consequence, practices locally vary hugely (Carmona et al. 2016). It has, nevertheless, given rise to significant innovation in some localities and to a diverse ecology of organisations – public, private, third-sector – operating in networked and public open governance modes. Tools being used are diverse.

Type 3: Guided network

Following their federal traditions, Germanic countries have adopted a networked approach to urban design governance. *Baukultur* policies at the national level exhort their constituent Länder/cantons to prioritise design quality with governments at this regional level setting up often diverse arrangements to deliver on their objectives. A notable example is the City of Vienna's local *Baukultur* policy (see Chapter 3), with the delivery of design quality focused around its strong tradition of organising design competitions managed by a specific department responsible for architecture and urban design policy (Bento and Laopoulou 2019). Federal-scale institutions are either within government, for example

Switzerland's Federal Office for Culture, or at arms-length, such as the German Federal Foundation of Baukultur (see Box 1, p. 117).

Type 4: Devolved local champion
In some countries a more explicitly devolved set of practices is apparent, with cities/regions adopting their own typically arms-length models. Sometimes this is because of the absence of a national role, such as in Belgium, and sometimes the national role is limited and clearly defined, including in the Czech Republic, creating space for practices to develop locally. The Prague Institute of Planning and Development (IPR), for example, is an arms-length management organisation funded by the city and ultimately responsible for guiding the city's urbanism, architecture and development (see Box 25). It uses a wide range of tools from practice guides to various forms of exploration and persuasion, such as its permanent information centre and exhibition space focused on enhancing public debate.

More common are units based around the authority of an individual – a state or city architect or Bouwmeester. For example, in September 2018 Sweden's government appointed its first national architect responsible for implementing the country's new national architecture

---

Box 25   Arms-length, but not: IPR Prague (Czech Republic)

The Prague Institute of Planning and Development (IPR) is an arms-length organisation funded by the City of Prague and responsible for developing the principles and guidelines for the city's urbanism, architecture and development (http://en.iprpraha. cz). IPR is responsible for strategic and spatial planning and development, transport, landscape and economic infrastructure. Key projects include the Metropolitan Plan and the implementation of the Prague Strategic Plan, but IPR also guides public space standards across the city – for example through its *Prague Public Space Design Manual* – and direct assistance to public-realm projects (see Figure 7.1). It conducts participatory planning and training, handles the processing of geographical data and information for Prague, conducts design competitions, and aims to raise public awareness through publications, exhibitions, lectures, workshops and other activities. In doing so it uses a wide range of both formal and informal tools of urban design governance.

Figure 7.1   IPR's guidance focuses on making Prague a pleasant city for pedestrians, with space for people, trees and commercial activities (a). A focus on the detail helps to reinforce Prague's unique character (b, bottom half of image) but as its guidance is informal, it is not always implemented (b, top half of image) (images: Matthew Carmona).

IPR represents Prague's attempt to follow the lead of other successful European cities by establishing a semi-independent body solely focused on the built environment, one that is closely connected, albeit not a part of, the local administration. It offers an alternative to a city architect although with the key difference that it is not structured around a single person. It also represents an alternative to the combination of a purely public local authority and a largely independent architectural centre. IPR operates in that middle ground, being involved in policy and regulations but also prioritising public-oriented outreach.

In September 2017 IPR opened the Centre for Architecture and Metropolitan Planning (CAMP), an information centre and exhibition space with the mission 'to improve the current form of public debate on the development of Prague'. CAMP provides a space to bring together the public, developers, local government, professionals, and so on through a library of relevant spatial information, exhibitions, educational programmes and public events. Various groups of stakeholders, from investors to students, are encouraged to use the facilities at CAMP, which is viewed as the city's main hub for all things urban- and space-related.

Figure 7.2 The Swedish National Architect will build upon the enviable reputation that the country already has as reflected in well-known projects such as Hammarby Sjöstad in Stockholm. This project is based on a clear but flexible urban design framework and detailed design codes to 'fix' the key design parameters at each phase, all delivered by a public-sector team with the means and capabilities to proactively engage through the full range of tools available to them. These include: powerful incentives vested in enlightened land ownership; the use of design competitions at each phase of the development; a rigorous design review and evaluation process; and partnerships between the city and local development teams (image: Matthew Carmona).

policy (see Figure 7.2). With a longer pedigree, the Belgian Bouwmeester positions are, in effect, government architects, but their independent status allows them to act as (semi-)autonomous experts to promote design quality in the built environment and high-quality public buildings (see Box 13, p. 172). Leading a small team and assisted by an expert group, they deliver this mission through a variety of informal design governance tools including support to public developers; exploration projects; design competitions; research by design, alliances, and general advocacy aimed at fostering a place-making culture. In doing so they contribute to the development of a long-term policy vision and advise on formal urban design governance tools.

Type 5: Ad hoc (sometimes innovative)

In some major countries practices have been little coordinated at a national level, and this has led to a fragmentation in local practices of urban design governance. While this means that practices are very variable, significant local innovation is still possible. In Italy and Portugal, for example, the Urban Maestro panorama revealed a number of practices at the city/regional scale, notably in Turin (see Box 26), Milan, Reggio Emilia and Lisbon (see Box 15, p. 181), with a particular focus on engaging local communities in establishing and driving forward positive local agendas on place quality through the co-governance of key urban assets. These more ad hoc practices may be changing following the increasing adoption of high-level architectural policies by national states across Europe.

Box 26   Co-governing the urban commons in Turin (Italy)

The Co-City project began as a response to the lack of public funds following the economic crisis of the 2010s. The approach utilised a shared-management approach to the city's 'urban commons', undertaken between the city's administration and a network comprising the Houses of the Neighbourhoods (Case di quartiere), the University of Turin, and ANCI (the association of Italian municipalities), in the process supporting new forms of citizen participation aimed at the regeneration of deprived neighbourhoods through their collaborative management.

This approach operated between 2017 and 2020 and was operationalised through the establishment of pacts of collaboration between the city's inhabitants and the city administration. Primarily these focused on transforming abandoned structures and vacant land into hubs of resident participation, with the aim being to foster community spirit as well as the creation of social enterprises that contribute to the reduction of urban poverty. The pacts represented legal tools through which the nature of the informal engagement was specified (stimulating collective use, management, ownership of urban assets, provision of services, infrastructure, and so on).

The project's approach aimed to foster urban innovation while also tackling social exclusion in some of the city's most challenging urban contexts. The structured process of co-creation and collaborative management ultimately improved the participation of residents in various parts of the city, fostering the commitment of the citizens towards a more inclusive and cohesive city (https://www.uia-initiative.eu/en/uia-cities/turin) (see Figure 7.3).

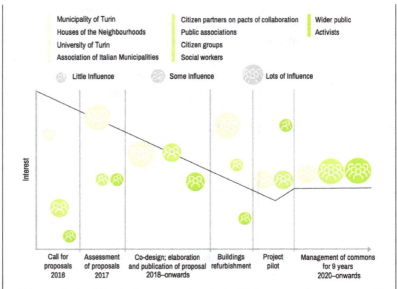

Figure 7.3 The influence of stakeholders over the course of the Co-City project Cumiana 15, Turin (image: Urban Maestro Masterclass).

Type 6: Development-focused

While the first five types are mutually exclusive, overlapping with each of these regimes as part of local diverse urban design governance landscapes are practices related to particular local development projects and the frameworks put in place to deliver them. Across Europe, large scale regeneration/development schemes are typically accompanied with defined public-sector quality aspirations, which are built into the way these are organised and managed by using urban design governance tools that go over and above the usual practices found in surrounding areas. Urban Maestro revealed that these additional layers of governance are often structured through public–private partnerships (see Chapter 6) associated with areas undergoing large-scale change. In such cases, the use of financial mechanisms – notably land value capture – with design strings attached help to deliver a comprehensive focus on design quality, as seen in examples such as HafenCity in Hamburg (see Box 27) or By&Havn in Copenhagen (see Box 23, p. 227). Inevitably, because such initiatives are geographically defined at a smaller spatial scale than a municipality, tools of urban design governance are used with a greater degree of discrimination, but also often with greater focus.

Box 27 Development-focused urban design governance in Hamburg (Germany)

At 220 hectares, HafenCity is one of the largest urban redevelopment projects in Europe, and is expected to run until 2030. The development is an international exemplar of urban regeneration with the former inner-city port being revitalised with new hotels, shops, office buildings and residential areas and with a strong focus on high-quality, resilient public spaces (https://www.hafencity.com/en).

The entire development area is under the ownership of the City of Hamburg, which formed HafenCity Hamburg GmbH (HCH) in 1997 (originally under a different name) to undertake the regeneration. HCH is the city's manager of development, property owner (through the special assets fund for city and port) and developer of public infrastructure (roads, bridges, parks, social and cultural developments) based on revenues from the sale of land.

The redevelopment project started with the approval of a masterplan by the Hamburg Senate in 2000, and since 2010 HCH has regularly released land for apartment buildings, sold in the market on the basis of a concept-tendering process (see Box 22, p. 215). For each individual housing plot a strict competitive bidding process is enforced in which the crucial factor for awarding the contract is the quality of the concepts submitted (worth 70 per cent of the evaluation) and not the highest bid (worth 30 per cent). After ratification by the City Land Commission, the process is followed by an exclusive option period with an obligation to plan, during which projects can be refined before the plot is formally sold.

The advantage of this process for the developer is that financing of the purchase price is postponed until after the building permit is granted. This gives time to refine the quality of the project, secure finance and acquire potential users. Throughout the whole process, HCH, the local authorities and the investors remain in constant dialogue to ensure a high-quality design (see Figure 7.4). For example, following tendering, the process requires investors to work in conjunction with the HCH to organise an architectural competition.

Figure 7.4   The Hamburg Kesselhaus in HafenCity is an information centre for the area and its regeneration, including a 1:500 scale model of the entire development (image: Matthew Carmona).

What sets HafenCity apart from the other major international urban waterfront developments is the high expectations on design quality – which include a mix of uses, high public-realm standards and ecological sustainability – and its innovative development process, which ensures that quality criteria are considered when selling public land. With the city taking the lead, HCH demonstrates how public and private sectors can successfully cooperate in a way that shifts the core of the risk profile to benefit both city and investors.

Deploying tools within the landscapes

The Urban Maestro project did not begin with the intention of determining if one set of arrangements were necessarily more effective than another. Each relate to long-term governance traditions that are still regionally defined across Europe and unlikely to change quickly. The project revealed, however, that it is possible to prioritise design/place quality within each of the six types and to deliver high-quality outcomes as a result. With this proviso, it is possible to offer three general conclusions:

- Judging by their dominance in the Urban Maestro panorama, dedicated organisations (however constituted and at whatever scale) seem particularly effective at ensuring that design quality is prioritised. They do this by bringing focus, innovation and what resources they have to bear on the design-quality challenges they face, often utilising multiple overlapping tools of urban design governance. The implication is that rather than burying the remit for delivering place quality within an organisation with multiple other (perhaps conflicting) responsibilities, it may be better to establish a dedicated unit.

- Whichever types (1–5) of urban design governance arrangements are adopted locally, there is the potential to overlay established practices with 'special' urban design governance arrangements focused on particular critical developments (type 6). Again, this allows for an increased focus on urban design quality alongside the leveraging of dedicated resources (from the development) to pursue it.

- Together urban design governance tools span the 'field of action' covered by urban design governance as discussed in Chapter 2, with numerous overlapping tools available to both build a culture of quality and facilitate its more reliable delivery (see Figure 7.5). Governance organisations therefore have a choice to make about which types of instruments to use and in which combinations. In making these choices some tools of urban design governance are already ubiquitous across Europe. Others are used heavily in some jurisdictions and not at all (or in a far more limited manner) elsewhere. Some are infrequently found. In part this reflects the fact that tools often travel regionally with common practices tending to group in a number of geographic poles: the Germanic countries, the Nordic countries, the British Isles, and the Benelux countries. France is its own pole, and practices in southern and eastern Europe tend to be more varied, with less obvious commonalities locally or transfer of practices between countries that have variously struggled to deal with the legacy of communism, rapid neoliberal restructuring and/or economic crisis (Rysler 2014: 10–11).

A comprehensive typology of urban design governance

Drawing from across the discussions in this book, four headlines can be confidently advanced:

- First, place quality is not produced by accident, or overnight, but requires ongoing determination and investment by all stakeholders to deliver better places for people than would otherwise be produced.
- Second, informal tools and processes of urban design governance can play a critical role in this, helping to establish a local culture of good design and the sorts of delivery tools that can help to shape places, projects and processes for the better.
- Third, soft powers can be harnessed quickly and cost-effectively and can be linked to formal tools and investment processes in a manner that focuses and enhances those tools to deliver design quality.
- Fourth, it is always better to do something than nothing, although there is no simple 'recipe' of urban design governance approaches that will be appropriate everywhere; context is critical and establishing the right mix of tools will depend on local circumstances, resources and practices.

While it acts with, for and among other stakeholders, the public sector nevertheless has a special responsibility for creating the conditions within which a high-quality built environment can flourish. Across Europe, the move to enhance design quality as a key policy ambition is increasingly being prioritised. Differences in political, legal, and administrative systems mean that variations in practice are large, and as has already been argued, it is difficult to determine the superiority of one approach over others. As with any policy arena, however, the concern for urban quality will only be delivered if properly resourced and effectively implemented. The range of tools developed and used in different jurisdictions offers an indication of this commitment.

The research has shown that a varied palette of informal tools of urban design governance is central to this drive. To facilitate discussion and allow comparisons to be made, a European typology of urban design governance was advanced, tested and found to be robust (see Figure 3.4, p. 79). Beginning with two key conceptual and practical distinguishing features of such tools – quality culture/quality delivery and formal/informal – these, in turn, define three categorisations of tool: i) informal quality-culture tools, ii) informal quality-delivery tools and iii) formal quality-delivery tools; nine tool types; and eventually 24 separate informal tools of urban design governance.

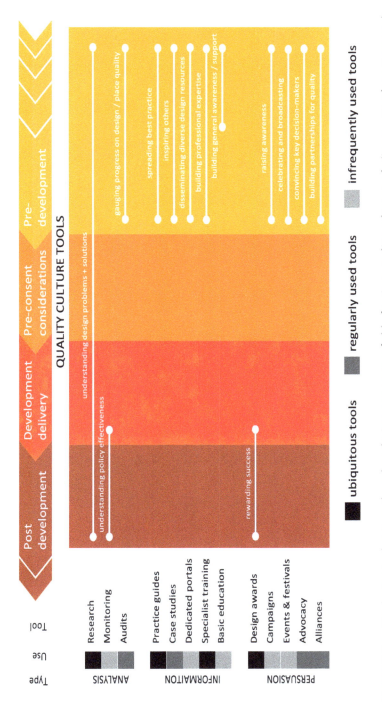

Figure 7.5a Deploying tools across the urban design governance field of action: quality-culture tools (image: Matthew Carmona).

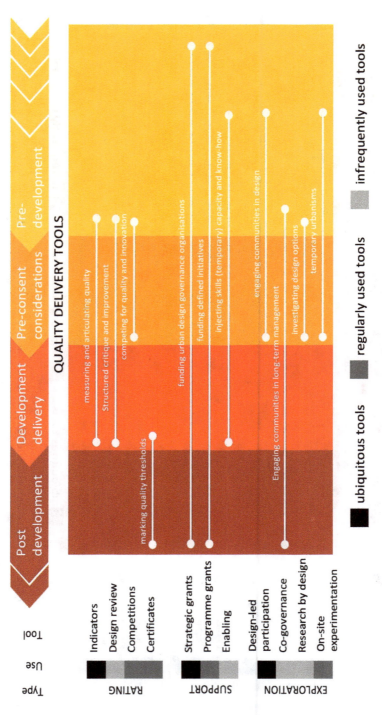

Figure 7.5b Deploying tools across the urban design governance field of action: quality-delivery tools (image: Matthew Carmona).

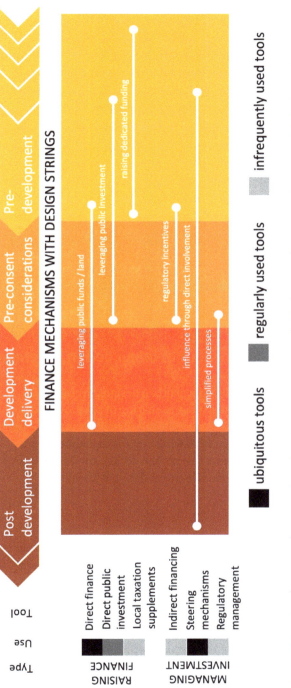

Figure 7.5c Deploying tools across the urban design governance field of action: finance mechanisms with design strings (image: Matthew Carmona).

Despite low levels of awareness regarding the potential linkage between urban design governance tools and finance mechanisms, the research also showed a clear potential to add design strings to financial mechanisms, particularly to those in the subcategories of direct financing instruments, direct public investment, indirect financing instruments, and steering mechanisms (see Figure 5.9, p. 220). Financial means could, for example, encourage the production and use of urban design governance tools and also promote the aspirations encompassed within them. Typically this occurs as part of a formal incentivisation process, but also occurs within the informal support category (see Figure 3.6, p. 83). These mechanisms have the potential to further reinforce the quality culture from which they emerge and may eventually even nullify the need for ongoing financial incentives and the design strings to which they are attached.

All these tools are brought together in a final comprehensive typology of European urban design governance tools as represented in Figure 7.6.

Six Cs: the fundamentals of urban design governance

Whatever the nature of the local urban design governance landscape and its tools, the extensive discussions, sharing of practices and analyses that underpinned Urban Maestro suggested that governments – national and local – might begin by reviewing six fundamental factors. In these concluding pages (and summarised in Figure 7.7 below) they are expressed as six Cs of effective urban design governance.

1. Culture of design quality

The quality of the built environment impacts profoundly on the social and economic opportunities available to citizens as well as on the health of the environment and local populations. Nurturing a shared desire to see high-quality architecture and streets and public spaces that support an inclusive urban life requires sufficient and predictable funding, a willingness to actively engage in shaping places, and an ability to persuade investors and citizens that such a commitment is worthwhile.

Producing a high-quality urban environment requires a culture change across the many people and institutions that together shape places

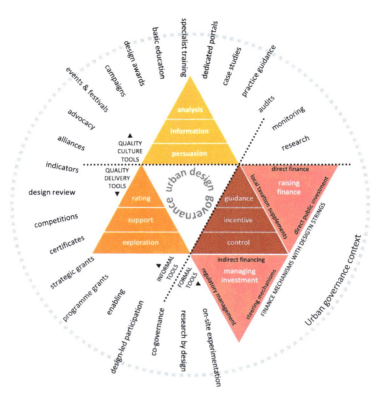

Figure 7.6 Comprehensive typology of urban design governance tools

1. Analysis tools – evidence about how and with what consequences the built environment is shaped.

2. Information tools – dissemination of knowledge about good (or poor) design practices and processes.

3. Persuasion tools – actively make the case for particular design responses in a proactive manner.

4. Rating tools – allow judgements about design quality to be made in a systematic and structured manner.

5. Support tools – directly assisting or enabling design / development teams with particular projects.

6. Exploration tools – hands-on design investigations and community engagement.

7. Guidance tools – formally set out operational design parameters to direct the design of development.

8. Incentive tools – direct and indirect economic stimulation by the state.

9. Control tools – development- and construction-related regulation and decision-making.

....

10. Raising finance – through subsidy and direct investment.

11. Managing investment – through process management, indirect economic stimulus and partnership working.

(image: Matthew Carmona).

The full value and potential of cities can be released by committing to build a culture of urban design quality

Putting in place the right structures and people is a key step to realising design quality ambitions

Learning and refining practices in the light of best practices and changing local circumstances is a continuous process

Bringing 'tools' together across hard- and soft-power categories is particularly effective for influencing design quality delivery

It is essential to consider how to tie design-quality aspirations to financial-incentivisation mechanisms and to private sector know-how

Developers, investors and citizens shall be engaged in an ongoing conversation about design quality

Culture of...
Continuity of...
Capacity for...
Design quality
Commitment to...
Coordination of...
Collaboration for...

Figure 7.7 The six Cs of effective urban design governance (image: Matthew Carmona).

and spaces. Places that have achieved it have typically worked to establish such a widely shared culture of quality, but a leap forward of this type is made of many small steps encompassed in numerous decisions associated with the delivery of individual plans, projects and spaces. It requires a continuity of effort – well beyond the duration of any political mandate – as well as many short-term actions that combine to deliver more than the sum of their parts. A culture change has been delivered when no one questions the need for design quality and when it is quite simply, the expectation.

2. Capacity for design quality

The most sophisticated governance of urban design starts with the public sector recognising its own huge potential to decisively shape new development and existing places for the better. A first key step is to put in place the necessary administrative structures or organisations to deliver on the ambitions and to invest in people with the right capabilities and commitment to command trust and wield authority when negotiating design outcomes.

This may involve enhancing the function of existing structures and arrangements or creating new ones, but any arrangements need to be suitably empowered in order to challenge existing practices and bureaucratic processes, particularly if they are leading to substandard outcomes. In doing so it may be wise to start small and build from there, selecting a single tool such as design review, design competitions, citizens juries, awards schemes, and so forth. If a tool works well, it is necessary to commit resources to it and make it economically sustainable, adding other tools as and when resources allow. Leadership is key and determining from who or where that is coming is critical.

3. Coordination of design quality

A culture of quality is underpinned by having the right tools in place to enable city authorities to encourage and require design quality consistently. Formal regulatory instruments are important, but so too are the sorts of informal and flexible tools such as design guidance, professional enabling, on-site experimentation, and so forth, which can leverage the expertise and creativity of motivated individuals and utilise the soft powers of the public sector to inform and actively engage key parties in the delivery of design-quality ambitions.

The most sophisticated approaches use a mix of tools, creating continuity in approaches and achieving success by aligning a diverse set of tools towards the same quality objectives. For example, traditional regulatory tools such as spatial development plans, construction regulations, and local taxation, can be given a quality dimension through combining them with softer approaches across the six categories of informal urban design governance tools. These are cost effective to deliver and, when used in combination with financial mechanisms, can help to maximise value from public resources by encouraging more informed and effective public spending.

4. Collaboration for design quality

A feature of much contemporary development is an imbalance of power in development processes. Informal tools of urban design governance can be particularly effective at garnering and amplifying community voices, and for motivating private interests to both engage in a conversation about the future of place and to commit to playing a role in delivering public design-quality ambitions and long-term visions. The quality of these conversations is critical for enriching understanding and mutual learning.

For example, urban design processes can be seen as political or developer-led processes, leaving residents feeling side-lined. Here soft-power tools such as co-creation and collaborative management can help to legitimise processes and inspire better outcomes. Similarly, economic resources and incentives can be fully integrated with design objectives when ambitions, methods and even languages are fully aligned. Demonstrating leadership on design is essential, and soft powers can facilitate this, but it requires listening, garnering support and recognising diverse private and public interests.

5. Commitment to design quality

Too often design quality is considered in a bubble separated from the economics of development. There is huge potential to incentivise the delivery of urban design quality, while saving on public funding, by linking any direct or indirect public sector financial contribution – land, loans, remediation, infrastructure, know-how, partnership, and so on – to the aspirations expressed through informal urban design governance tools. Land value capture and public–private partnerships have particular potential to make this link (see Chapter 6).

These tools offer tried and tested means to fill the public-funding gap and align private actions to community-wide quality objectives. They are not just concerned with capturing private sector finance, but also private expertise to complement public and community knowledge and resources. Tying design strings to such financial commitment can help to ensure that outcomes meet public-quality aspirations and deliver long-term place value to all.

6. Continuity of design quality

Everywhere is different, and practices that might be right for one municipality won't be right for another. As this book has shown, there is great potential to learn from practices in cities that have made the transition to a culture of urban design quality. In this respect, it is easier to transfer practices that use the soft powers of the state because usually they work independently of defined legislative and governance regimes and can be adapted to diverse and changing local contexts.

Soft powers can facilitate innovation, allow adjustment when outcomes are disappointing and the rapid commitment of more resources and political capital when practices succeed. But there is a need to create space (and time) for experimentation, incorporating continuous learning and refining of practices. Such local scale innovations – both inside and outside public administrations – can then be scaled up to inform more general and formal policies. The question is how to create a stronger drive in the public sector and maintain such a continuous learning process. In this context there may be need for what one commentator at the final Urban Maestro Policy Dialogue defined as a seventh C to add to the list: 'Come on!' – an inspirational call to cities to get going. This book demonstrates how.

Unanswered questions

Urban Maestro was a deliberately ambitious project, scanning the whole of Europe to find, explore and understand practices of urban design governance. A decision was taken early on that in order to explore the full diversity and scope of practices, depth of understanding (of individual practices) would need to be sacrificed for breadth of coverage and a broad understanding. Inevitably this leaves unanswered questions, among which are:

- A deep dive: Few of the individual tools explored by Urban Maestro at the pan-European scale have been explored comprehensively. An exception is the area of design competitions, which have been the focus of a number of recent studies (see Chapter 4), as – to a lesser degree – has design review. Other tools have yet to benefit from a deep dive in order to reveal comparative experiences and lessons for improving practice.
- Beyond Europe: A relatively minor aspect of the Urban Maestro project was to look beyond Europe to understand if concepts of urban design governance have relevance in the global South (see Chapter 6). The answer to this relatively narrow question was 'yes': the concepts and practices are relevant, but the very different contexts found in developing parts of the world clearly need far deeper investigation and understanding in order to answer the question 'how?'
- The economics of design: A more significant theme explored by Urban Maestro was the relationship between urban design governance tools and financial instruments. Repeatedly this aspect of the research came up against the unseen barrier that seems to exist between the worlds of economics and that of design. While a positive connection was revealed by the research, several aspects merit further in-depth investigation: how this works, how barriers can be overcome, and what the conceptual relationships are between design and economics.

- Place value: Repeatedly, the Urban Maestro team heard about the economic, social and environmental value delivered by better design and therefore by the practices being investigated. In Europe, with the instigation of the New European Bauhaus (see Chapter 1), this case seems to be in the ascendancy, but how urban design governance processes influence and deliver these forms of value remains to be fully traced and proven.

These are just some of the many unexplored lines of enquiry for other projects to investigate …

References

Books, reports and articles

Academy of Urbanism (2012) *The Freiburg Charter for Sustainable Development*, Freiburg: Academy of Urbanism. https://issuu.com/theaou/docs/aou_freiburg_charter_final_print.

Acampa, G. (2019) 'European guidelines on quality requirements and evaluation in architecture', *Valori e Valutazioni* 23: 47–56.

Adam, R. (2013) *The Globalisation of Modern Architecture: The impact of politics, economics and social change on architecture and urban design since 1990*, Newcastle upon Tyne: Cambridge Scholars Publishing.

Adams, D. and Tiesdell, S. (2013) *Shaping Places: Urban planning, design and development*, London: Routledge.

Antonelli, A., Nictolis, E. D. and Iaione, C. (2021) 'Promoting urban co-governance: towards just and democratic ecological and digital transition in cities'. https://urbanmaestro.org/wp-content/uploads/2021/03/urban-maestro_promoting-urban-co-governance-by-a-antonelli-e-de-nictolis-c-iaione.pdf.

Architect's Council of Europe (2016) 'Recommendations for Architectural Design Contests (ADC)'. https://www.ace-cae.eu/uploads/tx_jidocumentsview/6.1.1_GA2_17_Compet-Rules.pdf.

Architectuur Lokaal (2017) *Competition Culture in Europe, 2013–16*, Amsterdam: Architectuur Lokaal. https://arch-lokaal.nl/wp-content/uploads/2017/07/Competition-Culture-in-Europe_Architectuur-Lokaal_web_compressed.pdf.

Architectuur Lokaal (2018) *EU Competition Culture Dictionary*, Amsterdam: Architectuur Lokaal. https://arch-lokaal.nl/wp-content/uploads/2020/12/180831-Competition-Culture-EU-Dictionary.pdf.

Architectuur Lokaal (2021) *Competition Culture in Europe, 2017–2020*, Amsterdam: Architectuur Lokaal. https://arch-lokaal.nl/wp-content/uploads/2021/01/Competition_Culture_in_Europe_2017_2020.pdf.

Ball, J. (2019) 'Housing as a basic human right: the Vienna model of social housing', *New Statesman*, 3 September. www.newstatesman.com/spotlight/housing/2019/09/housing-basic-human-right-vienna-model-social-housing.

Barth, L. (2015) 'Leadership, design and value', *Urban Design* 135: 32–4.

Baukultur Bundestiftung (2015) *Baukultur Report 2014/15: Built living spaces of the future*, Potsdam: Baukultur Bundestiftung. https://www.bundesstiftung-baukultur.de/fileadmin/files/medien/78/downloads/baukultur-bericht-e.pdf.

Beatley, T. (ed.) (2012) *Green Cities of Europe,* Washington, DC: Shearwater Books.

Bedrone, R. (2011) 'L'esperienza Francese dei CAUE', *Giornale dell'Architettura* Vol. 2.

Ben-Joseph, E. (2005) *The Code of the City: Standards and the hidden language of place making*, Cambridge, MA: MIT Press.

Bento, J. (2012) *Survey on Architectural Policies in Europe*, Brussels: European Forum for Architectural Policies. http://www.efap-fepa.org/docs/EFAP_Survey_Book_2012.pdf.

Bento, J. (2017) 'Architecture as Public Policy – the Role and Effectiveness of National Architectural Policies in the European Union: The cases of Ireland, Scotland and The Netherlands', PhD thesis, London: University College London.

Bento, J. and Laopoulou, T. (2019) *Spatial Design Leadership: The role, instruments and impact of state architect (or similar) teams in fostering spatial quality and a place-making culture across five European states*, Tallinn: Government Office of Estonia.

Berni, M. and Rossi, R. (2019) 'Considering the quality of projects in relation to the common good', *Valori e Valutazioni* 23: 57–64.

Biau, V., Weber, B. and Zetlaoui-Léger, J. (2020) 'The architecture competition: a beauty contest or a learning opportunity? The French case in the light of European experiences', *Footprint* Spring/Summer: 83–98.

Biddulph, M., Hooper, A. and Punter, J. (2006) 'Awards, patronage and design preference: an analysis of English awards for housing design', *Urban Design International* 11: 49–61.

Bishop, P. and Williams, L. (2020) *Design for London: Experiments in urban thinking*, London: UCL Press.

Block, I. (2021) 'Biden revokes Trump's "beautiful" architecture executive order', 25 February. https://www.dezeen.com/2021/02/25/biden-revokes-trumps-beautiful-architecture-executive-order/.

Boys Smith, N. (2018) *More Good Homes: Making planning more proportionate, predictable and equitable*, London: Legatum Institute.

Brennan, T. and Tomback, D. (2013) *The Use of Historic Buildings in Regeneration*, London: Historic England.

Building Better, Building Beautiful Commission (2020) *Living with Beauty: Promoting health, well-being and sustainable growth*. https://assets.publishing.service.gov.uk/government/uploads/system/uploads/attachment_data/file/861832/Living_with_beauty_BBBBC_report.pdf.

Bulkeley, H., Marvin, S., Voytenko, Y., McCormick, K., Breitfuss-Loidl, M., Mai, L., Von Wirth, T. and Frantzeskaki, N. (2019) 'Urban living laboratories: conducting the experimental city', *European Urban and Regional Studies* 26 (4): 317–35.

Bund Deutscher Architekten (BDA) (2011) *Gestaltungsbeiräte: Mehr Kommunikation, mehr Baukultur*, Berlin: BDA. https://www.bda-bund.de/wp-content/uploads/2016/06/Gestaltungsbeir%C3%A4te.pdf.

Campos, V. and Ferrão, J. (2015) 'O Ordenamento do território: uma perspetiva genealógica' (ICS Working Papers, 1). Lisbon: Instituto de Ciências Sociais da Universidade de Lisboa.

Carmona, M. (2001) *Housing Design Quality: Through policy, guidance and review*, London: Spon Press.

Carmona, M. (2003) 'An international perspective on measuring quality planning', *Built Environment* 29 (4): 281–7.

Carmona, M. (2009) 'The Isle of Dogs: four waves, twelve plans, 35 years, and a renaissance ... of sorts', *Progress in Planning* 71 (3): 87–151.

Carmona, M. (2011) 'Goodbye CABE ... long live CABE', *Urban Design Matters* blog. 24 May, https://matthew-carmona.com/2011/05/24/goodbye-cabe-long-live-cabe/.

Carmona, M. (2012) 'The London way: the politics of London's strategic design', *Architectural Design* 82 (1): 36–43.

Carmona, M. (2013) 'By design – bye bye', *Urban Design Matters* blog. 14 January, https://matthew-carmona.com/2013/01/14/by-design-bye-bye/.

Carmona, M. (2014a) 'The place-shaping continuum: a theory of urban design process', *Journal of Urban Design* 19 (1): 2–36.

Carmona, M. (2014b) 'Re-theorising contemporary public space: a new narrative and a new normative', *Journal of Urbanism* 8 (4): 373–405.

Carmona, M. (2016) 'Design governance: theorizing an urban design sub-field', *Journal of Urban Design* 21 (6): 705–30.

Carmona, M. (2017) 'The formal and informal tools of design governance', *Journal of Urban Design* 22 (1): 1–36.

Carmona, M. (2018) 'Marketizing the governance of design: design review in England', *Journal of Urban Design* 24 (4): 523–55.

Carmona, M. (2019) 'Place value: place quality and its impact on health, social, economic and environmental outcomes', *Journal of Urban Design* 24 (1): 1–48.

Carmona, M. (2020a) 'Do zoning and design codes offer a fast track route to beauty?', *Urban Design Matters* blog, 20 August. https://matthew-carmona.com/2020/08/10/74-do-zoning-and-local-design-codes-offer-a-fast-track-route-to-beauty/.

Carmona, M. (2020b) 'Planning for an uglier future', *Urban Design Matters* blog, 27 March. https://matthew-carmona.com/2020/03/27/70-planning-for-an-uglier-future/.

Carmona, M. (2021a) *Public Places Urban Spaces: The dimensions of urban design*, New York: Routledge.

Carmona, M. (2021b) 'Design quality: have we reached a moment of national change?', *Urban Design Matters* blog, 1 February. https://matthew-carmona.com/2021/02/01/78-design-quality-have-we-reached-a-moment-of-national-change/.

Carmona, M., Alware, A., Giordano, V., Gusseinova, A. and Olaleye, F. (2020) *A Housing Design Audit for England*, London: Place Alliance.

Carmona, M., Clarke, W. and Giordano, V. (2018) *Reviewing Design Review in London*, London: Place Alliance, Urban Design London and Mayor of London.

Carmona, M., de Magalhaes, C. and Edwards, M. (2001) *The Value of Urban Design*, London: CABE.

Carmona, M., De Magalhães, C. and Natarajan, L. (2016) *Design Governance: The CABE experiment*, London: Routledge.

Carmona, M. and Giordano, V. (2021) *The Design Deficit: Design skills and design governance approaches in English local authorities*, London: Place Alliance. http://placealliance.org.uk/wp-content/uploads/2021/07/Design-Skills-in-Local-Authorities-2021_Final.pdf.

Carruth, S. and Stokholm, K. (2022) 'Green thresholds', *Urban Design* 161: 21–4.

Castree, N. (2008) 'Neoliberaling nature: the logics of deregulation and reregulation', *Environment and Planning A* 40: 131–52.

Champy, F. (2001) 'Sociologie de l'architecture', *La Découverte* 45 (3): 1–128.

Cities Climate Finance Leadership Alliance (CCFLA) (2015) *State of City Climate Finance 2015*, New York: Cities Climate Finance Leadership Alliance. www.citiesclimatefinance.org/wp-content/uploads/2015/12/CCFLA-State-of-City-Climate-Finance-2015.pdf.

Conference of Ministers of Culture (2018) *Davos Declaration: Towards a European vision of high-quality Baukultur*. https://davosdeclaration2018.ch/media/Context-document-en.pdf.

Corr, P. and Plagnol, P. (2018) *Behavioral Economics: The basics*, New York: Routledge.

Cravinho, J. (2017) 'Descentralização e Ordenamento do Território', Ad Urbem annual meeting minutes, Coimbra, Almedina.

Crespo, J. L. and Cabral, J. (2010) 'The institutional dimension to urban governance and territorial management in the Lisbon metropolitan area', *Análise Social* 45 (197): 639–62.

Cuthbert, A. (2006) *The Form of Cities: Political economy and urban design*, Malden, MA: Blackwell.

Dings, M. (2009) 'Historic Perspective 1900–2010. In Ovink, H. and Wierenga, E.(eds.) *Design and Politics*, Rotterdam: Nai010.

Directorate General for the Territory (2021) *Relatorio de Avaliacao PNAP 2016–2020*, Lisbon: Ministry of the Environment.

Ellin, N. (ed.) (1997) *The Architecture of Fear*, New York: Princeton Architectural Press.

ESPON (2018) 'Governance, planning and financial tools in support of polycentric development'. https://www.espon.eu/sites/default/files/attachments/Policy%20Brief%20Polycentric%20development%20tools.pdf.

European Commission (2009) *Guide to the Commission's Architectural Policy*, Brussels: European Commission.

European Commission (2021) COM(2021) 573 final: New European Bauhaus, Beautiful, Sustainable Together. https://europa.eu/new-european-bauhaus/system/files/2021-09/COM%282021%29_573_EN_ACT.pdf.

European Environment Agency (2019) *The European Environment: State and Outlook 2020*, Luxembourg: Publications Office of the European Union.

European Forum for Architectural Policies (EFAP) (2007) *European Forum for Architectural Policies: A chronological history*, Brussels: European Forum for Architectural Policies. http://sadas-pea.gr/archive/2000-2011/EFAPhistory.pdf.

European Forum for Architectural Policies (EFAP) (2008) *Manifesto for European Cities*, Brussels: European Forum for Architectural Policies.

European Union (2001) Council Resolution of 12 February 2001 on Architectural Quality in Urban and Rural Environments (2001/C73/04), Brussels: European Union.

European Union (2007) *Leipzig Charter on Sustainable European Cities*, Brussels: European Union.

European Union (2008) 'Council conclusions on architecture: culture's contribution to sustainable development (2008/C319)', Brussels: European Union.

European Union (2021) 'Council conclusions on culture, high-quality architecture and built environment as key elements of the New European Bauhaus initiative (2021/C501/03)', Brussels: European Union.

Falk, N. (2011) 'Masterplanning and infrastructure in new communities in Europe'. In Tiesdell, S. and Adams, D. (eds.) *Urban Design in the Real Estate Development Process*, Chichester: Wiley-Blackwell.

Falk, N. (2020) 'Applying land value capture tools: lessons from Copenhagen and Frieburg'. https://urbanmaestro.org/example/applying-land-value-capture-tools/.

Federal Chancellery of the Republic of Austria (2017) *Austrian Federal Guidelines for Building Culture*, Vienna: Federal Chancellery of the Republic of Austria.

Figueiredo, S. M. (2010) 'Going Dutch: the NAi and the search for quality architecture in the Netherlands', *Conditions* 5/6: 30–5.

Ford, H. and Sawyers, B. (2003) *International Architecture Centres*, Chichester: Wiley-Academy.

Forte, F. (2019) 'Architectural quality and evaluation: a reading in the European framework', *Valori e Valutazioni* 23: 37–45.

Freestone, R., Davison, G. and Hu, R. (2019) *Designing the Global City: Design excellence, competitions and the remaking of central Sydney*, Singapore: Palgrave Macmillan.

Fröbe, T. (2020) *Architectural Policy in Finland: Architecture as civic education*, Berlin: Jovis.

Gleeson, D. (2015) 'City planning as initiator, enabler, regulator', *Urban Design* 135: 12–14.

Gospodini, A. (2004) 'Urban morphology and place identity in European cities: built heritage and innovate design', *Journal of Urban Design* 9 (2): 225–48.

Hack, G. and Sagalyn, L. (2011) 'Value creation through urban design'. In Tiesdell, S. and Adams, D. (eds.) *Urban Design in the Real Estate Development Process*, Chichester: Wiley-Blackwell.

Hall, P. (2014) *Good Cities, Better Lives: How Europe discovered the lost art of urbanism*, Amersham: Routledge.

Harris, E. (2005) *Democracy and Rule of Law in Classical Athens*, New York: New York University Press.

Harris, R. (2019) 'Call in and recovered appeals 2018–19: a controversial year!'. https://www.landmarkchambers.co.uk/wp-content/uploads/2019/12/Secretary-of-State-Recovered-Appeals-and-Call-In-Decisions.pdf.

Harvey, L. (2013) 'Imperial Rome: a city of … rental property'. https://www.academia.edu/33603849/Imperial_Rome_A_City_of_Rental_Property.

Haughton, G. and Allmendinger, P. (2007) 'Soft spaces in planning', *Town and Country Planning* 76 (9): 306–8.

Hebbert, M. (1998) *London: More by fortune than design*, Chichester: John Wiley and Sons.

Hood, C. (1983) *The Tools of Government*, London: Chatham House Publishers.

Howlett, M., Ramesh, M. and Perl, A. (2009) *Studying Public Policy: Policy cycles and policy subsystems*, Oxford: Oxford University Press.

Imrie, R. and Street, E. (2009) 'Regulating design: the practices of architecture, governance and control', *Urban Studies* 46 (12): 2507–18.

Katsakou, A. (2013) 'The competition generation. Young professionals emerging in the architectural scene of Switzerland through the process framework of housing competitions: a case study'. In Andersson, J. E., Zettersten, G. B. and Rönn, M. (eds.) *Architectural Competitions: Histories and practice*, Stockholm: Royal Institute of Technology and Rio Kulturkooperativ.

Kayden, J. (2005) 'Using and misusing law to design the public realm'. In Ben-Joseph, E. and Szold, T. (eds.) *Regulating Place: Standards and the shaping of urban America*, New York: Routledge.

Kononenko, V. (2021) 'The New European Bauhaus must transform beauty into public good', 19 May. https://www.euractiv.com/section/energy-environment/opinion/the-new-european-bauhaus-must-transform-beauty-into-public-good/.

Kowalczyk, M. (2018) 'Architectural design contest with social participation as a part of building culture in Europe', *Journal of Education, Culture and Society* 2: 195–200.

Kresse, K. (2016) 'Dutch architecture policy and institutional infrastructure since the 1990s', *Architectural Research* 18 (2): 49–58.

Ladi, S. and Tsarouhas, D. (2017) 'International diffusion of regulatory governance: EU actorness in public procurement', *Regulation and Governance* 11 (4): 388–404.

La Rosa, D., Privitera, R., Barbarossa, L. and La Greca, P. (2017) 'Assessing spatial benefits of urban regeneration programs in a highly vulnerable urban context: a case study in Catania, Italy', *Landscape and Urban Planning* 157: 180–92.

Lees, L. (2008) 'Gentrification and social mixing: towards an inclusive urban renaissance?', *Urban Studies* 45 (12): 2449–70.

Lehrer, U. (2011) 'Urban design competitions'. In Banerjee, T. and Loukaitou-Sideris, A. (eds.) *A Companion to Urban Design*, New York: Routledge.

Leinberger, C. (2005) 'The need for alternatives to the nineteen standard real estate product types', *Places* 17 (2): 24–9.

Leinberger, C. (2008) *The Option of Urbanism: Investing in a new American dream*, Washington, DC: Island Press.

Licka, L. and Rode, P. (2014) 'Open spaces in Vienna's subsidised housing', *Urban Design* 130: 25–7.

Liefooghe, M. and Van den Driessche, M. (2019) *Open Call: 20 Years of Public Architecture* (Visitor's guide), Brussels: Atelier Vlaams Bouwmeester.

Linder, S. and Peters, G. (1989) 'Instruments of government, perceptions and contexts', *Journal of Public Policy* 9 (1): 35–58.

Lloyd-Jones, T. (2004) *Urban Design for Sustainability: Final report of the working group on urban design for sustainability to the European Union expert group on the urban environment*. http://www.evonymos.org/files1/333SUSTAINABLE%20DESIGN.pdf.

Local Government Association (2019) *Attracting Investment for Local Infrastructure: A guide for councils*. https://www.local.gov.uk/sites/default/files/documents/5.54_Supporting_Councils_14.pdf.

Local Government Lawyer (2021) 'London borough in judicial review challenge after Mayor of London approves 514-home scheme', 13 May. https://localgovernmentlawyer.co.uk/planning/401-planning-news/47062-london-borough-in-judicial-review-challenge-after-mayor-of-london-approves-514-home-scheme.

Loew, S. (ed.) (2012) *Urban Design Practice: An international review*, London: RIBA Publishing.

Lung-Amam, W. (2013) 'That "monster house" is my home: the social and cultural politics of design reviews and regulations', *Journal of Urban Design* 18 (2): 220–41.

Madureira, A. M. (2014) 'Physical planning in entrepreneurial urban governance: experiences from the Bo01 and Brunnshög projects', *European Planning Studies* 22 (11): 2369–88.

Mangen, S. (1999) 'Qualitative research methods in cross-national settings', *International Journal of Social Science Methodology* 2 (2): 109–24.

Mathieson, J. and Verlan, T. (2019) 'The far right's obsession with modern architecture', 11 September. https://failedarchitecture.com/the-far-rights-obsession-with-modern-architecture/.

Mayor of London (2020) *2020 Placeshaping Capacity Survey*. https://www.london.gov.uk/sites/default/files/2020_placeshaping_capacity_survey.pdf.

Medeiros, E., Brandão, A., Pinto, P. and Lopes, S. (2021) 'Urban planning policies to the renewal of riverfront areas: the Lisbon metropolis case', *Sustainability* 13: 5665.

Meijer, H. (1999) 'Safeguarding the quality of the built environment in Rotterdam', *Urban Design International* 4 (1/2): 3–4.

Mélice Dias, A. and Marat-Mendes, T. (2020) 'The morphological impact of municipal planning instruments on urban agriculture', *Cidades* 41. http://journals.openedition.org/cidades/2991.

Metzembaum, J. (1957) 'The history of zoning: a thumbnail sketch', *Case Western Reserve Law Review* 9 (1): 36–42.

Ministers of Culture and Communications (MCC) (2002) 'A Resolution for Architectural Quality in Europe', Paris: Ministère de la Culture et de la Communication, Direction de L´Architecture et du Patrimoine.

Ministry of the Environment (2007) *Programa Nacional de Politica de Ordenamento do Território*, Lisbon: Ministry of the Environment.

Ministry of the Environment (2015) *Política Nacional de Arquitectura e Paisagem*, Lisbon: Ministry of the Environment. https://pnap.dgterritorio.gov.pt/sites/default/files/livro_pnap.pdf.

Ministry of Housing, Communities and Local Government (2019) *Public Attitudes to House Building: Findings from the 2018 British Social Attitudes Survey*. https://assets.publishing.service.gov.uk/government/uploads/system/uploads/attachment_data/file/841815/BSA_House_building_report.pdf.

Ministry of Housing, Communities and Local Government (2020) *A National Design Guide*. https://www.gov.uk/government/publications/national-design-guide.

Ministry of Housing, Communities and Local Government (2021a) 'All new developments must meet local standards of beauty, quality and design under new rules', 30 January. https://www.gov.uk/government/news/all-new-developments-must-meet-local-standards-of-beauty-quality-and-design-under-new-rules.

Ministry of Housing, Communities and Local Government (2021b) *National Model Design Code, Part 1: The coding process*. https://assets.publishing.service.gov.uk/government/uploads/system/uploads/attachment_data/file/1009793/NMDC_Part_1_The_Coding_Process.pdf.

Ministry of Regional Development (2021) *Architecture and Building Culture Policy of the Czech Republic, Implementation Evaluation to 2020*. https://www.mmr.cz/getmedia/2ac8283c-8b04-4df6-ad9d-3eb87960f936/Architecture-and-Building-Culture-Policy-CZ-Implementation-Evaluation-to-2020.pdf.aspx?ext=.pdf.

Ministry of Welfare, Health, and Public Affairs (VROM) (1991) *Space for Architecture*, The Hague: VROM.

Nadin, V. and 35 others (2018) *COMPASS: Comparative analysis of territorial governance and spatial planning systems in Europe. Applied research 2016–2018: Final Report*, Luxembourg: ESPON and TU Delft.

Nadin, V., Hawkes, P., Cooper, S., Shaw, P. and Westlake, T. (1997) *The EU Compendium of Spatial Planning Systems and Policies*, Luxembourg: European Commission.

Nagel, R., Lesch, M. and Schacht, F. (2020) 'Biennial *Baukultur* reports: communicating high-quality planning and impacting public discourse'. https://urbanmaestro.org/example/biennial-baukultur-reports/.

Naujokaitytė, G. (2021) 'Commission puts flesh on New European Bauhaus plans', 17 September. https://sciencebusiness.net/climate-news/news/commission-puts-flesh-new-european-bauhaus-plans.

Nelissen, N. (1999) 'Preliminary conclusions: ten megatrends in aesthetic control in Europe', *Urban Design International* 4 (1/2): 77–8.

Nelissen, N. and De Vocht, C. (1991) 'Aesthetic control in Europe', *Netherlands Journal of Housing and the Built Environment* 6 (4): 347–61.

Netto, V. (2017) *The Social Fabric of Cities*, Abingdon: Routledge.

OECD (2017) *Land-Use Planning Systems in the OECD: Country fact sheets*, Paris: OECD Publishing.

OECD (2020) *Innovative Citizen Participation and New Democratic Institutions*. https://www.oecd.org/gov/innovative-citizen-participation-and-new-democratic-institutions-339306da-en.htm.

Office Fédéral de la Culture (1918) 'Davos Declaration, Swiss Confederation'. https://davosdeclaration2018.ch/media/Brochure_Declaration-de-Davos-2018_WEB_2.pdf.

OMC (Open Method of Coordination) Group of EU Member State Experts (2021) *Towards a Shared Culture of Architecture: Investing in a high quality living environment for everyone*. https://op.europa.eu/en/publication-detail/-/publication/752b8b71-2680-11ec-bd8e-01aa75ed71a1/language-en.

Order of Architects of Romania (OAR) (2019) *The Architecture Stamp Duty: A community resource. Cultural and editorial projects 2015–2018*. https://oar.archi/wp-content/uploads/2021/02/oar_timbruldearhitectura20152018_pdf_1570533027.pdf.

Ottenhyem, K. and De Jonge, K. (eds.) (2013) *The Low Countries at the Crossroads: Netherlandish architecture as an export product in early modern Europe (1480–1680)*, Turnhout: Brepols.

Parkes, S., Marsden, G., Shaheen, S. and Cohen, A. (2013) 'Understanding the diffusion of public bikesharing systems: evidence from Europe and North America', *Journal of Transport Geography* 31: 94–103.

Patti, D. (2013) 'Governance in the metropolitan region: the Vienna-Bratislava case'. In Schrenk, M., Popovich, V., Zeile, P. and Elisei, P. (eds.) *Proceedings REAL CORP*, Rome: Tagungsband.

Phillips, E. (1973) 'The Roman law on the demolition of buildings', *Latomus* 32: 86–95.

Pierre, J. (1999) 'Models of urban governance', *Urban Affairs Review* 34 (3): 372–96.

Pierre, J. (2014) 'Can urban regimes travel in time and space? Urban regime theory, urban governance theory, and comparative urban politics', *Urban Affairs Review* 50 (6): 864–89.

Pierre, J. and Peters, B. G. (2000) *Governance, Politics and the State*, Basingstoke: Macmillan Press.

Platform Baukulturpolitik (2017) *3rd Austrian Building Culture Report. Scenarios and Strategies for 2050*, Vienna: Federal Chancellery of Austria.

Platform Baukulturpolitik (2021) *4th Austrian Building Culture Report. Concrete Building Culture Policy: The way to an agency for building culture policy*, Vienna: Federal Chancellery of Austria.

Punter, J. (1994) 'Design control in Europe', *Built Environment* 20 (2): 84–7.

Punter, J. (1999) 'Improving the instruments, processes and products of aesthetic control in Europe', *Urban Design International* 4 (1/2): 79–99.

Punter, J. (2007) 'Developing urban design as public policy: best practice principles for design review and development management', *Journal of Urban Design* 12 (2): 167–202.

Purkarthofer, E. (2016) 'When soft planning and hard planning meet: conceptualising the encounter of European, national and sub-national planning', *European Journal of Spatial Development* 61: 1–20.

Radcliffe, J., Stubbs, M. and Keeping, M. (2021) *Urban Planning and Real Estate Development*, 4th Edition, New York: Routledge.

Rapoport, E. (2013) 'Globalising sustainable urbanism: the role of international masterplanners', *Area* 47 (2): 110–15.

Reynolds, F. (2016) *The Fight for Beauty: Our path to a better future*, London: Oneworld.

Rogers, E. (1995) *Diffusion of Innovations*, New York: The Free Press.

Rybczynski, W. (1994) 'Epilogue'. In Scheer, B. C. and Preiser, W. (eds.) *Design Review: Challenging urban aesthetic control*, New York: Chapman and Hall.

Rysler, J. (2014) 'Urban design in central and eastern Europe', *Urban Design* 130: 19–21.

Rysler, J. (2019) 'Northwestern Europe', *Urban Design* 150: 19–21.

Salamon, L. (2000) 'The new governance and the tools of public action: an introduction', *Fordham Urban Law Journal* 28 (5): 1611–74.

Salet, W., Thornley, A. and Kreukels, A. (2003) *Metropolitan Governance and Spatial Planning: Comparative case studies of European city regions*, London: Spon Press.

Sawyers, B., Morishima, H. and Mayer, K. (2002) 'The value of architecture centres' (European Architecture Centres Briefing Document), London: Architecture Foundation and Office of the Deputy Prime Minister.

Schultz, B., Keiner, M. and Schmid, W. (2003) 'Measuring quality in cantonal guiding planning in Switzerland', *Built Environment* 29 (4): 327–35.

Scruton, R. (1994) *The Classical Vernacular: Architectural principles in an age of nihilism*, Manchester: Carcanet Press.

Scruton, R. (2009) *Beauty*, Oxford: Oxford University Press.

Siodmok, A. (2017) 'Mapping service design and policy design', *Policy Lab* blog, 22 September. https://openpolicy.blog.gov.uk/2017/09/22/designing-policy/.

Squires, G., Hutchison, N., Berry, J., Adair, A., McGreal, S. and Organ, S. (2015) *Innovative Financing for Real Estate Development in Pan-European Regeneration*, London: RICS (Royal Institution of Chartered Surveyors). https://www.isurv.com/downloads/download/1999/innovative_finance_for_real_estate_development_in_pan-european_regeneration_rics.

Stad Wein (2014) *Baukultur Wien: ein Programm für die Stadt*, Vienna: Stad Wein.

Strebel, I. and Silberberger, J. (2017) *Architecture Competitions: Project design and the building process*, London: Routledge.

Swiss Federal Office of Culture (2021a) 'Davos *Baukultur* Quality System: eight criteria for a high-quality *Baukultur*'. https://davosdeclaration2018.ch/media/DBQS-en.pdf.

Swiss Federal Office of Culture (2021b) 'Davos *Baukultur* Quality System: eight criteria for a high-quality *Baukultur* – the whole story'. https://davosdeclaration2018.ch/media/DBQS-the-whole-story-en.pdf.

Tait, M. and Jensen, O. (2007) 'Travelling ideas, power and place: the cases of urban villages and business improvement districts', *International Planning Studies* 12 (2): 107–27.

Talen, E. (2012) *City Rules: How regulations affect urban form*, Washington, DC: Island Press.

Temel, R. (2020) *Baukultur for Urban Neigbourhoods: Process culture through concept tendering*. https://www.bbsr.bund.de/BBSR/DE/veroeffentlichungen/sonderveroeffentlichungen/2020/konzeptvergabe-langfassung-dl-en.pdf?__blob=publicationFile&v=4.

Thompson-Fawcett, M. (2003) 'A new urbanist diffusion network: the Americo-European connection', *Built Environment* 29 (3): 253–70.

Tiesdell, S. (2011) 'Design champions: fostering a place-making culture and capacity'. In Tiesdell, S. and Adams, D. (eds.) *Urban Design in the Real Estate Development Process*, Chichester: Wiley-Blackwell.

Tiesdell, S. and Adams, D. (2011) 'Real estate development, urban design and the tools approach to public policy'. In Tiesdell, S. and Adams, D. (eds.) *Urban Design in the Real Estate Development Process*, Chichester: Wiley-Blackwell.

Tonkiss, F. (2013) *Cities by Design: The social life of urban form*, Cambridge: Polity Press.

Trigg, M. (2017) 'Baukultur: the term everyone should know', 10 March. https://www.linkedin.com/pulse/baukultur-term-everyone-should-know-matthew-trigg.

United Nations (2017) 'New urban agenda', Habitat III. https://habitat3.org/the-new-urban-agenda/.

UN-Habitat (2015) *Global Public Space Toolkit: From global principles to local policies and practice*. https://unhabitat.org/global-public-space-toolkit-from-global-principles-to-local-policies-and-practice.

UN-Habitat (2016a) *HABITAT III, 2016: The United Nations Conference on Housing and Sustainable Development. Conference Report*. https://habitat3.org/documents-and-archive/final-reports/the-conference-report/.

UN-Habitat (2016b) *Finance for City Leaders Handbook*. https://unhabitat.org/finance-for-city-leaders-handbook.

UN-Habitat (2020) *Governance Assessment Framework, for Metropolitan, Territorial and Regional Management*. https://unhabitat.org/sites/default/files/2020/10/gaf-mtr.pdf.

UN World Tourism Organization (2018) *European Union Tourism Trends*. https://www.e-unwto.org/doi/pdf/10.18111/9789284419470.

Urban Design London (2020) 'London design review story'. https://www.urbandesignlondon.com/documents/1115/Design_Review_in_London_fs6s5k0.pdf.

Vale, L. (2013) *Purging the Poorest: Public housing and the design politics of twice-cleared communities*, Chicago: University of Chicago Press.

Van Assen, S., Van Campen, J. and Stolk, E. (2018) 'Q-factor: Dutch spatial quality advisory practices', AESOP Congress, Gothenburg.

Van Doren, P. (2005) 'The political economy of urban design standards'. In Ben-Joseph, E. and Szold, T. (eds.) *Regulating Place: Standards and the shaping of urban America*, London: Routledge.

Van Ginneken, S. (2008) *Q-Team Almere: het Geweten van het Stadshart*, Almere: Gemeente Almere.

Van Ulzen, P. (2007) *Imagine a Metropolis: Rotterdam's creative class, 1970–2000*, Rotterdam: 010.

Visscher, H. and Meijer, F. (2005) 'Professional experience for young architects', Delft: OTB Research Institute for Housing, Urban and Mobility Studies, Delft University of Technology.

Von der Leyen, U. (2020) 'A new European Bauhaus', 15 October. https://ec.europa.eu/commission/presscorner/detail/en/AC_20_1916.

Wesener, A. (2011) 'Improving quality of place: strategic approaches in Germany and the UK', *Proceedings REAL CORP* 2011: 425–35.

White, J. and Punter, J. (2017) 'Toronto's "Vancouverism": developer adaptation, planning, responses and the challenge of design quality', *Town Planning Review* 88 (2): 173–200.

Willacy, S. (2022) 'Community engagement in Aarhus', *Urban Design* 161: 31–3.

Zeayter, H. and Mansour, A. M. H. (2017) 'Heritage conservation ideologies analysis: historic urban landscape approach for a Mediterranean historic city case study', *HBRC Journal* 14 (3): 345–56.

Websites

All websites accessed and operational April 2022

http://en.iprpraha.cz
http://beexemplary.brussels
http://www.landluft.at/
http://www.versounaleggeperlarchitettura.it/
http://www.builtforlifehomes.org
https://arch-lokaal.nl
https://architektura.um.warszawa.pl/baipp
https://www.bak.admin.ch/bak/en/home/baukultur/service/kontakte-und-organigramme.html
https://bma.brussels/en/
https://byoghavn.dk
https://charleslandry.com/themes/creative-bureaucracy/
https://davosdeclaration2018.ch
https://europa.eu/new-european-bauhaus/index_en
https://farrells.com/publications/type/research
https://finnisharchitecture.fi
https://garagemsul.ccb.pt
https://leyarquitectura.mitma.es/
https://placealliance.org.uk
https://placemaking-europe.eu
https://pnap.dgterritorio.gov.pt
https://oar.archi/en/timbrul-de-arhitectura/about-the-architectural-stamp-duty/

https://ohpraga.pl/?locale=en
https://q-factor.info/en/home/
https://stadmakersfonds.nl
https://uia2023cph.org/the-guides
https://urbanmaestro.org
https://urbanroomsnetwork.wordpress.com
https://webarchive.nationalarchives.gov.uk/ukgwa/20110118095359/http://www.cabe.org.uk/
https://www.architecture.com/awards-and-competitions-landing-page/competitions-landing-page
https://www.ads.org.uk/inspiring-learning-spaces-toolkit/
https://www.arkki.com/
https://www.baukulturpolitik.at
https://www.big.at
https://www.bjorvikautvikling.no/portfolio-item/information-in-english/
https://www.bmk.gv.at/ministerium/staatspreise/staatspreis_architektur.html
https://www.bundesstiftung-baukultur.de/en/
https://www.collegevanrijksadviseurs.nl/projecten/panorama-nederland
https://www.dgterritorio.gov.pt
https://www.dqi.org.uk
https://www.europan-europe.eu/en/
https://www.faireparis.com/en/
https://www.fncaue.com/?page=home
https://www.fncaue.com/dossiers-thematiques/
https://www.hafencity.com/en
https://www.hofvancartesius.nl
https://www.iledenantes.com
https://www.london.gov.uk/what-we-do/regeneration/advice-and-guidance/about-good-growth-design
https://www.miesarch.com/
https://www.nextroom.at
https://www.oecd.org/cfe/cities/land-value-capture.htm
https://www.pavillon-arsenal.com/en/
https://www.placestandard.scot
https://www.publicpractice.org.uk
https://www.publicspace.org/the-prize
https://www.semanaarquitecturamadrid.com
https://www.thefulcrum.eu
https://www.uia-initiative.eu/en/uia-cities/turin
https://www.urbandesignlondon.com
https://www.vlaamsbouwmeester.be/
https://www.vlaamsbouwmeester.be/nl/subsite/bouwmeester-scan

Index

References to images and tables are in *italics*.

acontextuality 7
active learning 125
ad hoc practices 272–3
aesthetics 5, 7, 38–9
alliance building 138
America's Cup Pavilion (Valencia) *54*
analysis tools 78, 115–17, 119–20, 122–3
ancient Greece 2
architects 44–5, 244, 270, 272
Architects (Registration) Act (1931) 18–19
Architects' Council of Europe 16, 26, 141
Architects Directive 17
architecture 15–18
    competitions 257–8
    in Lisbon 84–7, 89, 92
    in London 99
    in Madrid 137, 138–9
    in The Netherlands 19–21
    policies 18–19, 21–3, 66–72
    quality 24–7, 30–41
    in Romania 206–7
    tools 232–3
    in Vienna 103, 105–7, 108, 111–12
*Architecture Guide to the UN 17 Sustainable
    Development Goals, An* 133, 134, *135*
Architecture Navigator 124–5
Arkki School of Architecture for Children and
    Youth 130–2
arts and crafts movement 15
audits 116, 119–22, 234
Augustus, Emperor 2
Australia 16; *see also* Sydney
Austria 33, 68, 247, 263
    analysis tools 122
    information tools 126, 129
    persuasion tools 143
    see also Vienna
    awards *see* design awards

Barcelona 56
Baukultur (building culture) 28, 32–6, 67, 71,
    269–70
    German reports 117–19, 122–3
    in Vienna 103, 105–7, 113
beauty 5, 7, 9, 27, 36, 38–40, 93, 195; *see also*
    aesthetics
Beaux Arts 15, 260
Belgium 22–3, 270
    exploration tools 183, 186–7
    rating tools 160, *161*

support tools 171–3, 176
    see also Bouwmeester Maître Architecte
    (BMA); Brussels
Biden, Joe 39
Birmingham *240*
bottom-up directive 269
Bouwmeester Maître Architecte (BMA) 58, 62,
    68, 262
    and architects 272
    and community participation 247
    and governance 244–5
    and tools 120, 232, 238
BREEAM (Building Research Establishment
    Environmental Assessment Method)
    152, 165
briefs (design and project) 30, 36, 47, 168,
    171, 176–7
    competitions, 227, 247
Brussels 58, 126, 245
Budapest 230, 252
budgets *see* funding
building culture *see* baukultur
Building for a Healthy Life (BfHL) 155
By&Havn 227–8

CABE (Commission for Architecture and the
    Built Environment) 21, 62–3, *66*
Cambridge 251, *252*
campaigns 120, 133, 137, 140–1, 174
case studies 63–5, 106, 124, 126, 129–30
CAUEs (Councils for Architecture, Urbanism
    and the Environment) 130, 173–5, 269
certification schemes 151–3, 155, 160, 162,
    165, 227
citizens assemblies 248
climate 1–2
climate change 5, 18, 196–7
co-design 40, 179, 230
co-governance agreements 179
Colombia 241; *see also* Medellín
commercialisation 6
community participation 67, 90, 109, 144,
    146, 179, 180–1, 190–1, 238, 247, 257,
    273
Competition Culture in Europe 155–6
competitions 34, 37, 48–9, 53, *54*, 68, 73, 86,
    108–10, 150–1, 155–6, 160–2, 164–6,
    168–71, 191–2, 212, 229, 232–3, 238–9,
    247–8, 257–60, 262–3, 269–70, 272
    in Madrid *264*
    subsidising 257–8
    in Sydney *259*

concept tendering 215–17, 253
Conclusions on Architecture: Culture's contribution to sustainable development 29
construction 5
Continuing Professional Development (CPD) programmes 126–7
control tools 77
Copenhagen *12*, 227–8, 254, 262
  Carlsberg City *242*
  development 274
  gentrification 245
  public spaces 234
Correa, Charles 89
corruption 246
countryside 2
Covid-19 pandemic 234, *236*, 239
Croatia 126
culture 1–2, 5, 18
  and design quality 223, 226–31
  in Lisbon 85, 86–7
  and sustainability 28, 29
  tools 73, 75, 77–8
  see also *Baukultur*
Cyprus 68
Czech Republic 169, 170–1, 229, 251, 258; see also Prague

Dancing House (Prague) *46*
Davos Declaration on *Baukultur* 33–6, 263
debt finance 199–200
defence 2
delivery 73
  analysis tools 116–17
  exploration tools 180–1, 183–4, 186, 189
  formal tools 75–7
  informal tools 78–80
  information tools 126–9
  persuasion tools 139–40
  rating tools 152–3, 155–8
  support tools 168–9, 171, 173
Denmark 30, 263
  analysis tools 120
  exploration tools 183, *184*
  information tools 133, 134
  rating tools 161, 165
  support tools 169
  see also Copenhagen
design 15–18, 47, 60–4
  finance 195–201, 203–6, 208, *209–13*, 218–20
  governance 10–11, 13–17, 43–4, 56–60
  housing *14*
  in Lisbon 87–92
  in London 93, *94*, 95, 97–102
  politics 9–10, 50, 52–3
  quality 55–6, 223, 226–31, 265, 283–6
  strings 217–18, 253–4
  in Vienna 107–12
  see also architecture; *Baukultur*; competitions; direct design; indirect design; urban design governance
design awards 27, 68, 137–8, 140–3, 161, 170–1, 284
design briefs see briefs
design competitions see competitions

design process 44, 48–50, 52–3, 60–1, 75, 78–80, 119, 124–5, 140–1, 149, 178, 189, 237–8
design review 14, 49, 98–101, 110–11, 120–1, 127–8, 150–1, 155–62, 165–6, 236, 238, 243, 247, 249, 263
development 5, 7–9, 10, 28–9, 48, 109, 147, 184–5, 196, 201, 245, 274–6
development management 43, 89, 100, 236, 240
development process 75, 77–8, 132, 140, 147, 158, 167, 177–9, 196, 233, 250, 285
devolved local champions 270–2
digitalisation 18
direct advocacy 138
direct design 44–9
direct investment 204
disability 4, 7
disease 4
Dublin *148*, *236*
Dundee *154*

economics 4, 5, 80, 250–9, 266, 287; see also finance
education 75, 87, 92, 111–12, 125–32, 128–31, 143, 174, 181, 271
EFAP see European Forum for Architectural Policies
engineers 45
England 21, 31, 32
  architectural policies 68, 69, 71
  Birmingham *240*
  CABE 62–3
  Design Network 130
  design review 243, 258
  place quality 58
  top-down discretionary 269
  see also Cambridge; London; Place Alliance
environment 5, 7, 38; see also sustainability
Estonia 30, 169
Europan 162, *163*, 164
Europe 1–2, 3–5, 15–18
  architectural policies 18–19, 21–30, 66–72
  design governance 43–9
  design quality 30–41
  post-war rebuilding 11, 13
  regulations 45
  spatial planning 53–6
  surveys 65–6
  unsustainability 7–9
  urban design governance landscape 60
  Urban Maestro project 60–4
  see also individual countries
European Council of Spatial Planners 16
European Forum for Architectural Policies (EFAP) 23, 24, 28–9, 30–1, 33
European Prize for Urban Public Space 27, 144–5
European Union (EU) 17–18, 23, 25–7; see also New European Bauhaus
events 137–8
exploration tools 79, 178–81, 183–4, 186, 189–91, 193–4

façades 2, *3*
fairness 4

festivals 99, 137–8, 141, 143
finance 195–201, 203–6, 208, *209–13*, 218–20
　　debt finance 196, 199–200, 214
　　in Germany 215–17
　　in the Netherlands 214–15
　　in Oslo 202–3
　　in Romania 206–7
　　see also funding; incentive; investment
Finland 22, 124–5, 130–2, 169, *199*
fire 2, 4
Flemish State Architect 172–3
Florenc 164
formal tools 50, *51*, 52–6, 75–7
　　urban design governance 234–7, 251,
　　　253–4
formative evaluation 150–1
France 3, 15, 19, 32, 262
　　analysis tools 120
　　architectural policies 66–7, 68
　　competitions 151, 166, 263, 269
　　exploration tools 180–1, 184, 186–8
　　persuasion tools 140, 142, 143
　　support tools 173–5
　　see also Paris
Freiburg 254, 255–6
funding 47, 167–9; *see also* financing

garden cities 15, 260
Gdansk *13*
Gehry, Frank *46*
Geneva *235*
gentrification 9, 192, 245
Germany 3, 15, 237
　　architectural policies 67
　　Baukultur 33, 117–19, 122–3
　　concept tendering 253
　　finance 215–17
　　Freiburg 254, 255–6
　　Hamburg 274–6
　　IBAs 183–4, 185–6
Gothenburg 25
governance 10–11, 13–17, 265
　　analysis tools 119–20, 122–3
　　design 43–4, 56–60
　　exploration tools 189–90
　　finance 200–1, 203, *209–13*
　　in Lisbon 82
　　in London 92–3, 95–9
　　persuasion tools 141–2
　　Urban Maestro project 60–4
　　in Vienna 102–3, 105
　　see also local governance; hierarchical
　　　governance; networked governance;
　　　public open governance; urban design
　　　governance
Graça, Carrilho da 89
grant-in-aid 167–9
Great Fire of London 2
green spaces 4
Grenoble 231
guidance tools 76
guided network 269–70

Hamburg 274–6
hard powers 50, *51*, 52–6, 58, 75, 97, 229–30,
　　234, 236, 238, 241, 261, 266–7

Haussmann, Baron 18
health 5, 6, 18, 98
height 1–2, *12*, *46*, 96
heritage 4–5, 7, 15, 22, 24, 28, 53, 85–6, 96,
　　103, 124, 183, 192–3, 208, 237, 259
　　in Lisbon 85, *86*
hierarchical governance 58
homelessness 7
homogeneity 6–7
Hong Kong 16
housing 5, *14*, 18–19, 49
　　in England 21
　　in Freiburg 255
　　in Geneva *235*
　　in Lisbon 86
　　in Malmö *219*
　　and Place Alliance 121
　　social 245, *246*
　　in Vienna 110, *111*
Housing and Town Planning Act (1909) 18
Hungary 67, 126; *see also* Budapest

incentive tools 76–7, 80, 205, 208–9, 213,
　　218–20, 237, 253, 267, 282
independent networks 143
India 16
indicator tools 150
indicators 73, 122, 150, 152–3, 160, 162, 165,
　　203, 215, 267
indirect design 44–9
inequity 7
influencing tools 50, 52, 75, 138, 147, 177, 266
informal arrangements 56
informal tools 50, *51*, 52–6, 57, 113
　　policies 72–4
　　quality culture 77–8
　　quality delivery 78–80
　　urban design governance 234–7, 239–40,
　　　247–9, 251–2
information tools 78, 123–34, 136
International Building Exhibitions (IBAs)
　　183–4, 185–6, 250, 257, 262
investment 197–8, 204–5, 208; *see also* finance
Ireland 22, 71, 129, 137, 169; *see also* Dublin
Italy 35, 67–8, 181
　　Architectural Festival 141
　　Quartiere delle Albere (Trento) *152*
　　Rome *246*
　　Turin 273–4

Japan 16
Johnson, Boris 98

Khan, Sadiq 98–9
Kigali 230, 238–9, 253
knowledge-sharing 124–5
knowledge transfer 221–3

land control 228–9
land ownership 47
land value capture (LVC) 254–7, 285
landscape architects 44–5
landscapes (urban design governance) 59–60,
　　74, 80–1, 112–13, 268–70, 272–3, 274,
　　276–7
language 15, 123, 191, 250, 269, 285

Latvia 30, 142, 262; *see also* Riga
Le Havre 53
LEED (Leadership in Energy and
    Environmental Design) 152
legal systems 55, 81–2
Leipzig Charter of Sustainable European Cities
    28
Levete, Amanda 89
Lisbon 82, *83*, 84–92, 112–13
    ad hoc practices 273
    BIP/ZIP Programme 181–2
    information tools 133
Lithuania 30, 151, 262
Livingstone, Ken 98
local governance 87–92, 190
    in London 99–102
    in Vienna 108–12
London 2, *3*, 92–3, *94*, 95–102, 112–13, 236
    Boroughs 92, 97–102, 112–13, 162
    Marble Arch Mound *242*
    UDL 127–8
Luxembourg 30

Madrid 248, *264*
    Architecture Week 137, 138–9
Malmö *219*, *249*
Malta 68
Manifesto about European Cities 29
manuals 124
materials 1–2
Mateus, Aires 89
mayors 92, 97–9, 112
Medellín 229, 253–4
Mendes da Rocha, Paulo 89
Middle Ages 2
Mies van der Rohe Award 26–7
Modernism 11, 15, 33, 38–9, 260
monarchy 18
monitoring 53, 116, 153, 168

Napoleon III 18
natural light 4
Nazi Germany 33
neglect 7
neighbourhoods 44, 89, 116, 118, 155, 189
    in Copenhagen 227–8
    in Lisbon 90–1, 181–2, 190
    in London 92
    in Malmö *219*
neoliberalism 6, 13, 55, 57, 93, 277
Netherlands 15, 18, 19–21, 22, 23, 262
    Citymaker Fund 214–15
    education 129
    Panorama Lokaal competition 155, 233
    persuasion tools 142
    Q-Teams 247, 252, 269
    Spatial Quality Teams 158–9
    support tools 176–7
networked governance 58
New European Bauhaus 18, 36–41, 263
New York City 3, 16
New Zealand 16
non-governmental organisations 108, 120,
    130, 183, 192, 238
    exploration tools 190–1
    persuasion tools 143

Northern Ireland 30
Norway *145*; *see also* Oslo

OMC (Open Method of Coordination) Group
    36–7
on-site experimentation 180, 183–4, 186,
    189
orientation 1–2
ornamentation 1–2
Oslo 202–3, 254

panorama 63, 114–15
Paris 10–11, *12*, 18, 145–7
Les Grands Voisins 186–8, 239–40
parking 10, *11*, 237
participation *see* community participation
persuasion tools 78, 136–44, 147–9
Piano, Renzo 89, *152*
Place Alliance 58, 93, 120–1, 143
place-shaping 79, 99–100, 140, 178
place-shaping continua 44, 60
Place Standard 153–4, 165, 250, 252, 262
place value 5–6, 7, 73, 120, 197, 218, 223,
    251, 265, 287
Placemaking Europe 16
planning 5, 15–17, 47–8
Poland *13*, 151, 192–93, *198*
Policy Lab 50, *51*, 52
politics 9–10, 50, 52–3, 229–31; *see also*
    governance
pollution 6, 18
population rates 18
Porto 236, *237*
Portugal 67, 141, 176; *see also* Lisbon; Porto
power 246–50, 265–6; *see also* hard powers;
    public power; soft powers
practice guides 124, 126, 129, 133, 270
Prague *46*, 119, 164
    Institute of Planning and Development
    (IPR) 270–1
Pretoria 233–4
privacy 1–2
private consultancies 190–1
private investment 197–8; *see also* investment;
    finance
privatisation 6
proactive engagement 179
process 48–9; *see also* design process
professional investigation 179–80
programme grants 168, 176–7
promulgation tools 137–8
protection 4
public buildings 110
public open governance 58
public power 57–8
public-private partnerships (PPPs) 205, 220,
    254–7, 266, 285
public sector 3–5, 13–14, 57, 74 , 164
    finance 198–200; *see also* finance, funding
    indirect design 45, 48
    in London 93, 100, 127–8
    persuasion tools 139
    rating tools 149, 156, 160, 161, 165–6
    support tools 167, 171, 175–7
    urban design governance 241–3, 257–8
public spaces 97–8, 109, 233–4

quality culture (and tools) 73, 75, 77–8, 103, 169, 177, 229, 232–3, 278, 282
quality delivery (and tools) 73, 75, 78, 278
Q-teams 158–9, 247, 252

rating tools 78, 149–53, 155–8, 160–2, 164–6
recreation 5
regeneration 5,44, 45, 82, 88, 100, 102, 148, 165, 181, 199, 201, 206, 273–6
regulation 2–3, 10–11, 12, 13–14, 26, 37, 45, 77, 108, 186, 229, 234–6, 241, 284
regulatory management 205
religion 2
research 116, 120–1, 179, 192, 243
research by design 179, 183, 189–91, 238–9, 272
Riga 142, 238
roads 2, 4, 45; see also street design
Rogers, Richard 21
Roman Empire 2
Romania 67, 116, 206–7
Rome 10, 11
Rotterdam 53, 230
Rwanda 241

Samoa Île de Nantes 230, 249
Scotland 21–2, 72, 126, 180
    Place Standard 153–4, 165
securitisation 7
site promoters 48
Slovakia 126
Slovenia 126, 262
social benefit 5
soft powers 50, 51, 52–6, 57, 236, 246, 260–1, 266, 285
soft spaces 56
Solon the lawgiver 2
South Africa 16, 233–4, 241
Spain 67–8, 184, 186; see also Barcelona; Madrid; Valencia
spatial planning 46–7, 53–6, 103
    in Lisbon 84, 87, 91
Spatial Quality Teams 158–9
specialist training 125; see also training
sport 5
Stadmakers Fonds 214, 253, 256
steering mechanisms 205, 208, 282
strategic grants 167–8
street design 97–8
summative evaluation 151–2
support tools 78–9, 167–9, 171, 173, 175–8
surveyors 2
surveys 63, 65–6, 72–4, 114–15
sustainability 27–9, 255, 256
    UN goals 133, 134, 135
    see also unsustainability
Sweden 22, 25, 32, 130
    national architect 35, 270, 272
    state architect 35
    see also Malmö
Switzerland 33, 35, 262
    analysis tools 123
    architectural policies 67
    Baukultur 234, 235, 269–70
    informal tools 263–4

rating tools 160–1, 165
    Zurich 245
Sydney 48–9, 259

tactical urbanism 180, 239; see also temporary urbanism
taxation 205, 206–8, 255–6
technology 1–2
teenagers 7
temporary urbanism 79, 178, 180, 184, 186–7, 191, 209, 209, 230–1, 234, 236, 241–2; see also tactical urbanism
terrorism 249
tools 62–3, 65–6
    finance 199–201, 203
    landscapes 276–7
    travel 260–4
    urban design governance 74–5, 80–2, 231–40, 265, 266–7
    see also analysis tools; exploration tools; formal tools; informal tools; information tools; persuasion tools; rating tools; support tools
top-down directive 269
Toronto 261
tourism 15, 18, 236
trade 2
traffic 6
training 128–30; see also specialist training
Trajan, Emperor 2
Transport for London 97–8, 99
transportation 5, 6
Trump, Donald 39
Turin 273–4
typology 63, 74–80
    urban design governance 277–8, 279, 282

ugliness 7
UN Sustainable Development Goals 133, 134, 135
United Kingdom 15–16, 18–19
    aesthetics agenda 39, 40
    housing developments 49
    tools 53, 161–2
    see also England; Northern Ireland; Scotland; Wales
United Nations 254
United States of America 16, 39; see also New York City
unsustainability 7–9
Urban Design for Sustainability 27–8
urban design governance:
    economics 250–9
    fundamentals 283–6
    governance 241–6
    in Lisbon 82
    people power 246–50
    propositions 264–7
    public sector 257–8
    tools 74–82, 231–40 see also tools
    travel 259–64
    typology 277–8, 279, 282
    see also landscapes (urban design governance)
Urban Design London (UDL) 127–8, 257

urban designers 45–8
urban development *see* development
Urban Maestro project 30, 41, 57, 58–9, 60–4
    finance 204, 220
    workshops 221–3, *224–5*, 226
    see also urban design governance
urban regeneration *see* regeneration
urban renewal 11
urbanism 15–18

Valencia *45*, *54*, 247
Vancouver 261
Vienna 102–3, *104*, 105–12, 113, 229, 269
Von der Leyen, Ursula 37

Wales 68, 120
Warsaw 192–3
waste disposal 2
water access 2
web portals 124–5
welfare 4
women 7
workshops 63, 221–3, *224–5*, 226
World Bank 254
Wren, Sir Christopher 18

zoning 3, 10, *46*, 53, 87–9, 110
zoning bonuses 205, 208

CPSIA information can be obtained
at www.ICGtesting.com
Printed in the USA
BVHW050135100723
666935BV00001B/1